Interactive Democracy

How can we confront the problems of diminished democracy, pervasive economic inequality, and persistent global poverty? Is it possible to fulfill the dual aims of deepening democratic participation and achieving economic justice, not only locally but also globally? Carol C. Gould proposes an integrative and interactive approach to the core values of democracy, justice, and human rights, looking beyond traditional politics to the social conditions that would enable us to realize these aims. Her innovative philosophical framework sheds new light on social movements across borders, the prospects for empathy and solidarity with distant others, and the problem of gender inequalities in diverse cultures, and also considers new ways in which democratic deliberation can be enhanced by online networking and extended to the institutions of global governance. Her book will be of great interest to scholars and upper-level students of political philosophy, global justice, social and political science, and gender studies.

CAROL C. GOULD is Distinguished Professor of Philosophy at Hunter College and in the Doctoral Programs in Philosophy and Political Science at the Graduate Center of the City University of New York. She is the author of *Globalizing Democracy and Human Rights* (Cambridge, 2004) and *Rethinking Democracy: Freedom and Social Cooperation in Politics, Economy, and Society* (Cambridge, 1988), and has edited and co-edited several books including *Cultural Identity and the Nation-State* (2003), *The Information Web: Ethical and Social Issues in Computer Networking* (1989), and *Women and Philosophy* (1976).

Interactive Democracy

The Social Roots of Global Justice

Carol C. Gould

CAMBRIDGE
UNIVERSITY PRESS

CAMBRIDGE
UNIVERSITY PRESS

University Printing House, Cambridge CB2 8BS, United Kingdom

Cambridge University Press is part of the University of Cambridge.

It furthers the University's mission by disseminating knowledge in the pursuit of education, learning, and research at the highest international levels of excellence.

www.cambridge.org
Information on this title: www.cambridge.org/9781107607415

© Carol C. Gould 2014

This publication is in copyright. Subject to statutory exception and to the provisions of relevant collective licensing agreements, no reproduction of any part may take place without the written permission of Cambridge University Press.

First published 2014

Printed in the United Kingdom by Clays, St. Ives plc

A catalogue record for this publication is available from the British Library

Library of Congress Cataloguing in Publication data
Gould, Carol C.
Interactive democracy : the social roots of global justice / Carol C. Gould.
pages   cm
Includes bibliographical references and index.
ISBN 978-1-107-02474-8 (hardback)
1. Democracy – Social aspects.   2. Social justice.   3. Human rights.   I. Title.
JC423.G665   2014
321.8 – dc23   2014014931

ISBN 978-1-107-02474-8 Hardback
ISBN 978-1-107-60741-5 Paperback

Cambridge University Press has no responsibility for the persistence or accuracy of URLs for external or third-party internet websites referred to in this publication, and does not guarantee that any content on such websites is, or will remain, accurate or appropriate.

For Michael Gould-Wartofsky
and in memory of Marx Wartofsky

Contents

Acknowledgements

My greatest debt is to my son Michael Gould-Wartofsky and to Marx Wartofsky, my late partner of blessed memory. My son Michael, a doctoral student at NYU and a published author in his own right, has provided constant inspiration and encouragement to me throughout the writing of this book. I have benefited greatly from his acute social understanding, his political engagement, his attunement to the arts of language, and his personal generosity and kindness. He shares these qualities with his father Marx, whom we call "our Marx." I learned much from Marx's profound philosophical insight and synthetic modes of understanding, and deeply admired the way he combined these with a humane appreciation of diverse perspectives in knowledge and in life, and a commitment to social justice.

Thanks are due to my colleagues at Hunter College and the Graduate Center of the City University of New York (CUNY), Temple University, and George Mason University for many helpful discussions over the past several years, and especially to Noel Carroll, Omar Dahbour, Adam Etinson, Virginia Held, John Lango, Peter Mandaville, Michael Menser, Joseph Schwartz, Sibyl Schwarzenbach, Arun Sood, John Wallach, and Shelley Wilcox.

I am grateful to my close colleagues in the profession with whom I have been privileged to collaborate on themes related to this work, including Tim Hayward, Alistair Macleod, and Sally Scholz.

I have had stimulating conversations with many friends and professional associates who have given me valuable feedback, including Daniele Archibugi, Seyla Benhabib, James Bohman, Bruce Baum, Deen Chatterjee, Tom Christiano, Frank Cunningham, Yossi Dahan, John Dryzek, Andreas Føllesdal, Rainer Forst, Leslie Francis, Nancy Fraser, Pablo Gilabert, Robert Goodin, Philip Green, Cindy Holder, Gregg Horowitz, Ioanna Kuçuradi, Anthony Langlois, Arto Laitinen, Matthew Liao, Jane Mansbridge, Raffaele Marchetti, William McBride, Darrel Moellendorf, Julie Mostov, David Reidy, Massimo Renzo, Fiona Robinson, Mortimer Sellers, James Sterba, Joan Tronto, Gülriz Uygur, and David Wood.

Acknowledgement is also due to colleagues and administrators who provided me with valuable time and opportunities to work on this book, including Frank Kirkland, Laura Keating, Joseph Rollins, Peter Stearns, Iakovos Vasiliou, and Thomas Weiss.

I have been fortunate to be able to present early versions of most of the chapters at conferences around the world and I am grateful to the sponsors and audiences for their insightful questions and comments. I also benefited from helpful comments and suggestions received from two anonymous reviewers of the manuscript for Cambridge University Press, as well as from my astute editor at the press, Hilary Gaskin.

My graduate students have helped me tremendously over the years, with probing questions and valuable insights. I am especially grateful to my Research Assistant Joshua Keton for his incisive comments and first-rate editorial assistance over the past five years. I received important editorial help from Chloe Cooper Jones. I would also like to thank the following students from the Graduate Center of CUNY in philosophy and political science for their comments: Brandon Aultman, Elvira Basevich, Kenneth Courtney, Emily Crandall, Laura Kane, Jamie Lindsay, John McMahon, Kamran Moshref, Kristopher Peterson-Overton, Carolyn Plunkett, and Gregory Zucker. I am grateful to my Temple students Francis Raven, Robert Gertz, Heather Coletti, and Matt Smetona, to Katherine Razzano from George Mason University, and to Matt Whitt from Vanderbilt. Finally, I have benefited from my interactions with my talented undergraduates at Hunter College, Temple University, and George Mason University.

I would like to give deep thanks to my nephews Andrew Gould and Jon Gould and their families for their generous, steady, and kind support over the years. I also want to express my appreciation to my good friend Eric Ross, and to Annie Gow, Bob and Claire Hotchkiss, Sol Macner, Rob Wurtzel, Paul Jenner, and my other friends in New York City and the Berkshires for the warm encouragement they have given me at various stages in this project.

Earlier versions of material in several of the book's chapters have appeared previously in the following publications, which I would like to acknowledge here:

"Approaching Global Justice through Human Rights: Elements of Theory and Practice," in *Global Justice and International Economic Law*, ed. Chi Carmody, Frank Garcia, and John Linarelli (Cambridge: Cambridge University Press, 2012), 27–43.

"Retrieving Positive Freedom and Why it Matters," in *Isaiah Berlin and the Politics of Freedom*, ed. Bruce Baum and Robert Nichols (New York: Routledge, 2013), 102–13.

"Reconceiving Autonomy and Universality as Norms for Global Democracy," in Global *Democracy and its Difficulties*, ed. Anthony J. Langlois and Karol Edward Soltan (London: Routledge, 2008), 160–72.

"Is there a Human Right to Democracy?" in *Human Rights: The Hard Questions*, ed. Cindy Holder and David Reidy (Cambridge: Cambridge University Press, 2013), 285–300.

"Transnational Solidarities," Special Issue on Solidarity, ed. Carol Gould and Sally Scholz, *Journal of Social Philosophy* 38, no. 1 (spring, 2007): 146–62.

"Recognition in Redistribution: Care and Diversity in Global Justice," *Southern Journal of Philosophy* 46, Supplement (2008): 91–103.

"Women's Human Rights as Equality through Difference," in *Gender Identities in a Globalized World*, ed. Ana Marta Gonzalez and Victor J. Seidler (Amherst, NY: Prometheus/Humanity Books, 2008), 35–52.

"Structuring Global Democracy: Political Communities, Universal Human Rights, and Transnational Representation," Special Issue on Global Democracy and Political Exclusion, *Metaphilosophy* 40, no. 1 (January, 2009): 24–46; republished as *Global Democracy and Exclusion*, ed. Ronald Tinnevelt and Helder De Schutter (Oxford: Wiley-Blackwell, 2010).

"Self-Determination beyond Sovereignty: Relating Transnational Democracy to Local Autonomy," Special Issue on Democracy and Globalization, ed. Carol C. Gould and Alistair Macleod, *Journal of Social Philosophy* 37, no. 1 (spring, 2006): 44–60.

"Regional vs. Global Democracy: Advantages and Limitations," in *Global Democracy: Normative and Empirical Perspectives*, ed. Daniele Archibugi, Mathias Koenig-Archibugi, and Raffaele Marchetti (Cambridge: Cambridge University Press, 2011), 115–31.

Introduction

Democracy in the twenty-first century has failed to live up to its promise. It is widely noted that democratic governments have grown increasingly detached from the governed and incapable of standing up to the powerful economic interests that tend to dominate everyday life. Indeed, these interests have come to permeate politics itself, appearing to render "rule by the people" a bare ideal, seemingly remote and out of reach. Pervasive and persistent inequalities mark contemporary economies, which, though they may produce a wide range of goods and make effective use of new technologies, nonetheless fail to provide many with adequate livelihoods or dignified conditions of work. Even in societies where multiple sources of gratification and fulfillment are available, the limits of the "private sphere" and the informal contexts of interpersonal relationships leave many people dissatisfied and disempowered, whether because of their inability to realize their goals or develop their capacities, or in virtue of residual forms of oppression, racism, and group hatreds. What can political philosophy contribute to understanding and helping to remedy these contemporary problems? Why has democracy, in particular, been unable to fulfill its potential? And is it possible to deepen democracy while also achieving greater degrees of economic justice, not only locally but also more globally? What would make those dual aims achievable?

   This book argues that to realize democracy and global justice we have to look beyond the strictly political forms and remedies to the underlying social conditions that would enable these norms to be met at local, national, and transnational scales. Democracy would have to be transformed from its static and purely formal state to a more dynamic, responsive, and interactive form of governance. And we would need to understand the ways that democracy is normatively connected to social justice, both at home and abroad. It is sometimes acknowledged that political equality among citizens presupposes a certain level of economic well-being, but it is equally the case, I will argue, that achieving global justice – say, through forms of aid or redistribution – requires democratic participation on the part of the people whom one proposes to help in these ways. To date, political philosophers have tended to focus on one or another of the norms of freedom, justice, human rights, and democracy, as if each operated independently of the other. Despite their abundant insights, however, these approaches have not been very effective guides to contemporary practice. I believe that to address these problems we need to understand how these various norms are interrelated, both in theory and in practice, and that progress in regard to one also requires some movement on the others.

A central thesis of this book is that democratic transformation is largely dependent on changes in and across society, and involves the cultivation of solidarities across borders, new social movements, innovative forms of managing economic life, along with institutional transformations in the political domain. We need to consider the motivations that might lead people to take seriously the human rights of everyone else – is reasoning sufficient or are caring and affective attitudes also necessary? If both are required, how are they related? Is it plausible to suppose that people can care about others at a distance, especially if it involves more than a few other people? If we want to aid these others and mitigate global poverty, do we need to hear from them about their needs, and introduce new forms of global democracy that would enable such input? How can democratic dialogue and deliberation across borders proceed in any case, given the continued pervasiveness of conflict, whether in the form of cultural misunderstanding, state violence, or gender violence? Can online networking and new social media help to facilitate the requisite communication transnationally, as well as within given political societies?

This work takes up and elaborates upon the emergence of a human rights framework worldwide, including the growing recognition of an economic right to the means of subsistence. It argues that the fulfillment of this right would be a crucial step toward global justice. But justice is not only an economic matter; it involves the recognition of people as equal, and, in the view here, gives rise to a requirement for democratic participation beyond existing electoral and representative forms. We have recently seen sustained efforts toward substantive democratic transformation in the Middle East and North Africa, and attempts to confront inequality and deepen democracy with the Occupy Wall Street movement in the United States and the *Democracia Real Ya* (Real Democracy Now) movement in Europe. But in the face of powerful institutions of global governance and the economic dominance of transnational corporations, can democracy be of any use in holding these institutions and governments accountable for the impacts of their policies on people's lives? What forms would such democracy have to take? Would new types of regional and global democracy be helpful in this regard, and if so, how could they be structured?

Building on my previous book *Globalizing Democracy and Human Rights*,[1] I propose that to get to the root of these pressing social and political problems, we need to take a distinctively *interactive* approach to understanding democracy. To this end, we need to start with a more interactive conception of individuals, social relations, and collective activity within a given society. This networking perspective is also important in comprehending how people can link up across borders, how movements can make a difference at a distance, and how contemporary democracies can function effectively with others in an increasingly interconnected world.

Going beyond liberal understandings of the individual (whether in terms of rational choice or utility maximization), the theory of social reality (or *social ontology*) that underlies this work takes people to be "individuals-in-relations." As subjects, they have a capacity for freedom, but also require a set of basic conditions to make this freedom effective, including equal forms of social recognition and access to the material means of life. The human rights that protect and give expression to their freedom go beyond bare legal requirements to moral desiderata; they serve as goals for developing political, economic, and social institutions that would help to fulfill them. They will be interpreted not only or mainly as rights of individuals against others or against the state, but as claims on others to cooperate in setting up, supporting, and sustaining these institutions.

Justice is understood in an egalitarian way to require equal rights of access to the basic conditions that people need for their self-transformative or self-developing activity throughout their lives; it is understood in terms of what I call "equal positive freedom." Although this conception makes room for the political claims of local communities and nation-states, justice extends beyond their borders in cosmopolitan or global directions. One of the most central of the conditions for people's freedom is, I argue, taking part in common or cooperative activities with others. Equal positive freedom as a principle of justice can thus be seen to require rights of democratic participation in determining the direction of the various common activities in which people engage.[2] In this view, democracy gains its significance not by instrumentally producing

---

[1] Carol C. Gould, *Globalizing Democracy and Human Rights* (Cambridge: Cambridge University Press, 2004).

[2] See Carol C. Gould, *Rethinking Democracy: Freedom and Social Cooperation in Politics, Economy, and Society* (Cambridge: Cambridge University Press, 1988), chapter 1.

just outcomes (though it may tend to do so), but because it is required by this equal freedom of persons, as active and social beings.[3] And the scope of democracy in this view is considerably broader than generally understood: It applies not only to politics but to institutions within economic and social life as well, supporting the development of new forms of democratic management, for example, within firms or workplaces.

I will argue that in order to achieve justice in its more global or cosmopolitan reach, we need to understand its social bases, and specifically, the types of interconnections among people and groups that it requires: first, the formation of *transnational solidarities*; second, forms of care and recognition across borders; third, the achievement of gender equality and the overcoming of oppressive social relations; fourth, the ways in which "power over" others can be replaced by "power-with" others; and fifth, the conditions for effective dialogue and deliberation, both online and off. Beyond deliberation, the possibilities that the Internet offers for more participatory forms of democracy will be explored, together with the problems it raises concerning control over information.

These various social factors will be seen to support a conception of *concrete universality*, in which norms are understood not only in their abstract significations extending across time and space but also in their diverse manifestations as they emerge from various social and historical contexts. Although, in a sense, norms are constructed over time, I will argue that this does not eliminate their universal import.

The term *interactive democracy* highlights certain crucial features of this new conception and the accompanying forms of practice that it needs: It speaks to the dependence of real democracy on cooperative relations in social life and on a social understanding of persons. It signifies the interdependence between political democracy and the organization of the economic, social, and personal spheres. It connotes the interrelations of participatory, deliberative, and electoral modes of democracy. And crucially, it takes seriously the emergence of cross-border, transnational, regional, and even global forms of community and governance, such that any one existing expression of political democracy has to be understood in connection with the others.

Conceptually, too, the term *interactive* suggests that democracy can only be understood in relation to other core social and political norms and values. Political theories have tended to emphasize only one of the relevant norms in the last decades, focusing on justice *or* freedom *or* human rights *or* democracy *or* care *or* recognition. This book regards each of these

---

[3] For a discussion of the relation between the norms of justice and democracy, see Gould, *Globalizing Democracy*, chapter 1.

an integrated theory of democracy, justice, & rights.

foci as having much to contribute to our social and political understanding of the problems we face and the alternative arrangements we wish to propose. It sees the strengths of the existing theories, which, however, have tended to contradict each other on key points. The methodology advanced here attempts to reconcile conflicting views but not by averaging them or seeking compromise. Instead, it aims to develop a broader or more comprehensive approach in which preexisting theoretical perspectives have their place. Despite its contemporary subject matter, this book follows a classical philosophical approach in self-consciously aiming to be systematic and in adopting what could be called a dialectical method. It draws on and integrates elements from a variety of traditions in political philosophy, including feminism, Marxian approaches, existentialism, and liberalism, along with participatory democratic and critical social theory. In doing so, it attends to the ways that aspects of these traditions can cohere with each other and thereby contribute to our understanding, by reinterpreting them within a new, more synthetic perspective.

The book will advocate a somewhat similar approach for practical dialogues and deliberation, so that seemingly divergent views can be related to each other across political and cultural traditions. Beyond calling for more open and inclusive attitudes on the part of the interlocutors, there may be new ways to highlight misunderstandings of the meaning of the terms and concepts employed in such dialogues. But emphasizing intercultural perspectives is not to say that we have to remain uncritical about oppressive practices, for example, regarding the treatment of women, whether within distant cultural contexts or our own. On the contrary, the discussion presupposes some measure of critical engagement within these dialogues.

To say that this work aims at conceptual coherence is not to claim that it is complete. The book notably lacks an adequate treatment of environmental and ecological matters. There is ample room for developing such an account within the theory proposed here, in light of the emphasis it places on the material conditions for human activity, its broad reading of justice (which would encompass environmental justice), and its grounding in a human rights framework, which would recognize a right to an environment adequate to support health and well-being.[4] The proposals offered for dealing with the crisis in democracy – along with attention to transnational communities and their alternative forms of decision-making – could facilitate the future development of a more effective and democratic response to the climate crisis. But a substantial account of

---

[4] See Tim Hayward, *Constitutional Environmental Rights* (Oxford: Oxford University Press, 2005), chapter 1.

this and other ecological challenges, along with the most effective ways of dealing with them through more global forms of cooperation, are not yet developed in the way these serious problems would merit.

The book is divided into three parts: The first lays out my theoretical framework and distinguishes my approach from alternative social and political theories; the second explores some of the social roots of global justice; and the third develops the idea of interactive democracy in several of its conceptual and practical dimensions. A brief overview of the chapter contents will give the reader a prospective look at the key problems to be taken up, the main theses, and the general line of argument.

Part I lays out the fundamentals of the theory and its accompanying practice. It begins by developing an approach to global justice premised on the realization of people's economic and social human rights; it then proceeds with some practical suggestions for institutional changes along those lines. It raises some conundrums, compares this understanding of global justice to other cosmopolitan theories, and shows how this human rights approach is broadly egalitarian but is also more practicable than some others in prioritizing the fulfillment of basic human rights. This part then moves to consider alternative ways of justifying human rights philosophically, taking up both individualist and social/practical understandings of them (Griffin, Gewirth, Habermas, Beitz). It goes on to propose a social ontological and relational basis for these rights, which takes them beyond their status as legal protections by nation-states. These rights are understood as cosmopolitan moral and social norms, and as goals for transnational institutions of social, political, and economic life.

The core concept of positive freedom (or effective freedom) is analyzed next and defended in the face of Isaiah Berlin's critique. Freedom is understood to presuppose the protection of liberties, as Berlin insisted, but also requires freedom from oppression and exploitation, as well as access to a set of enabling material and social conditions. Inasmuch as the freedom in question is that of "individuals-in-relations" and is given a dynamic reading in which it develops over time, the conception goes beyond standard notions of autonomy and even the feminist conception of relational autonomy. The historical emergence of the norms of freedom and human rights is considered as well, as is the challenge of interpreting them from a variety of cultural perspectives. Here, too, will be noted the relation between my conception of positive freedom and the capabilities approach of Sen and Nussbaum.

The part concludes with an argument for democracy as a human right, defending that view against critics like Joshua Cohen. It gives an initial account of two criteria for determining the proper scope of democratic decision-making – "common activities" and "all-affected" – and then shows how they apply to emerging transnational communities, in the first case, and to the exogenous effects of policies and decisions on people outside a given community, in the second. The question arises whether equal rights of participation are possible here or only lesser forms of democratic "input."

Part II of the book addresses the fundamentally social bases of the norms of global justice. It starts with a conceptual analysis of solidarity in networked transnational contexts, contrasting it with humanitarian aid, and connecting it to notions of "fellow feeling," as well as those of mutual concern and mutual aid. It considers the sense in which transnational solidarity networks are helpful for fulfilling such norms, or whether a more unified form of solidarity within a global community would be needed to support global redistributive justice. Given that a truly global solidarity is likely unachievable, and may not even make sense, would that vitiate the possibility of achieving global justice as well? It will also be of interest to consider whether solidarity is required beyond justice, as an additional value to be realized in its own right.

The role of care and care work in global contexts is considered next, with attention to new ways of supporting this work politically. Forms of recognition needed for global justice are analyzed, along with the relations between care, empathy, and the recognition of equal dignity that is presupposed in respecting others' human rights. We also ask whether care as a basic condition of life is adequately recognized within the existing international human rights documents, and whether there is a human right to care per se. The book then broaches some hard questions and political paradoxes concerning gender equality and women's human rights, in view of the practices of cultural or religious groups that do not recognize such equality. The idea of using human rights as a limit on tolerating cultural practices is proposed, but the complication concerning the status of alternative cultural interpretations of these human rights and varying views on their priority has to be analyzed as well. This cross-cultural variability is illustrated with two cases of human rights adjudication that bear on women's freedom and their equality in public and private realms.

Next, we turn to the conditions for communicating across cultures, which come to the fore when we focus on the case of humor, and specifically the sociality of jokes. The connection of jokes to a particular audience that can understand them, and to which they are directed, will be seen to raise interesting questions both of inclusion and exclusion that are relevant to social and political uses of speech. Can jokes be understood across cultures? Hard cases of misunderstanding and of hate via humor are considered, exemplified by the case of the 2005 Danish cartoons depicting the Prophet Muhammad. Other uses of political humor in the context of protest and resistance can also shed light on unexplored social dimensions of speech and the prerequisites for effective communication transnationally.

This second part of the book concludes with an elaboration of the notion of "power-with" and a consideration of the ways in which it may be mobilized to help address transnational forms of violence. Building on the work of Hannah Arendt and Iris Young, it analyzes the contrast they drew between power and violence, and takes up its implications for democracy. The part concludes with an argument that recognizing a human right to democracy in practice (while also addressing economic rights) can help in the mitigation of violence. The discussion of the collaborative and cooperative potential of new forms of "power-with" to replace existing forms of power over others points ahead to the notion of interactive democracy.

Part III draws out the import of the earlier sections for theorizing democratic participation and deliberation in interactive forms beyond the nation-state – at transnational, regional, and possibly global levels. It begins by considering how democratic deliberation and dialogue across borders can be enhanced both online and off, and calls attention to the problem of misunderstanding terms and concepts in cross-cultural contexts. It goes on to analyze the role of social media and mobile technologies in democratic transformations, beginning with their use in the Arab Spring of 2010–11 and the Occupy Wall Street movement of 2011–12. The focus here is on how new media may enable participatory modes of democratic protest and organization – beyond e-government or e-voting or even "crowd-sourcing" – by way of new opportunities for collaboration, decentralized communication, and user-generated content. Some of the dangers and dilemmas of networking are discussed, as are issues of open access to information, surveillance, and the role of anonymity in online politics.

This part goes on to elaborate the two criteria for extending democracy beyond the nation-state – rights of participation in new transnational communities and rights of input into the policies of global institutions on the part of all those importantly affected by them – and discusses their connection to regional and global human rights frameworks. It then moves to consider some new directions for facilitating democratic input into the "epistemic communities" of global governance institutions and developing forms of transnational representation at that level. The possibility of introducing deeper, broader forms of democratic management within firms is then explored and justified philosophically. The import of such innovations is assessed for an understanding of workers' labor rights around the world (currently limited to the prevention of exploitation and

the protection of collective bargaining). The book concludes with an evaluation of the alternate emphases on regional vs. global democratization
as possible frames for the future development of interactive democracy.
The concern in both of these directions would be to find ways to give
people more input into the growing number of transnational decisions
and policies and the power structures that affect them.

By way of these arguments, this book thus aims to develop an integrative normative approach that can overcome existing theoretical conundrums, while helping to frame our increasingly transnational relations in
the coming period. The hope is to show how we can expand the scope
of democracy and make it more responsive, at the same time that we
address our global responsibilities to support institutions that fulfill people's human rights and meet their basic needs. This new approach arises
not only through reflections on alternative theories, but also by drawing
on ideas that have emerged from social networks, social movements, and
other elements of contemporary life. Its success, too, will depend on the
degree to which people will find it useful as a guide to their own practice,
above all in their common action.

nothing succeeds like success, nothing
fails like failure.

Part I

A theoretical framework

1   A human rights approach to global justice: elements of theory and practice

Introduction

Philosophers operating within a cosmopolitan framework have made powerful claims regarding what global justice requires of us. Beginning from the premise of the fundamental equality of persons, whether understood primarily in terms of interests, agency, or dignity, it is argued that there are strong requirements to more equally distribute wealth, resources, or opportunities so as to alleviate poverty, or to meet basic needs, or to develop people's capabilities so they can be relatively equally agential in the course of their lives.[1] Although drawing on different philosophical frameworks – consequentialist, contractarian or contractualist, capabilities and positive-freedom based – these approaches can be highly demanding in requiring massive aid to the poor, or else comprehensive redistributive schemes at the global level, or at the very least intensified forms of development assistance. They may also call for the introduction of institutional frameworks to effect these distributions and to promote development, and they may contain innovative proposals for changes to the international system.

Among the prominent approaches is Peter Singer's call for affluent people to donate a substantial percentage of their income to poverty relief,[2] more institutionally oriented calls for the implementation of a global difference principle, as in the early work of Charles Beitz,[3] or

---

[1] See, for example, Peter Singer, "Famine, Affluence, and Morality," *Philosophy and Public Affairs* 1, no. 3 (1972); Charles Beitz, *Political Theory and International Relations* (Princeton, NJ: Princeton University Press, 1979); Thomas Pogge, *World Poverty and Human Rights* (Cambridge: Polity Press, 2002); Darrel Moellendorf, *Cosmopolitan Justice* (Boulder, CO Westview Press, 2002); Simon Caney, *Justice Beyond Borders* (Oxford: Oxford University Press, 2005).

[2] Singer, "Famine, Affluence, and Morality"; Peter Singer, *Practical Ethics*, 2nd edn. (Cambridge: Cambridge University Press, 1999), 246; Peter Singer, *One World: The Ethics of Globalization*, 2nd edn. (New Haven, CT: Yale University Press, 2004), 187–9.

[3] Beitz, *Political Theory and International Relations*, Part III, and Thomas Pogge, *Realizing Rawls* (Ithaca, NY: Cornell University Press, 1989), Part III.

Thomas Pogge's proposals for a global resource dividend.[4] Again, cosmopolitan luck egalitarians concerned with the deep economic inequalities at the global level may propose achieving genuinely equal opportunity by correcting for the unchosen features of people's circumstances such as the availability of natural resources, since these so affect their life chances. Alternatively, they may focus on the way that existing institutions function to transform natural facts about people or their environment into social disadvantages and on institutional ways of correcting that in the interest of equality.[5]

These various approaches have in common a commitment to cosmopolitanism along with calls for strongly redistributive schemes in global contexts, at least in terms of what justice requires normatively. Many of the objections to such schemes – where they do not simply reassert the prerogatives of contemporary capitalist neo-liberalism – consist in challenging their exclusively cosmopolitan premises and insisting instead on the priority or importance of one's fellow co-nationals or of other particularistic obligations (for example, to family or community), or of the right to national self-determination.[6] Alternatively, the objections may focus on the excessively ideal and (putatively) unrealizable character of these demanding approaches. To this, the theorists in question sometimes respond by showing how their conclusions are required by even much weaker assumptions about justice, for example, Pogge's claims that his view follows from elementary libertarian requirements to avoid causing preventable harm to others.[7]

In terms of normative commitment, I side with the cosmopolitans, at least in the ethical domain. And I argue for a strongly egalitarian principle of justice, namely, what I have called equal positive freedom (EPF).[8] However, I propose here that when understood in its connection to human rights (on a certain interpretation of them) we get an approach that is not only theoretically strong but one that can provide practical and realizable guidance for moving towards global justice. I suggest then that approaching global justice in terms of human rights can avoid the sometimes excessively utopian character of some of the other views, while adhering to a firmly egalitarian framework. Moreover, I believe that this

[4] Pogge, *World Poverty and Human Rights*, chapter 8.

[5] Kok-Chor Tan, *Justice, Institutions, & Luck* (Oxford: Oxford University Press, 2012).

[6] See, for example, David Miller, "National Self-Determination and Global Justice," in *Citizenship and National Identity*, ed. David Miller (Cambridge: Polity Press, 2000), and David Miller, "Against Global Egalitarianism," *The Journal of Ethics* 9 (2005).

[7] Pogge, *World Poverty and Human Rights*, and Thomas Pogge, "Severe Poverty as a Violation of Negative Duties," *Ethics & International Affairs* 19, no. 1 (2005).

[8] For a discussion of this principle, see Gould, *Rethinking Democracy*, especially chapters 1 and 5, and Gould, *Globalizing Democracy*, chapter 1.

existing approaches to global justice

approach makes room for diverse and particular communities while at the same time arguing for strengthened global commitments (although I will not be able to develop this particular feature of the approach in much detail in this chapter).

In what follows, I lay out some of the key theoretical elements of this framework, which privileges human rights, including economic and social ones, noting in passing its difference from Pogge's conception of such rights,[9] and then indicate some of the main practical directions by which such rights can be institutionalized in more effective ways than they are at present. It will be apparent that both the theoretical and practical conceptions of human rights presented here go beyond their current interpretations in international law and practice, but I suggest that they constitute plausible developments of these conventional understandings. In the course of this analysis, I will also be concerned to address a few of the key objections that can be posed to this philosophical approach and some of the main difficulties that confront it in practice.

Equal positive freedom, social ontology, and a philosophical conception of human rights

Without attempting to present a fully developed philosophical justification, we can say that the account of justice recommended here emerges from what can be called the positive freedom tradition, associated, for example, with the work of C. B. Macpherson,[10] following earlier accounts by Karl Marx, the British Hegelians, and some American pragmatists like John Dewey, and more recently elaborated in a distinctive way by Amartya Sen and others.[11] As we shall see, however, the account I propose is a synthetic one centering on a conception of agency that brings together several features often treated discretely in various modes of thought. It seeks to interpret agency in a way less strongly tied than usual to liberal individualist premises, so that the understanding here remains open to multiple cultural interpretations.

---

[9] For an analysis and critique of Pogge's approach, see Carol C. Gould, "Coercion, Care, and Corporations: Omissions and Commissions in Thomas Pogge's Political Philosophy," *The Journal of Global Ethics* 3, no. 3 (2007).

[10] C. B. Macpherson, *Democratic Theory: Essays in Retrieval* (Oxford: Oxford University Press, 1973).

[11] Amartya Sen, "Equality of What?" in *Tanner Lectures on Human Values*, ed. S. McMurrin (Cambridge: Cambridge University Press, 1980); Amartya Sen, "Well-Being, Agency, and Freedom: The Dewey Lectures of 1984," *Journal of Philosophy* 82, no. 4 (1985); Amartya Sen, "Capability and Well-Being," in *The Quality of Life*, ed. Martha Nussbaum and Amartya Sen (Oxford: Oxford University Press, 1993).

To explain some of these various claims: In a series of books and articles, dating from *Marx's Social Ontology*, I have argued for a conception of agency that involves not only the capacity for choice, but also a process of the development of capacities and the realization of long-term projects over time, as well as the cultivation of relationships.[12] Such agency centrally presupposes freedom from domination, but is not limited to this negative notion, and in this way the account differs from some recent republican theories. Rather, the theory takes a quasi-Aristotelian turn in conceiving agency as requiring not only the absence of this sort of constraining condition, along with freedom from interference with basic liberties, but also sees it as requiring the availability of positive or enabling conditions if people are to be able to transform or develop themselves effectively. The character of this agency can be either individual or collective, as what I have called common activity or joint activity.[13] In these cases, the activity is oriented to shared ends or goals, and the social group is understood as constituted by individuals in their relations rather than as existing holistically above or beyond them.[14] This notion of agency is analyzed more fully in Chapters 2 and 3.

When characterized in these ways, the freedom of agents, understood as not only negative but also positive, and as involving transformation over time, in social as well as individual contexts, can be distinguished from classical liberal conceptions of autonomy, even when the latter are interpreted in terms of newer ideas of relational autonomy, as I show in Chapter 3. Along these lines, it is interesting to note in passing that the term *positive freedom* is finally coming back into its own, after falling into unjustified disrepute because of Isaiah Berlin's rejection of it,[15] which presupposed his giving it a strangely statist interpretation. From the standpoint of the account here, the focus on capabilities in Sen and Nussbaum[16] is important though I think better conceived in terms of what I called the development of capacities, which I interpret as including general capabilities as well as individualized capacities as an aspect of a process of self-transformation over time.[17] Yet these cannot be the entire story with respect to positive freedom. As noted, the realization of long-term projects also has a place in this conception, and even the

[12] Carol C. Gould, *Marx's Social Ontology* (Cambridge, MA: MIT Press, 1978), and developed at some length in Gould, *Rethinking Democracy*.
[13] Gould, *Rethinking Democracy*, chapter 1.
[14] Carol C. Gould, "Group Rights and Social Ontology," *The Philosophical Forum*, Special Double Issue on Philosophical Perspectives on National Identity, 28, nos. 1–2 (1996–7).
[15] Isaiah Berlin, "Two Concepts of Liberty," in *Four Essays on Liberty*, ed. Isaiah Berlin (Oxford: Oxford University Press, 1969).
[16] For Nussbaum's account, see Martha Nussbaum, *Women and Human Development: The Capabilities Approach* (Cambridge: Cambridge University Press, 2001).
[17] Gould, *Rethinking Democracy*, chapter 1.

notion of basic interests can be brought in, though this account eschews the conception of a person as simply a "bundle" or aggregate of interests, a notion that often afflicts interest-centered approaches.

The social ontology operative in this conception is one that takes as its basic entities what I have called *individuals-in-relations*,[18] in recognition not only of the importance of agency but also of the fundamental fact of social interdependence. This sociality plays a role in the centrality of common activities, and in the reciprocal recognition of each one's agency, as a core notion, along with the need for institutional and associational frameworks of social cooperation in economic, social, and political life. The idea of reciprocal recognition here, while derived partly from the Hegelian and Marxist traditions (especially in the Kojèvian interpretation that foregrounds the master–slave dialectic),[19] does not take such recognition to be constitutive of agency or of people's rights, but sees recognition instead as required by the equality of people as agential beings. Although human agency takes a great variety of forms and is elaborated variously, nonetheless it evidences a fundamental equality in the capacity for self-transformation – again, whether taken in a collective sense as in the production of culture, or in an individual sense, in the phenomenon of choice and self-development.

does it?

Observe the importance here of the conditions of agency, both negative and enabling. If each person is equally an agent and if their agency requires access to conditions for it to be effective at all, as well as for them to flourish, where such self-transformation constitutes the full meaning of freedom and is a normative imperative posited in their activity itself, then it follows from the recognition of their fundamental equality that people should have prima facie equal access to the conditions of their agency.[20] This constitutes the principle of equal positive freedom, which serves as an egalitarian principle of justice. The approach I take thus starts with the fundamental recognition of people's equality as agents but goes on to argue that their agency is empty or purely formal without access to the conditions that can make it effective. People's equality therefore extends to their access to a range of conditions necessary for their transformative activity.

When agency is taken relationally in these ways, as operating in conditions and as in many ways socially constituted, we can derive a powerful emphasis on the availability of a set of material and social conditions, in addition to the absence of some constraining conditions. Some of these

---

[18] Gould, *Marx's Social Ontology*, chapter 1; Gould, *Rethinking Democracy*, chapter 2.
[19] Alexandre Kojève, Introduction à la Lecture de Hegel, 2nd ed. (Paris: Gallimard, 1947).
[20] For a fuller development of this argument, see Gould, *Rethinking Democracy*, chapters 1 and 3.

conditions for agency are basic in that they are required for any human life activity whatever, for example means of subsistence, security, and basic liberty, along with freedom from domination, while some of these are enabling conditions for people's fuller flourishing. Even the basic conditions are understood as required for distinctively *human* life activity (i.e., as free life activity).[21] Likewise, emphasizing the socially related character of this activity, we can propose that some conditions are required for the very possibility of any sort of relatedness whatever, while others provide a basis for the fuller flourishing of our various relationships.

In my view, these various conditions are specified in human rights, both basic and nonbasic. As suggested earlier, they include the absence of constraints such as threats to bodily security, or restrictions on liberty (including freedom from domination), as well as a set of enabling material and social conditions, such as means of subsistence and health care, the provision of education and support for crucial social relationships (e.g., in childcare), along with access to the means of cultural development. Thus an articulated account of both civil and political human rights and economic, social, and cultural ones is important, in my view.[22]

Since everyone needs access to these conditions for their agency, the recognition of people's equality in the situation of interdependence requires that we cooperate to provide for their fulfillment. People have mutually valid claims on these fundamental conditions of agency and development, where the notion of a valid claim is equivalent to the idea of a right. This account is reminiscent in some ways of Alan Gewirth's, but in fact importantly differs from his, as we see in Chapter 2.[23] I am not arguing that we can reason from the importance of the conditions of agency for ourselves to their importance for others, but that the normatively required recognition of others as equally agents and the fact of our fundamental interdependence establish the validity of our mutual claims to these fundamental conditions of agency.[24]

The sort of claims involved here are not understood in the first place as legal claims on others, but as social and moral demands or expectations of mutual aid, and only derivatively as legal claims. It is in virtue of our fundamental interdependence that we can expect the cooperation

---

[21] See also the discussion of human rights and their relation to equal positive freedom in *ibid.*, chapter 8 ("What are the Human Rights?"), and Gould, *Globalizing Democracy*, especially chapter 1.

[22] Not all of the relevant human rights have thus far been recognized in the international documents or interpretations (e.g., freedom from oppression is obviously not included there). The connection of the philosophical account of human rights to their legal recognition will be discussed in Chapter 2 and elsewhere in this work.

[23] Alan Gewirth, *Reason and Morality* (Chicago, IL: University of Chicago Press, 1980).

[24] See also the discussion of Gewirth's view in Gould, *Rethinking Democracy*, chapter 1.

of others in meeting basic needs. And indeed, I suggest that in principle, human rights hold on all others. But, in practice, they must be satisfied through more delimited forms of social, economic, and political institutions. Yet such human rights, in this philosophical interpretation of them, have only contingently come to be seen as holding against states in the first instance. Human rights have a more general, interpersonal significance, to use Pogge's terms,[25] as well as an institutional one. They are institutional because they are interpersonal – or better, based on our fundamental social relations of interdependence – but they can only be realized institutionally.[26] The institutions that they hold against are not only the state, but also economic, social, and cultural institutions. Note how suitable this approach is for the current development of globalization, in which transnational communities are coming to prominence, along with new institutions of global governance. The view I present is consonant as well with feminist approaches that seek to "bring rights home," as it were, and to see them as extending to the private and not only the public sphere.[27] It also supports the new ways in which human rights are being applied to a range of nonstate actors in current developments in international law. We can say, too, that care and solidarity are necessary to such a relational view of rights, by way of the motivation for them, as well as for their diffusion, and for their fulfillment; the arguments for these claims are developed in later chapters of this work.

Although the conditions for agency included in the list of human rights are general or widely applicable, they do not have to be interpreted in precisely the same way in all cultural and institutional contexts. They may vary to a degree nationally or regionally, as well as socially and culturally, though the basic rights (e.g., security and means of subsistence) would likely be subject to less variability in interpretation than the nonbasic. Certainly, too, the justice principle of equal positive freedom itself should not be taken as one that counsels sameness in distribution or rigorously equal shares. Further, the modes of realizing the various conditions specified in lists of human rights require a degree of

---

[25] Pogge, *World Poverty and Human Rights*, chapter 2.
[26] See also the discussion in Gould, "Coercion, Care, and Corporations."
[27] See, for example, Hilary Charlesworth, "What Are 'Women's International Human Rights'?," in *The Human Rights of Women*, ed. Rebecca J. Cook (Philadelphia, PA: University of Pennsylvania Press, 1994); Celina Romany, "State Responsibility Goes Private: A Feminist Critique of the Public/Private Distinction in International Human Rights Law," in *Human Rights of Women*, ed. Rebecca J. Cook (Philadelphia, PA: University of Pennsylvania Press, 1994), and Donna Sullivan, "The Public/Private Distinction in International Human Rights Law," in *Women's Rights, Human Rights*, ed. Julie Peters and Andrea Wolper (New York: Routledge, 1995).

differential specification depending on the particularities of social context, and also require substantial innovation in reforming existing institutions and developing new ones. Such reform can variously extend also to property law, to new modes of democratic procedure, and to a new emphasis on the provision of care and support for those who provide it. Dialogic forms of interpretation, including intercultural ones, necessarily play a role in their interpretation and casuistic application to particular contexts and practices – a theme that is taken up in some later chapters.

One final implication of this philosophical approach can be noted before considering the two conundrums sketched at the outset. From the principle of equal positive freedom, we can derive strong rights of democratic participation, as will be elaborated in Chapter 4. These rights pertain not only to participation within political institutions but in the range of institutions in economic, social, and cultural life. The argument is that taking part in common activities is one of the main conditions for freedom, as we have seen in this social account. And if people are not to be dominated by others within these common activities, they must have equal rights to codetermine these activities, that is, rights to participate in determining the goals and the course of the activities. Obviously, this presupposes a substantive and not only procedural conception of democracy in which deliberation plays an important role, and where majority voting, while usually required in large organizations, does not exhaust the meaning of the concept.

Human rights and global justice

I now want to suggest how this account – which foregrounds human rights in a certain interpretation of them – provides a way to break through two of the conundrums that have afflicted most discussions of global justice. I will also elaborate the elements of the approach somewhat further and consider certain objections to it at the theoretical level. In the last section of this chapter, I briefly sketch some practical directions for institutionalizing human rights, particularly those closely relevant to achieving justice.

As noted at the outset, the global justice discussion has often been framed as an opposition between cosmopolitan egalitarian views that require global aid or redistribution and alternative conceptions that privilege national political societies as the appropriate arena for redistribution.[28] Such antithetical formulations pose for us the first

---

[28] It should be noted that cosmopolitans can accept that there are duties that apply at levels or associations below the global order. But the problem of reconciling these with

the grounds & scope of justice.

problems of positive freedom?

conundrum: between the global claims of universal personhood or global interconnectedness on the one hand, and the nation-state or compatriot priority for economic distribution and redistribution on the other. The global claims can be understood in rigorously cosmopolitan terms founded in a notion of the equal consideration or distribution owed to each person worldwide, or instead may be rooted in the increasing social interconnections that are in fact emerging with globalization, where these interconnections themselves are regarded as a basis for newly global, or at least transnational, social responsibilities of justice. The first option is illustrated in some individualist global difference principle accounts, certain human rights approaches, and in luck egalitarian views applied globally.[29] The second variant is exemplified in Iris Marion Young's social connections model,[30] and to a degree in Pogge's account of the obligations resulting from the West's coercive imposition of exploitative systems on developing countries, although Pogge's commitment to human rights pulls somewhat in a more strictly cosmopolitan direction. The alternative emphasis on political society as a basis for redistribution is found in Thomas Nagel's reliance on systems of reciprocity as sources of obligation and in the accounts of David Miller and others that emphasize national ties or civic solidarity.[31] These latter views do not require that there be no duties of assistance or aid abroad, but may well be compatible with such duties, as is evident in Rawls's account[32] and Nagel's as well.[33]

The second conundrum is what may be characterized as the "demandingness" of egalitarian cosmopolitan approaches.[34] Approaches like luck egalitarianism or a difference principle applied globally pose this problem

the global ones remains, I suggest, insofar as it is a matter of which sort of duty or obligation should be privileged and also inasmuch as the contrasting approaches may involve different presuppositions about the priority of individuals globally or instead of nation-state groups.

[29] For the latter, see Tan, *Justice, Institutions, & Luck.*

[30] Iris Marion Young, "Responsibility and Global Labor Justice," *Journal of Political Philosophy* 12, no. 4 (2004); Iris Marion Young, "Responsibility and Global Justice: A Social Connections Model," *Social Philosophy and Policy* 23, no. 1 (2006).

[31] Thomas Nagel, "The Problem of Global Justice," *Philosophy & Public Affairs* 33, no. 2 (2005); Miller, "Against Global Egalitarianism."

[32] John Rawls, *The Law of Peoples* (Cambridge, MA: Harvard University Press, 1999).

[33] Nagel, "The Problem of Global Justice."

[34] In a certain sense, the first conundrum could be conceived to raise core concerns of demandingness as well, especially inasmuch as the obligations to those close to us are seen as compelling and as sufficiently challenging in themselves. However, my concern in articulating the first conundrum was to focus on the general tension between cosmopolitan and nation-state claims, which goes beyond issues of the demandingness of the cosmopolitan perspective. The conundrum of "demandingness," as described here, focuses on the issue of the stringency of the requirements of global justice.

statists.   cosmopolitans

Nagel Rawls Miller   Young Pogge Beitz Singer.

more of a continuum? (e.g. Young on social interactions),

not only practically but also theoretically. How can people's situations be compared across national and cultural borders and what mechanisms are to be used to affect the redistributions, presumably without making use of excessively coercive devices? Should these redistributions focus on resources, or goods, or opportunities, or the development of capabilities? What weight is to be given to people's own contributions to the production of the goods to be redistributed? (One would think that such contributions should count for something, after all.) And what about the various dis-utilities that global transfers can produce? How should these be put in the balance?

To begin with this second conundrum, we can observe that problems of demandingness would also affect the full implementation of the principle of justice that I have proposed – that is, the principle of equal positive freedom, understood as requiring prima facie equal access to the conditions of self-transformation or self-development. Yet, I would suggest that this principle, along with the theory that frames it, has advantages over some of the others in several respects: in putting the focus on both the negative and positive (or enabling) conditions for agency, in building difference into its understanding of people's expressions of agency in various cultural contexts, in its openness to both capacities and projects, and in the space it makes for collective or shared activities. Further, the principle in question already qualifies strictly equal access with the notion of "prima facie," in recognition of the weight that sometimes should be given to other, perhaps consequentialist, considerations and principles of contribution or desert. These come into play when this sort of principle is applied in actual political economies, where there may well be a need for some differential rewards for special skills and cultivated abilities. Despite these qualifications and putative advantages, it must be admitted that this principle would also be subject to a charge of demandingness if applied globally, since it would require the achievement of substantial levels of equality across nation-states and cultures, in the difficult context of economic globalization.

Even granting its "demandingness" in this sense, however, I believe that the principle of equal positive freedom can nonetheless serve as a useful goal or *heuristic* for the evolution of national and global institutions toward greater equality over time. Most significant, in distinction from other approaches, this one has the advantage of providing a *principled* way of prioritizing certain claims of global justice over others and thus provides the basis for a strategy for making progress in this domain. It does so by privileging human rights as those conditions most in need of being available to people worldwide. Further, among these rights, it distinguishes between basic and nonbasic ones, and in this way posits the fulfillment of the rights that protect or fulfill basic human needs as realizable goals for the nearer term. It thus takes a more practical, though not minimalist, approach to the realization of the more maximalist requirements of strongly egalitarian principles.

Among the basic conditions for any human activity whatever is access to means of subsistence. Yet, as noted, human rights are not to be taken as claims on others for direct provision but rather as goals and guides for the development of institutional frameworks that would realize them for everyone. Given the centrality of work to human existence, both as necessary for the provision of these means of subsistence and as a central source of meaningful activity in itself, this economic right gives rise in the first instance to a requirement that people be able to work (if they can) so as to meet their basic needs, or if they cannot do so, then other ways have to be found to make these means available to them, presumably through a system of welfare or of basic income.[35] I will point to some of the complexities in the implementation of such rights in the third section.

For now, we can note that aside from its philosophical strengths, a great advantage of a human rights approach is that it is already recognized in international law, including the economic and social rights. It was an important step forward, I think, for human rights to be enunciated in 1948 in the Universal Declaration of Human Rights (UDHR) and subsequently elaborated in the various UN Covenants and other agreements. These practical recognitions of their importance make the philosophy of human rights less of a pipedream, and provide a basis for sketching a path to their fuller realization. Of course, a great deal remains that is problematic in these international formulations. Several of the covenants have been ratified only by a subset of states. Notably, the United States is mostly absent with regard to the economic and social rights, the Convention on the Elimination of Discrimination against Women (CEDAW), and other important agreements. The list of rights covered is somewhat haphazard (there is the controversial right to a paid vacation)[36] and the prevailing doctrine of the interdependence of all the rights makes it very difficult to prioritize basic from nonbasic. Moreover, these rights have largely been given a statist interpretation, which they are only now slowly beginning to lose. That is, human rights were held to apply within states and, in some sense negatively, against the state. Thus their original

---

[35] For a proposal on basic income, see Philippe Van Parijs, *Real Freedom for All* (Oxford: Oxford University Press, 1995), chapter 2.

[36] International Covenant on Economic, Social and Cultural Rights, Art. 7(d). Of course, this is primarily to be understood as a means toward the availability to persons of some sort of leisure time and a break from constant work.

designers called for their constitutionalization exclusively at the level of nation-states.[37]

Despite these drawbacks, we can appreciate the significance of the recognition of basic human rights in international law. Economic rights are included in Article 25 of the UDHR as a person's "right to a standard of living adequate for the health and well-being of himself and of his family, including food, clothing, housing, medical care and necessary social services, and the right to security in the event of unemployment, sickness, disability, widowhood, old age or other lack of livelihood in circumstances beyond his control." A right to work is included among the provisions of the UDHR in Article 23. These rights are incorporated in international law in the International Covenant on Economic, Social and Cultural Rights, and specified in several articles there, especially Article 11. Of course, these rights are often honored in the breach, but at least their outlines are reasonably clear in principle and in law.

We can now comment on the first conundrum noted earlier, between global claims of universal personhood or global interconnectedness on the one hand, and nation-state priority for economic distribution and redistribution on the other. The view developed here is clearly on the cosmopolitan side, in insisting on the recognition of the claims of all to the basic conditions of life activity. Nonetheless, we need to give some weight to what is due to people in virtue of their participation in cooperative processes of production and also what is due to political communities more generally, where their legitimate claims may include also economic and cultural factors. The social connections model, in particular, recognizes these sorts of ties but sees them as increasingly extending more globally as contemporary economic relations expand across borders.

The overall theory I have developed attempts to incorporate all three of these factors in a coherent fashion – the cosmopolitanism of human rights, the claims of (democratic) political and other more local communities (including cities and subnational regions), and the growing social relatedness given globalization. Here, we can more narrowly frame the issue in terms of the sort of human rights approach the theory entails and its implications for global justice. First, human rights hold not only against states but, as goals, they require the development of a range of economic, social, and political institutions that would realize them. There is no reason to restrict these to institutions within the nation-state; transnational institutions and networks are required as well. Moreover, without going so far as to use human rights to cover all laws and rules of

---

[37] I later consider the new moves to regionalize human rights, and I have noted the fact that increasingly they are held to apply to nonstate actors.

whatever sort, we can see that such rights are increasingly being taken, correctly, to hold against institutions below as well as across the level of nation-states. Correlatively, we can propose that the redistributive effects we seek, aimed at alleviating global poverty and the elimination of exploitation, will require developing solutions that are not exclusively statist in their focus, but engage this variety of cross-border associations and networks.

Political and other communities also come into play if democracy is recognized as itself a human right, as I argue that it should be in Chapter 4. Although the UDHR and the International Covenant on Civil and Political Rights use the language only of political participation and free elections, a right to democracy is increasingly being recognized in international law.[38] Moreover, self-determination is recognized in the Covenant in its first article.[39] In addition, as I have argued in *Globalizing Democracy and Human Rights*, there are other important interconnections between human rights and democratic participation, beyond that these rights can serve to constrain democratic decisions.[40] As Henry Shue observed in his early work *Basic Rights*, democratic participation importantly works to implement and preserve economic rights.[41] I have argued that to determine what the impacts of policies are on people's human rights we need to hear from those affected and not only imagine these impacts, in a way that implicates forms of democratic input, if not full-scale democratic participation.[42] As I will note again in the final section, this supports new requirements of democratic accountability in the institutions of global governance and of transnational representation, if we are to fulfill people's human rights.[43] In general terms, I propose that wherever decisions or policies prospectively impact the possibilities for people to fulfill their basic rights they ought to be able to provide input into these decisions.

The emphasis on democratic participation suggests a role for political communities within global distributive processes, a role that moderates a thoroughgoing cosmopolitanism. Moreover, from the standpoint of

---

[38] Gregory H. Fox and Brad R. Roth, *Democratic Governance and International Law* (Cambridge: Cambridge University Press, 2000).

[39] While differing in meaning from democracy, self-determination is itself increasingly being understood in terms of democratic self-determination. For a discussion, see Carol C. Gould, "Self-Determination Beyond Sovereignty: Relating Transnational Democracy to Local Autonomy," *Journal of Social Philosophy* 37, no. 1 (2006).

[40] Gould, *Globalizing Democracy*, chapters 8 and 9.

[41] Henry Shue, *Basic Rights* (Princeton, NJ: Princeton University Press, 1980).

[42] Gould, *Globalizing Democracy*, chapter 9.

[43] Carol C. Gould, "Structuring Global Democracy: Political Communities, Universal Human Rights, and Transnational Representation," *Metaphilosophy*, Special Issue on Global Democracy and Political Exclusion, 40, no. 1 (2009).

economic justice, some recognition is required of the work and other contributions to productive processes that are made by members of a given economic community. Thus we cannot view the results of such production as simply open to redistribution to meet human rights criteria without considerable qualification.

Finally, in order to frame the issue of implementing these principles, it is important to emphasize the way in which nonstate actors can themselves support the achievement of global justice in such a human rights approach. This would involve the usual emphasis on civil society organizations like international nongovernmental organizations (INGOs) in their role in influencing the institutions of global governance and in representing people from the global south, but it equally emphasizes the role of social movements oriented to global justice. Besides this, as I propose in Chapter 5, solidarity networks of a new transnational sort can play a crucial role in working to eliminate oppression and aid others at a distance. These particularistic networks and associations, arising from social empathy with the situation of distant people and oriented to justice, importantly supplement a human rights approach based on the universalist recognition of people's equality and dignity.[44]

Before proceeding to propose some practical directions for moving to global justice, we can address an additional philosophical objection that may be posed to a human rights approach based on equal positive freedom. The objection could arise precisely from its claim to represent a more practicable approach to global justice than do theories that advocate a more stringent form of global redistributive egalitarianism. Does this practicability by way of a focus on human rights mean that the approach is no longer fully egalitarian, that it is merely sufficientist? The latter characterization designates principles or approaches to distributive justice that advocate meeting a certain threshold, say, one in which basic human needs are met, rather than aiming at full equality among persons. In the global distributive justice context, such sufficientist approaches are likely to privilege eliminating poverty rather than requiring a more thoroughgoing redistribution of wealth and income. It will be helpful, then, to indicate the ways in which the understanding of global justice here in terms of equal positive freedom, with its priority to meeting human rights, remains broadly egalitarian rather than merely sufficientist.

I understand equal positive freedom to be a cosmopolitan principle of justice that calls for prima facie equal rights of access to the

---

[44] Carol C. Gould, "Recognition in Redistribution: Care and Diversity in Global Justice," *Southern Journal of Philosophy* 46, Supplement (2007); Carol C. Gould, "Transnational Solidarities," *Journal of Social Philosophy*, Special Issue on Solidarity, ed. Carol Gould and Sally Scholz, 38, no. 1 (2007).

conditions of self-development or self-transformation. It can be observed that this principle operates at a more general level than many principles that are concerned only with distributive economic justice, whether within nation-states or more globally. The EPF principle does not only pertain to this aspect of justice. Even if the concern is with economic distribution alone, we can observe that this distribution depends not only on the redistribution of income, say, through systems of taxation, but is also centrally dependent on the organization of production processes. Thus even principles of economic justice per se need to be taken in the context of political economy as a whole and need to be as concerned with production as with distribution. They need to address exploitation and issues of property and democracy as they bear on production, along with the standardly discussed issues of how income, wealth, and other goods are to be distributed or redistributed. Crucially, the question of whether the production process is organized more democratically than at present has important implications for distribution (and more generally for people's equal agency and well-being), and thus needs to be part of a theory of economic justice.

The way production is organized is not just an instrumental matter for the possibility of achieving egalitarian distributions. In my view, the elimination of exploitation and of oppressive relations more generally themselves constitute elements of a just form of social, political, and economic organization, and they are directly required by the principle of equal positive freedom. So concerns about what has been called relational equality loom large in this account, but they are not seen here as being in conflict with requirements of economic justice (distributive or otherwise). Both of these are conditions for full justice on this account. Accordingly, the realization of rights to means of subsistence is not to be understood merely as a condition for the equality of citizens (whether national or global). It is required for the equal freedom that justice requires in my account. (Some of the important relations between recognition and redistribution are explicitly addressed later in this work, especially in Chapter 7.)

It is certainly the case that giving priority to basic human rights involves privileging the achievement of a certain threshold of well-being for people worldwide, and although less demanding than directly egalitarian principles of global distributive justice, accomplishing that level even of basic subsistence and a fortiori of an adequate level of well-being is surely demanding enough and would be a great accomplishment. Nonetheless, while prioritizing the basic human rights, the principle of equal positive freedom calls for the fulfillment of nonbasic but still essential human rights that specify conditions for people's fuller flourishing, including their development and cultivation of capacities, relationships, and projects beyond bare levels of free life activity. The realization of all these human rights requires both the transformation of existing institutions that currently block their fulfillment and the introduction of new ones to facilitate their achievement. As already intimated, and as will be developed in later chapters, it will require also the introduction of new forms of democratic participation in the range of these institutions – political, economic, and social. Further, the claims of democratic communities themselves can sometimes legitimately qualify the requirements of global distributive justice, though on the view here, the basic human rights of people globally should presumably have highest priority of fulfillment from a normative standpoint, even if particular democratic communities may not recognize it.

In these ways, then, a conception of equal positive freedom serves as a helpful heuristic or guiding principle for understanding these various requirements and for planning new directions to achieve them. As a regulative principle, it is firmly egalitarian, inasmuch as it calls for equal access to the conditions of self-development. However, this does not always require access to the very same set of conditions, and the qualification by "prima facie" recognizes that the application of the principle can occasionally be qualified by the need to take into account other relevant principles and practices. The principle can be expected to have somewhat more stringent application at the nation-state level than globally, as things are presently constituted, because some weight needs to be given to the claims of democratic political communities, as I have suggested. Nonetheless, I believe that the principle retains an important role as a regulative ideal, and also helpfully indicates the relation between various features of equality – equal liberties and freedom from oppression, and egalitarian distribution in the context of more egalitarian and democratic social, political, and economic processes. Most specifically for purposes of this chapter, it gives a key role to economic and social human rights, along with the traditional ones, in ways I have indicated here. The deeper philosophical basis of these human rights and the conception of the equality of agents that they entail will receive further attention in the second chapter of this work.

Some practical directions for implementation

In this final part, I want to propose, by way of a list, some suggestions for innovations in public policy and institutional reforms that would advance global justice through a human rights approach. The first three of these directions specifically concern human rights implementation, and the last set concern what could be regarded as conditions for fulfilling human rights more globally. A full answer to the question of how to realize economic and social rights worldwide would require addressing the current political economy in ways that are beyond the scope of this work. Strategies would have to be devised to deal not only with the financial and other economic crises that are more global than heretofore, but also with the growing inequalities that globalization is engendering, and to figure out how to implement access to basic income or other modes of provision for subsistence needs globally. But I will not be able to consider those here, limiting myself instead only to the elements of a human rights approach. In the list that follows, I emphasize directions that supplement existing ones like foreign aid in innovative ways, bypassing those that are stressed in the existing literature.

The first and easiest reform would be the introduction of what I have elsewhere called Human Rights Impact Assessments.[45] These can be required of all important actors in the global arena, including the institutions of global governance, and multinational corporations. Such human rights assessments can be modeled on current environmental impact or technology assessments, but would focus instead on the expected consequences of a decision, policy, or activity for the human rights (or at least the basic human rights) of those likely to be importantly affected. This would require that efforts be made to determine these impacts and, to the degree possible, enlist in this process those affected or their representatives, to provide the needed input. The assessments would have to show how basic human rights are not violated and instead protected, or enhanced if possible. This constitutes a rather minimal requirement in comparison with the scope of the global justice problem, but it can be implemented immediately, at least on a voluntary basis. It could be expected to help establish human rights standards – including the critical economic and social rights – as directly applicable to corporate conduct and to policy making by global institutions.

A second direction would encourage the further constitutionalization and more general juridification of human rights, including the economic and social rights. Economic and social rights, known as "second generation" rights, have already been incorporated into some constitutions, most notably, that of South Africa, which has also taken the lead in their judicial enforcement. These moves represent a promising direction that

---

[45] Gould, "Structuring Global Democracy." See also Ronald K. Mitchell, Bradley R. Agle, and Donna J. Wood, "Toward a Theory of Stakeholder Identification and Salience: Defining the Principle of Who and What Really Counts," *Academy of Management Review* 22 (1997); Robert A. Phillips, "Stakeholder Legitimacy," *Business Ethics Quarterly* 13, no. 1 (2003), and the discussion of these views in Bert van de Ven, "Human Rights as a Normative Basis for Stakeholder Legitimacy," *Corporate Governance* 5, no. 2 (2005).

suggestions for reform
– but who will enact them?

other states can emulate, and some have. Of course, this is not to say that constitutionalization is sufficient without actual efforts to promote the realization of human rights through legislative action and decisions by other policy-making bodies.

Third, regional human rights agreements need to be developed; they need to be adopted where they currently do not exist, and implemented where they do exist. Regionalization is an important current trend in global politics, and not only in its main exemplar, the EU (despite its recent economic travails). Economic regional arrangements are already reasonably developed, if not always well-functioning. Such regionalism has much to commend it in terms of human rights protections as well. Given the emergence of new cross-border local communities, broader region-wide human rights agreements can be used to protect the rights of the members of such communities (as discussed in Chapter 13). Furthermore, regional agreements on human rights allow some scope for diversity in the interpretation of these rights. For example, property rights can be subject to considerable variation in interpretation in this way. But we should also note the dangers in such variability, particularly in regard to women's rights. Europe, and more recently the EU, constitutes the most prominent regional arena for human rights protection and, increasingly, provision, and its courts of human rights have been path breaking in allowing citizens to appeal even against the laws and decisions of their own governments. Africa and the Americas also have regional agreements in place.[46] We can propose the development of such human rights agreements in other regions and also try to find new ways to make them really effective.

Turning now to the broader political economic context for the reduction of global inequalities and the provision of means of subsistence, we can propose, fourth, the need for new forms of global taxation, as well as measures to reform the existing tax system. This is a major area for further research and of course would be challenging to implement. As Gillian Brock notes, good arguments can be given for carbon taxes, Tobin-type taxes on global financial transactions, taxes on arms trades, and aviation fuel taxes.[47] She also argues effectively for multinationals to

---

[46] These regional instruments include the European Convention on Human Rights (1950) with its five protocols, along with the European Court of Human Rights; the American Convention on Human Rights (Pact of San Jose, adopted by the Organization of American States [OAS] in 1969), supervised by the Inter-American Commission on Human Rights and the Inter-American Court of Human Rights; and the African Charter of Human and Peoples' Rights of the African Union (1981).

[47] Gillian Brock, "Taxation and Global Justice: Closing the Gap between Theory and Practice," *Journal of Social Philosophy* 39, no. 2 (2008).

pay their fair share of taxes, with attendant requirements to eliminate tax havens, tax evasion, and deceptive transfer pricing schemes, along with requiring transparency in regard to the revenues paid for resources in developing countries.[48]

A fifth direction is the need to make international labor standards effective rather than merely enunciated. The human rights connection is given in the right to work and in the requirement of Article 23 of the UDHR for "just and favourable conditions of work," among other provisions of the Declaration and the International Covenant on Civil and Political Rights. These provisions call for the elimination of exploitative working conditions, which some have incorrectly regarded as justifiable as a way to eliminate global poverty, and which may instead contribute to its continuation. But the International Labor Organization (ILO) thus far establishes only requirements of "good practices" and has little enforcement capacity. Voluntary efforts by corporations as in the UN Global Compact are useful to a degree but are far from sufficient. I suggest that new regulatory mechanisms have to be devised in this domain. International labor standards are considered further in connection with democratic management at work, in Chapter 14 of this book.

The final directions for human rights implementation are tied to the key role played by democratic participation in the approach I have laid out. Thus, sixth, we need to increase democratic accountability in the institutions of global governance. While most International Relations theorists seem satisfied with aiming at lesser forms of accountability for such institutions, denying the relevance of democratic accountability in this context,[49] I believe that new ways have to be found to enable input into the policy making of these institutions by those affected by these policies. There are numerous proposals along these lines, for example by Joseph Stiglitz, Peter Willetts, and others, and these often focus on requirements of transparency as well as the representation of these affected people by INGOs.[50] Beyond this, I think we can look to Internet forums that would open the deliberations of the "epistemic communities" within these institutions to contributions from credentialed representatives of

---

[48] *Ibid.*

[49] Ruth W. Grant and Robert O. Keohane, "Accountability and Abuses of Power in World Politics," *American Political Science Review* 99, no. 1 (2005).

[50] Joseph E. Stiglitz, *Globalization and Its Discontents* (New York: W. W. Norton, 2002); Joseph E. Stiglitz, "Globalization and Development," in *Taming Globalization*, ed. David Held and Mathias Koenig-Archibugi (Cambridge: Polity, 2003), and Peter Willetts, "Remedying the World Trade Organisation's Deviance from Global Norms," in *Free and Fair: Making the Progressive Case for Removing Trade Barriers*, ed. P. Griffith and J. Thurston (London: Foreign Policy Centre, 2004).

broader publics.[51] And there is probably a role for even more open participation through wikis and other means. Some of these possibilities are explored in Chapter 12 on emancipatory networking.

Finally, we can mention two additional directions regarding democratization that are more far-reaching, but that are important for undergirding the proposals about human rights considered here. The first is the long-term need to devise new forms of transnational representation, extending even beyond the current institutions of global governance. Such forms of democratic representation would be important in order to provide the input into those institutions as I have proposed. In addition, while it is possible to adopt the various measures presented here by way of agreements among nation-states, in the longer run the growth of transnational communities and the enhancement of regionalization will require some procedures to assure the legitimacy of transnational regulation and law, including human rights law. This requires that we start thinking about new forms of transnational governance, perhaps primarily focusing on the regional, rather than global, level, as considered in the concluding chapter of this book.

A second democratic innovation, which I can only mention here, is perhaps the most difficult, though it can be implemented starting now. Effective respect for and fulfillment of the range of human rights in my view requires the democratization of the institutions of economic and social life, as well as the range of political associations and institutions. If human rights are to be recognized by nonstate actors and if the list of human rights also itself includes a right to democratic participation, it is reasonable to expect that such opportunities for participation would be introduced very generally, and not only at the level of nation-states. I have stressed this democratic direction in previous work[52] and it will come up for discussion in later chapters of this book as well.

Although the new practical directions sketched here may seem like something of a grab bag, I hope it can be seen that they are in fact based in a coherent philosophical approach to human rights and global justice. But I have also proposed that this philosophical approach itself will only work as a guideline for practice if it is a reasonably open conception in

---

[51] Carol C. Gould, "Global Democratic Transformation and the Internet," in *Technology, Science and Social Justice, Social Philosophy Today*, ed. John R. Rowan (Charlottesville, VA: Philosophy Documentation Center, 2007).

[52] See the arguments in Gould, *Rethinking Democracy*, and Carol C. Gould, "Economic Justice, Self-Management, and the Principle of Reciprocity," in *Economic Justice: Private Rights and Public Responsibilities*, ed. K. Kipnis and D. T. Meyers (Totowa, NJ: Rowman & Allanheld, 1985). Cf. David Schweickart, *After Capitalism* (Lanham, MD: Rowman & Littlefield, 2002).

its account of agency and its conditions and if it provides adequate space for diversity in interpretation and implementation. I suggest that such a philosophical approach needs to be responsive to current developments and to the real possibilities and challenges ingredient in contemporary social reality.

2   A social ontology of human rights

Introduction

The individualism of human rights has been regarded as both their strength and their weakness. As claims that individuals can make against the state and even perhaps against all other individuals for their fulfillment, these rights centrally appeal to an important notion of the inviolability of persons. Further, as pertaining to each individual simply in virtue of that person's humanity, such rights have a universalistic, and in this respect an egalitarian, dimension, stretching in a cosmopolitan way across time and place. Nonetheless, this strength has at the same time been held to constitute a profound weakness in the very conception of a human right. Insofar as such rights assert basic claims of each individual against others, an emphasis on human rights is thought to neglect our social nature, and the need for social cooperation for the achievement of most human goods. This putative asociality would also divert attention from the problematic power relations and forms of oppression that most urgently need to be redressed in contemporary forms of society.

In this chapter, I consider the philosophical basis for human rights and argue – in contrast to such views – that human rights are in important ways based on sociality and are themselves fundamentally social or relational conceptions, in ways that existing interpretations of them most often fail to recognize. Such relationality at the root of human rights will be seen to go beyond the correlativity of rights to duties or of rights to responsibilities. Further, when properly interpreted, the fulfillment of human rights, when understood in connection with the central norm of equal freedom, is implied by any critique we might give of domination and exploitation. The recognition of human rights, I suggest, can foster social cooperation while at the same time preserve an important regard for individuality. In order to develop these sizable claims, I will appeal

34

against atomism.

to what I have previously called social ontology[1] and show its import for our understanding of human rights norms.

In proposing this revisionist understanding of the philosophical basis of human rights, the investigation that follows goes beyond understanding these rights as primarily legal ones that hold against nation-states. The account focuses on their fundamental moral and social dimensions, which I believe can also serve to provide guidelines for interpreting and expanding existing legal notions of human rights. Within the moral sphere itself, it will be evident that we need to go beyond the idea, originally powerfully articulated by Henry Shue, that "human rights are the morality of the depths."[2] Rather, the suggestion will be that these norms can and should play a much broader role within social and political life. Further, while traditional views most often take human rights to protect individuals against grave wrongs perpetrated against them by their own nation-states or their governments, for example in the case of torture, or the abrogation of freedom of speech, or unreasonable search and seizure, the perspective here follows recent developments in political philosophy that take human rights to require wider-ranging institutional structures (including economic, as well as political, ones), along with transnational, rather than strictly national, institutions, if the rights are to be adequately fulfilled.

Likewise, human rights will be understood to range over a variety of economic and social rights, as well as civil and political ones. The UDHR provides a useful starting point for this sort of broad legal/moral account (despite its unsystematic and rather too extensive list), and many theorists have followed its approach by regarding the various enunciated rights as mutually interdependent. On this issue, I instead maintain the distinction I introduced in previous work between basic and nonbasic human rights,

---

[1] I originally used this term and elaborated a conception of social ontology in a short course on *Marx's Social Ontology* at the Graduate Center of the City University of New York in 1975, and subsequently in the book of the same title (Cambridge, MA: The MIT Press, 1978). A work that influenced me in constructing the term was Georg Lukács, *Zur Ontologie Des Gesellschaftlichen Seins*, 3 vols. (Neuwied: Luchterhand, 1971–3). It has recently come to my attention that the term social ontology was used by Joseph Gittler in 1950 in, "Social Ontology and the Criteria for Definitions in Sociology," *Sociometry* 14, no. 4 (1951): 8. In recent decades, the term, as well as the general project to which it refers, has become a commonplace in social philosophy. It has, of course, been variably interpreted, from views that seek to place sociality in the context of material factors to more phenomenological approaches. My own account takes social ontology as a theory of the nature of social reality, in terms of its basic entities, relations, and processes, and operates within an experiential or phenomenological framework. It is to be understood as a regional ontology rather than as a metaphysical theory.

[2] Shue, *Basic Rights*.

not human rights as rights against the state — in a negative sense.

keeping in mind that the latter remain essential, if not primary.[3] This distinction between basic and nonbasic human rights makes a human rights framework considerably more practicable than if all the rights are taken as wholly interdependent.

In what follows, I delineate key features of my own approach by way of a critical review of a few of the prominent accounts of human rights, focusing on how those accounts either incorporate or fail to adequately incorporate a conception of human sociality. Specifically, I raise some concerns about the otherwise strong agency approaches of James Griffin and Alan Gewirth, which, I suggest, at important junctures end up not being social enough, and I consider my own alternative in relation to theirs. I then turn to two (disparate) approaches that emphasize sociality or certain social and legal practices as at the basis of human rights – those of Jürgen Habermas and of Charles Beitz – but suggest that these views are (in different ways) ultimately unable to give an account of human rights as well-supported and fully universalist norms.

These critical considerations pose two large and difficult problems for the alternative account proposed here. First, and rather generally, how is it possible to preserve notions of agency and individuality while giving a stronger account of the interdependence of individuals? And second, how is it possible to give a universalist account that nonetheless recognizes varying historical and cultural understandings of human rights? Although these questions are too large to be adequately dealt with in the short frame of this chapter, I point to some directions for their resolution. First, I suggest that an effective constructive account will need to operate with a more open and relational conception of agency than on existing views. And second, it will need to add a conception of what I have called *concrete universality* to the abstractly universal approaches to human rights that have been traditionally advanced as their foundation. The challenge in that connection is to develop a view that gives weight to social practices without making human rights relative to existing, and perhaps pernicious, practices. I suggest that what I have called a "quasi-foundational" social ontological (though not "metaphysical") perspective is best able to mediate between the various desiderata of agency and relationality, and between historicity and normativity. Although I am unable to fully articulate this basis here, I hope to sketch some of its features as a springboard for further research.

---

[3] Gould, *Rethinking Democracy*, chapter 7, and Gould, *Globalizing Democracy*, chapters 1 and 9.

a. individualism v. communitarianism

b. universalism v. particularism.

Strongly individualist accounts of the basis for human rights

One theory that aims to provide a foundation for human rights is that of James Griffin in his *On Human Rights*. Griffin regards his approach as a "bottom up" one, inasmuch as it reflects on human rights as they are conceived in law and society and as they have historically come to be recognized since the Enlightenment. His theory articulates a conception of individual "personhood" as the justificatory core of the human rights idea, and he articulates this in terms of a conception of "normative agency," and as involving autonomy, liberty, and a minimum provision of goods necessary for such agency. The main notion is that persons are agents in having "a conception of a worthwhile life" (which is to be distinguished from having a single "plan of life"). In Griffin's terms, "what we attach value to, in this account of human rights, is specifically our capacity to choose and to pursue our conception of a worthwhile life."[4] He regards such normative agency as typical of adult human beings, and stipulates that children are only potential agents in this sense, while some disabled adults lack even that potential. Thus human rights on his view pertain to normative agents in this rather restrictive sense. Griffin suggests that limiting human rights in this way avoids the indeterminateness that has afflicted alternative accounts of them, as well as their inflation in some recent discourse to cover the entire moral realm. Of course, children and disabled adults have other moral rights, but not human rights (though he acknowledges that children could also plausibly be held to have human rights, although he opts for the view that they lack them).[5]

There are several issues to focus on in Griffin's account. The most obvious one, though not the most central to the theme of this chapter, is his restriction of human rights to a subset of humans (in a way reminiscent of Kant's account of moral personhood). Griffin's exclusionary account strikes me as problematic, since it loses the very force of the notion of the human that makes human rights norms such powerful instruments of social and legal change worldwide (at least potentially, given that this power is far from fully actualized). While it is true that boundary and extension issues inevitably arise with notions of the human, it seems clear that human rights, in their root conception, should pertain to all and only humans. I think we need to take an inclusionary approach, such that the conception of human rights sees them as fundamentally

---

[4] James Griffin, *On Human Rights* (Oxford: Oxford University Press, 2008), 45.
[5] *Ibid.*, chapter 2.

Griffin:
i) human rights pertain to those with normative agency.
ii) children & severely disabled lack this agency.
∴ iii) children & severely disabled lack human rights.

applying to children and to adults with disabilities, and in short, to all humans from birth to death. It is beyond the scope of this chapter to go into the issues surrounding who or what to call potential persons, but I think that Griffin goes astray in regarding children as only potential persons, rather than restricting this latter notion to embryos and fetuses. Even small babies display a sort of agency, though not the rich sense of normative agency that Griffin feels grounds human rights norms, in which such agents must have a "conception of a worthwhile life."

Significant for our purposes, here, is this high-level conception of personhood itself and the interpretation it gives of agency. Any account that builds a notion of "having a conception" into the basic idea of human agency is bound to exclude some humans. Having a conception of a good life is a fairly developed accomplishment. Moreover, the formulation itself seems distinctively liberal individualist in a way that is not obviously cross-cultural.

Yet, in some other important ways, Griffin's account is consonant with the one I gave of agency and human rights in my own *Rethinking Democracy* (1988).[6] I believe that a comparison of the approaches would be helpful to delineate some important similarities but also differences. My own view of agency and its conditions, I have claimed, is better able than Griffin's to support our attribution of human rights to all humans from birth to death, and also offers a more social account than Griffin's own, as well as one that is more open to the full range of human action and cultural expression. We can note that Griffin's emphasis on the high-level notion of normative agency does enable him to incorporate some of the richness and multiplicity of contemporary human rights norms, which more minimal accounts of agency open to all humans (e.g., those emphasizing negative liberty) would seem not to support. Thus because Griffin's approach includes the prerequisites for people to pursue their conception of the good, it requires not only basic civil and political rights, but also rights to a level of welfare. However, I think there is a better way of keeping human rights open to all humans while at the same time making room for this multiplicity of human rights, including the more demanding ones included in the UDHR.[7] In the course of the subsequent discussion here, I will point to that approach, elaborated in my previous work, including my *Globalizing Democracy and Human Rights* (2004). It is an approach that distinguishes basic agency, taken in an open and inclusive sense, from the development or flourishing of this agency, but at the same

---

[6] Gould, *Rethinking Democracy*, especially chapters 1, 3, and 7.

[7] This is not to say that all those rights are always optimally formulated in the international documents and not open to future reinterpretation or revision.

time ties these two aspects of agency together. Such an account is able to support a useful distinction between basic and nonbasic (though still essential) human rights. I also suggest that this sort of approach enables us to accommodate the important emphasis on both freedom and dignity that pervades the international human rights documents.

My account of agency with its accompanying understanding of human rights is developed most fully in *Rethinking Democracy*, on the basis of a social ontology of what I call "individuals-in-relations," a conception I introduced originally in *Marx's Social Ontology*.[8] This conception of agency appeals to a norm of positive freedom, interpreted in a different way from the notion of positive liberty that liberals such as Isaiah Berlin were at pains to criticize. I distinguish a basic sense of agency characteristic of human beings, and consisting in intentionality or choice as a feature of human action, from the exercise of this agency in the development of capacities or the realization of long-term projects or goals. The first sense is not to be taken as restricted to purely conscious or conceptual activity but I suggest is evident in human life activity as a mode or way of being. I characterize the latter sense of agency in terms of a notion of self-development or self-transformation, which can take both individual and collective forms, and emphasize that such self-transformation is a process that transpires over time. If we say that basic agency involves intentional action or choices, we can see that self-development presupposes this capacity for choosing. However, beyond this, a process of self-development (or "freedom to" and, in this sense, positive freedom) requires that choices be effective and involves also the cultivation of capacities, both distinctively individual ones and more generalized social ones. For this agency to be effective and to develop in these ways, a set of concrete conditions are needed, including both freedom from constraints on one's choices (including the negative liberties and also freedom from domination), as well as the positive availability of what I have called enabling conditions of action (both material and social).[9] I have suggested that human rights specify these necessary conditions of action. Where these are conditions for any human life activity whatever (e.g., security of the person, subsistence, and liberty), we have basic human rights, which presumably should have priority for fulfillment. Beyond this, the essential conditions for fuller flourishing or for self-development constitute the nonbasic, though still important, human rights.

[8] Gould, *Rethinking Democracy*, especially chapters 1 and 2, and Gould, *Marx's Social Ontology*, especially chapter 1.

[9] For a fuller discussion of this distinctive sense of agency and of self-development, including the limits there may be on it, see Gould, *Rethinking Democracy*, especially chapter 1.

for rights to be meaningful, the bearers of rights must be understood as socially embedded.

agency depends upon conditions. but the realisation depends upon agency.

The distinctive advantage of this view, vs. that of Griffin, is that the notion of basic agency is open and inclusive whereas his is exclusionary. Inasmuch as choice or intentionality is taken as characteristically human, it applies to humans as a class and thus can more easily support the universality necessary for an adequate account of human rights. Nonetheless, the account here also emphasizes that this bare capacity of choice is insufficient without the conditions for its exercise. It articulates a richer conception of freedom as self-development or self-transformation of persons (including the development of capacities and realization of goals), understood as a "normative imperative" posited in free human activity at the more basic level. Griffin, by contrast, is forced to introduce a single, high-level, notion of personhood as the justification for human rights, inasmuch as he sees that many of those rights are rather demanding and involve a complex exercise of capacities. Unfortunately, as we have indicated, Griffin is thereby forced to exclude a large number of humans from having human rights, including not only infants, but also children, as well as many people with disabilities. My account, by contrast, takes the basic conception of human agency as what we recognize when we say that human beings have human rights, but also holds that such agency must be cultivated or elaborated in the course of our lives, which I have emphasized requires a substantial set of conditions.[10] Unlike in Berlin's own account, however, these conditions are not just externally necessary for the achievement of freedom, but are integral to the overall conception of positive freedom itself, since human action always operates on such conditions, or takes place within them.

As I have indicated, among these conditions are social requirements of freedom from domination and oppression, as well as the need for recognition and the provision of care, welfare, and education over the course of a life. Thus the account here is able to make room for both traditional civil and political rights, and the newer social, economic, and cultural rights. The requirement for people to be free from constraint supports both liberty and nondomination, while the broader emphasis on freedom in the positive sense goes beyond security of the person as customarily understood to encompass also the newer requirements for what has been called human security. We can suggest too, but without elaborating it here, that these human rights can be construed as required for the full recognition of the dignity of persons as well, given the close

---

[10] While Griffin is able to recognize a number of demanding human rights as well (though not all of them in the Universal Declaration of Human Rights), my suggestion here has been that he is able to do so only by positing an overly restrictive basis for human rights, in his account of personhood.

connection between the notion of agency, taken as free in the twofold sense discussed here (namely, freedom as the capacity of choice and its development in forms of flourishing) and the understanding of dignity in the human rights documents. The latter goes beyond respect for purposes to an appreciation of the conditions that make people's lives bearable and indeed potentially flourishing.

It is worth noting as well that the distinction between conditions necessary for human life activity in an ongoing manner and those required for its flourishing, including in diverse social and political contexts, helps to clarify how basic human rights apply to all humans in roughly similar ways, while political and social rights can reasonably take more specific forms (as they do in the international documents) and also can vary to a degree in their application in diverse forms of social and cultural organization. Taking human rights to include both primary (basic) and secondary (nonbasic) rights has the further advantage of retaining the highest urgency for the protection and provision of the basic conditions for life and liberty, while also including among the human rights themselves certain important conditions that are often relegated to optional status as merely civil matters, to be decided by particular nation-states. In this way, this approach explicitly seeks to push human rights theory and practice to go beyond a minimalist account and to devise ways of institutionalizing the richer set of rights pointed to in the UDHR and other documents. Yet, the distinction between most urgent rights and other of the human rights also suggests how their fulfillment can proceed in a practicable and effective way.

The central understanding of individuals as interdependent proposed in this approach, that is, understood as individuals-in-relations, leads not only to differences in what are taken to be human rights (that is, in the list of such rights), but also affects the basic justification that can be given of human rights, which here appeals to a norm of equal freedom and the conditions needed for making freedom effective. In this proposed approach to justification, we can see a distinction not only from Griffin's theory, but also from Alan Gewirth's, to whose approach the view here is similar in some ways (particularly in interpreting rights in terms of the necessary conditions for agency).

In his influential approach to justifying human rights, in *The Community of Rights* and elsewhere, Gewirth formulates an argument for human rights as moral rights to freedom and well-being, which he thinks each agent must recognize in others on pain of logical inconsistency. Without reviewing the argument in detail, or the various criticisms that have been advanced against it, we can note that Gewirth operates with a conception of people as "prospective purposive agents" who act for goals that they regard as good.[11] He holds that they must claim for themselves freedom and well-being as necessary conditions of their action. Gewirth further argues that this "must" supports a claim on the part of agents to their having a right to these conditions. Beginning from this prudential perspective of a single agent, Gewirth believes that we can universalize this claiming in that it is a matter of logical consistency that any other agent, similar in all relevant respects, would equally require these conditions. Gewirth suggests that this universalization yields a moral perspective in which all other human beings also have rights to freedom or well-being, as human rights.

Gewirth tends to think that these rights do not apply to infants or to people who are severely cognitively disabled, which is a problem for his view. Although his account of purposive activity is somewhat less demanding than Griffin's, it nonetheless is more robust than the emphasis on choice or intentional activity as a basis for universal recognition that I suggest. But apart from this, the justification Gewirth offers differs at crucial points from the one I would give. Gewirth has been criticized especially for the transition he makes from "must" in the prudential perspective of the agent in which the agent must (i.e., needs to) have freedom and well-being as conditions to the idea that the agent has rights to these conditions in that it is not permissible for others (seemingly a different sense of must) to interfere or that they have duties not to interfere.[12] Equally problematic for my purposes is Gewirth's move from the prudential to the moral perspective. That is, universalizing my claiming freedom and well-being as rights might only amount to the idea that I recognize that others will likewise claim freedom and well-being, but not yet amount to their having a right to those conditions of action.[13]

The account I gave in *Rethinking Democracy* proceeds rather differently. It argues that the moral perspective requires a stronger and preexisting commitment to the sociality of individuals if the requisite rights are to be generated. It proposes not only that people are agential in the open sense specified earlier but also that they are fundamentally interdependent. The social ontology of individuals-in-relations sees these relations as constitutive of individuals in the sense that they become who they are in and through these relations, to put it in quasi-Hegelian terms. But it crucially differs from holistic social accounts, in which individuals are

---

[11] Alan Gewirth, *The Community of Rights* (Chicago, IL: University of Chicago Press, 1998), 16–19.

[12] See James Nickel and David A. Reidy, "Philosophical Foundations of Human Rights." See also Jamie Lindsay, "Gewirth's Argument to the Principle of Generic Consistency" (Unpublished manuscript, 2011).

[13] Nickel and Reidy, "Philosophical Foundations of Human Rights."

wholly constituted by their relations or by the community of which they are a part, inasmuch as I locate the power of change as arising from individuals as agents. That is, individuals remain capable of choosing and changing their relations (though often only through collective rather than individual action), but are then formed or constituted by these relations (as well as by previous ones).

In my view, the process of recognizing other human beings as basic agents (i.e., recognizing them as manifesting intentional activity) is already a feature of everyday experience. It is evident, for example, in the reciprocity of greetings ("Hello, how are you?" "I'm fine thanks, how are you?"), and in such elementary experiences as avoiding bumping into each other on the street (by meeting the other's glance and moving in an appropriate direction), which Goffman explicated as an instance of his account of the interaction of pedestrians as "vehicular units."[14] It is also evident in the reciprocity of discourse, as Habermas has emphasized. The basic forms of equality and reciprocity posited in these customary and practical (and most often embodied) interactions, whether verbal or not, are elaborated in other forms of reciprocity, including widespread instrumental ones (e.g., "tit for tat," or exchange for mutual benefit), along with more robust social forms of reciprocal respect and the reciprocity involved in group action oriented to shared goals, and ultimately in forms of genuinely mutual aid.[15] I suggest that such stronger forms of recognition of others as equals are previsioned in the elementary practices of everyday life, which involve reciprocally regarding others as agents, at least in the basic sense, that is, as choosers who manifest intentionality in their life activity (but who do so in diverse ways).

Needless to say, elementary experience can also include forms of misrecognition, in which denigrating views of others are often built into our ordinary interactions as well. Thus it is certainly possible to internalize and to manifest attitudes that stereotypically downgrade others or display oppressive attitudes of other sorts. In extreme cases, we can almost convince ourselves that the others are no better than animals or things to dispose of, or more weakly and commonly, are simply instrumental to our purposes. So I do not wish to imply that ordinary experience is fully egalitarian by any means. Actual relations of oppression and domination can inform that experience and our modes of perception so that we grasp

---

[14] Erving Goffman, *Relations in Public: Microstudies of the Public Order* (New York: Basic Books, 1971), 5–18.

[15] Carol C. Gould, "Beyond Causality in the Social Sciences: Reciprocity as a Model of Non-exploitative Social Relations," in *Epistemology, Methodology and the Social Sciences: Boston Studies in the Philosophy of Science*, ed. R. S. Cohen and M. W. Wartofsky (Boston and Dordrecht: D. Reidel, 1983).

others as lesser, in very immediate and almost automatic ways. However, it seems to me that the basic idea of recognizing the other as a human being is evident in germ despite that fact. As Hegel early observed in his account of mastery and servitude along somewhat similar lines, the master cannot succeed in subordinating others whom he regards as not fully human in a way that is satisfying (precisely because in their subjugated state they are regarded as lesser and unworthy, and thus incapable of fully recognizing the master as free).[16]

However, beyond the basic recognition of others in ordinary experience, we can come to see that the choice or intentional activity that grounds it is insufficient or ineffective without access to the conditions that support the development of people's various capacities and the realization of longer-term goals, as well as the cultivation of relationships (what I have called positive freedom). Taken without these conditions, choice remains bare or abstract, without consequence. This recognition of the importance of the prerequisites for effective freedom is not just a rational matter. Instead, in virtue of our interdependence and embodiment, we each necessarily and *ab initio* make social claims on others for the fulfillment of these conditions of activity.

But what supports the validity of these claims that we make on each other, that is, their moral status as valid claims or rights? My suggestion is that we cannot get to this dimension of rightness by supposing that we reason from what we need as individuals with specific goals to what others similarly situated need (seemingly involving an argument by analogy), along Gewirthian lines. This would yield only the observation that others make similar claims rather than that they have valid claims, although the recognition of equal status implied in that argument is an important feature and needs to be retained. Moreover, the Gewirthian argument appears to mistakenly suppose that the individual's interests and goals, as well as the conditions for action can be identified in this elaborated form prior to the recognition of other individuals, whereas, in fact, the individual in this strong sense (which goes beyond bare choice and intentionality) is already socially constituted. Instead, I think we recognize the basic agential power in others, which is equally characteristic of each of them. Beyond basic agency, we can come to recognize that the

---

[16] G. W. F. Hegel, *Phenomenology of Spirit*, trans. A. V. Miller (Oxford: Oxford University Press, 1977), 111–19 ("Independence and Dependence of Self-Consciousness: Lordship and Bondage"). For Hegel, the achievement of mutual rather than one-sided recognition was a product of a historical development. In the account in this chapter, reciprocal recognition is understood as posited in germ in certain everyday practices, though it remains far from a robust recognition of each as free and is consistent with the prevalence of forms of domination.

agency of each is inadequate without access to conditions and without the elaboration of social support through systems of mutual aid that we all need, and that shape us, whether in particularistic or more universal ways.

The argument for equally valid claims here, that is, *prima facie* equal rights of access to the conditions (following Feinberg's account of rights as valid claims) therefore involves several features beyond those appealed to in Gewirth's account:

(1) The idea is that our experience as agents is already normative, that is, endowed with values and is value endowing. More precisely, on my view this agential power is a source of value and this agency also affirms itself as valuable in the process of self-transformation or self-development. In this sense, the social ontology pointed to here is already normative.

But:

(2) This creative and valuing agency is also interactive and socially constituted. It is essentially open to others and expresses our need for and dependence on each other. Such interdependence and mutual neediness involve elements of both inter-constitution through processes of recognition and the necessity for collective rather than only individual action for the realization of many aims and goals.

(3) The everyday recognition of basic agency as free and thus as equal in a minimal sense is the germ of the elaborated recognition that each must not be dominated or oppressed, if their capacities are to be developed, their goals realized, and their relationships allowed to flourish. Such freedom from domination and the positive freedom to transform ourselves (individually or in common activity with others) involve claims we make on each other both for recognition of our agency and for the positive provision of means of action.

(4) Given the importance not only of interdependence but also embodiment, a set of such means or conditions of action, including basic life and liberty and extending to means of subsistence and other social and economic factors, are needed by each and realizable only jointly.

From these various presuppositions, then, we can see that people can be said to make not only claims but also valid claims on others for the fulfillment of the basic conditions of action. This follows from the normative fact of their equal (basic) agency and from the deep features of mutual neediness and embodiment. In contexts in which there is a need to recognize and adjudicate among the various claims that each makes on others, we can recognize that no one has more of a claim on these conditions for action than any other (by virtue of the equality of their basic agency ingredient in their human status), and they each need to be free from domination for self-transformation (individually or collectively). Their sociality signifies that they necessarily depend on each other and are inter-constituting, such that their agency is what it is only in a social context of cooperation (whether implicit or explicit). Inasmuch as they are equally agents, where this agency is valuable and where it operates necessarily through structures of interdependence, no one has a right to dominate others and they equally require access to the conditions of self-transformation, material and social. The value of access to the conditions arises from the value of free agency as such, which though recognized in germ, that is, in its basic forms, necessarily aims at further transformation and development by way of institutional structures of interdependence (and especially economic and political institutions, at least in modern forms of society), as well as particularistic forms of care. In my view, while the features of agency and interdependence are given in the basic structure of experience and obtain elemental recognition there, in order that these features can come to be widely acknowledged to extend to the broad requirements of universal human rights, historical processes of development are needed.

For the various reasons given above, the normativity of equal claims such as is involved in human rights as moral and ultimately as legal rights cannot therefore be derived simply from a first-person perspective coupled with a process of reasoning about its universality, as in Gewirth's account. Rather it only seems to be derivable in this way if we abstract from the feature of interdependence, which, like that of free activity, is a fundamental aspect of human action and interaction. Recognizing interdependence, however, does not mean that the power of agency, evident in ordinary experience and developed over time, can be reduced to any particular set of social relations; rather, it is also capable of transforming the very conditions of agency – material and social – though often only jointly with others. (Of course, this is not to say that this transformation is bound to occur; only that it is a possibility or potentiality of human action.) We can observe too that reason plays a role in this recognition of the equal agency of each, as Gewirth emphasizes, but that empathy and solidarity are also important, both as aspects of such processes of recognition, and in the emergence and development of individuality itself.

On the view presented here, then, the equality of agents can be seen to be the reverse side of the critique of domination or oppression. In order to be able to criticize the latter forms, we need the recognition of the value of agency and of its status as a characteristic feature of humans. I have suggested that when human activity is seen as free, presupposing both intentionality and its elaboration in processes of capacity formation, realizing individual and collective ends and cultivating relationships, we can find a basis for the critique of misrecognition and of one-sided forms of recognition. However, such equal agency has hardly been overtly acknowledged in any more than the barest and implicit forms. Even in contemporary societies, there is regrettably considerably more oppression, domination, or exploitation, than equal treatment or reciprocal recognition of agency. This raises for us the need to articulate how the relevant human rights norms are related to social and historical practices, and to further develop the social aspects of human rights and more generally the ways they can be said to be relational.

Social and practice-oriented conceptions of human rights

I would like now to briefly turn to the more social account of human rights found in Jürgen Habermas and to the practice-oriented one advanced by Charles Beitz. I want to consider some of the implications of their approaches for the question of the basis of human rights, as well as to take note of the differences of the account proposed here from theirs.

In Habermas's relatively late magnum opus, *Between Facts and Norms*, human rights are given an importance beyond that found in his earlier works.[17] In a way that partly contrasts with the approach here, Habermas conceives of human rights as emerging in the sphere of law rather than morality. I propose instead that human rights as fundamental normative claims of each on others ground human rights as legal rights. But these are not moral rights in Habermas's sense, taken as strictly individualistic duties towards others. Rather, I want to interpret these basic claims in social terms, though still normative ones. In Habermas's conception, while law and politics are capable of being organized normatively in terms of the discourse principle, that legal-political sphere, as including both democracy and rights, is now understood as separate from the moral domain. For Habermas (at least in *Between Facts and Norms*), as in prevailing understandings of human rights, the classic rights of life, liberty, and property pertain to citizens within a democracy, and he sees these rights as coming into being along with popular sovereignty or political autonomy itself. Popular sovereignty, for Habermas, gives his core discourse principle a legally institutionalized form, which is at the same time the "logical genesis of rights."[18] According to Habermas, "This

---

[17] Jürgen Habermas, *Between Facts and Norms: Contributions to a Discourse Theory of Law and Democracy*, trans. William Rehg (Cambridge, MA: MIT Press, 1996), especially chapter 3.
[18] *Ibid.*, 121.

system [of rights] should contain precisely the rights citizens must confer on one another if they want to legitimately regulate their interactions and life contexts by means of positive law." He refers to such rights as "conditions for a discursive exercise of political autonomy."[19]

In this way, for Habermas, human rights hold against nation-states, as in the classical models, though they presumably could be constitutionalized at supranational levels as well. On such an interpretation, however, it is not clear how they can gain a fully universalist dimension as rights of everyone worldwide, which seems to me a great strength of this concept, along with their resulting transnational critical dimension. Habermas indicates that the rights will, to a degree, be specific to each political community. While this allows for some helpful diversity of interpretation and application, it does not explain their transnational or fully cosmopolitan dimension. Clearly, Habermas is concerned to emphasize a postmetaphysical justification for rights, and to eschew any notion of them as natural, or even as necessarily founded in structural features of human action. But given their tie to legality and democracy in his view, it remains unclear what their basis or justification is beyond the requirement that they are required by formal and procedural principles of law and democratic discourse. Habermas's guidance is to say that they arise from "applying the discourse principle to the general right to liberties – a right constitutive of the legal form as such."[20] Inasmuch as they accord with the discourse principle, these rights are understood to arise in a communicative and socially interactive context, and, as he says, concomitantly with political autonomy, as two sides of the same coin, so to speak. His account is thus a social one, but one in which rights are taken as emerging in post-conventional legal contexts, and pertaining primarily to nation-states. Aside from not doing justice to the cosmopolitan appeal of human rights, this view cannot account for the urgent need to fulfill human rights precisely where states are weakest or even absent.[21]

Like many other theorists, Habermas understands human rights as primarily civil and political rights, which is not surprising, given that he sees human rights as being tied to political democracy and political autonomy. Partly as a consequence, his view treats economic and social rights as secondary, and they come in as conditions for effective political democracy. This reflects a common, though I think mistaken, view of social and economic rights, as required for the sake of political equality, rather than for fulfilling basic human needs. It is partly to accommodate

[19] *Ibid.*, 122.   [20] *Ibid.*, 121.
[21] Cf. Jeffrey Flynn, "Habermas on Human Rights: Law, Morality, and Intercultural Dialogue," *Social Theory and Practice* 29, no. 3 (2003).

the latter requirement, now recognized in many countries worldwide, that I think we have to introduce a more general and fundamental conception of human rights.

The sociality of Habermas's view more generally, arises primarily from the way it connects law to the Discourse principle, that is, the principle that: "Just those action norms are valid to which all possibly affected persons could agree as participants in rational discourses."[22] What human rights norms protect are both liberties and political rights that are important to citizens within a democratic state, and which they can discursively justify to each other, in a way required by their communicative freedom in that context. The conditions of discourse are expressed in historically changing forms, however, rather than being understood as protections of fundamental agency, taken apart from or prior to or other than this discursive context, which Habermas understands here as a specifically legal one. In this way, Habermas's view contrasts with the standard liberal view, which presupposes individual agency as fundamental.

With his emphasis on communication, whether understood in "quasi-transcendental" or in a wholly nonfoundationalist fashion, Habermas's view is on the side of those who emphasize the justifications or rational arguments we can give each other to be fundamental.[23] Indeed, Habermas seems to see the rights themselves as emerging in a historical context, and thus capable of a reconstructive account. This contrasts with an account of human rights as conditions for human life activity or agency and as involving centrally the fulfillment of needs, including bodily ones. Habermas's approach also privileges one dimension of social practice and interaction, namely communication and discourse, and delimits that to the legal and political domain. In contrast, I seek to build on more recent expanded interpretations of human rights as centrally including social and economic rights that address our embodied and relational existence. I see their basis not only in discourse, communication, and justification, but in the fundamental social claims we make on each other to cooperate to meet needs and common goals, as well as in our caring relations with each other. In such contexts, we recognize each other as agents, yet not only as individualized but as socially related and mutually dependent.

Despite its great strengths, then, a Habermassian account is limited in the above ways. I have elsewhere focused on the exclusionary aspects of a view that privileges discourse in this way, and have suggested difficult sorts of circularity that are evident in discursive approaches to

---

[22] Habermas, *Between Facts and Norms*, 107.
[23] See also Rainer Forst, "The Justification of Human Rights and the Basic Right to Justification: A Reflexive Approach," *Ethics* 120, no. 4 (2010).

justifying norms.[24] An implication for human rights, however, is that the freedom and equality of participants in discourse (or politics) are not seen as independently required by their agency but as justified as conditions for discourse (and more specifically in the context of law). But it is then unsurprising that the norms that emerge in such discursive contexts would turn out to include the very freedom and equality already presupposed in discursive practices themselves.

An alternative practice-based account of human rights is advanced by Charles Beitz in his influential book *The Idea of Human Rights*.[25] Without elaborating his theory here, we can note that at least relative to the moral individualist views considered earlier, his account is rather deflationary, and emphasizes the contemporary practice of human rights enunciation and protection in the context of international relations. Beitz presents a model of that practice, understanding human rights as the protection by nation-states of important human interests as a matter of international concern. The account articulates human rights in terms of the norms ingredient in that practice, with attention focused on the way human rights operate in that international domain, in a way that is consonant with Rawls's approach if not directly parallel to it. But there is also, perhaps inevitably, an appeal to notions of fundamental human interests, which we will presumably agree on cross-culturally, though Beitz seeks to distance himself from agreement views in the first part of his work, along with giving criticisms of what he terms naturalistic approaches that elaborate contemporary versions of natural rights theory.[26]

The restriction to contemporary international human rights practice lends the account specificity but also raises questions concerning whether such an approach can retain the important critical and normative edge of human rights as fully cosmopolitan norms. Beitz holds that these norms do preserve that edge, as is evident in his discussions of their role in calling for the elimination of global poverty and in requiring women's human rights. But I suggest that they do so for him only by means of a tacit appeal to a notion of fundamental human interests, comparable to the way universalistic notions of this sort are appealed to in foundational (or in his terms, naturalistic) approaches to human rights. Moreover, to

---

[24] See Carol C. Gould, "Democracy and Diversity: Representing Differences," in *Democracy and Difference: Changing Boundaries of the Political*, ed. Seyla Benhabib (Princeton, NJ: Princeton University Press, 1996), and Gould, *Globalizing Democracy*.

[25] Charles Beitz, *The Idea of Human Rights* (Oxford: Oxford University Press, 2009).

[26] For Beitz, agreement views understand human rights as the product of overlapping cultural perspectives and gain their authority from that intercultural agreement. Naturalistic conceptions for him conceive of human rights as possessed by all humans, simply in virtue of their humanity, rather than as a matter of legal enactment. *Ibid.*, 49–50, 73–4.

the degree that his discussion limits itself to contemporary human rights practice and the norms ingredient in it, we can ask why this practice should be taken to have this sort of priority and why its norms should be adhered to in the first place. Moreover, while Beitz gives a critique of what he calls naturalistic and agreement views, it is not clear that the interpretation he gives of those are the strongest existing versions available, particularly of the foundationalist approaches.

In any case, I suggest that the account I propose here is not simply naturalistic in Beitz's terms and certainly does not follow natural rights theory per se. Rather, it aims to combine both given and social understandings of agency and interaction, and also assigns a role to practices, as well as to cross-cultural dialogue. The practices I draw on are more basic social ones, rather than simply those evident in current international relations and law. I believe that only such a view is capable of guiding the further development of human rights in a way that is relevant to the emerging regionalization in world politics, as well as to controlling the economic forces of globalization in democratic and rights-respecting ways. It remains unclear to me how an analysis of the norms of contemporary practice can have this sort of critical role (beyond holding those who have already subscribed to them to account for these norms). Moreover, it is not clear how, despite its strengths in modeling contemporary practice, such an account can escape a problematic historicism in regard to norms and be able to succeed in providing guidance for future development of either the human rights conception generally or more specific concepts of human rights that articulate features of fundamental human interests.

The universality of human rights

I have questioned whether either of these social or practice-oriented conceptions is able to give sufficient weight to human rights as fundamental protections of individuals. We need an adequate basis for regarding human rights as more than contingent or relative to a given time and place. And we should have reason to expect that human rights will retain their importance even if states became transformed into less state-like entities, such that these rights give us legitimate claims on others in a more cosmopolitan framework. Thus they cannot be only protections given by our citizenship or our political community, but more fundamentally call on us to devise institutions that may serve to realize them, whether those institutions take the form of states or not.

The question is, then, how an account can be adequately *historical* and attentive to divergent contexts of practice and the emergence of norms,

practice-dependence?

without at the same time being *historicist*, such that these norms would be conceived as relative to time and place. As we have seen, this historicism can be a problem for views that place exclusive emphasis on practices, to the degree that they are limited to holding a given practice to the norms implicit in it. Alternatively, procedural approaches to norm discovery may covertly introduce those very norms or values into the process itself and thereby rather too easily achieve the universal range they aspire to. I have suggested that this problem can afflict counterfactual strategies that propose to rely on what people would agree to under ideal conditions, inasmuch as prerequisites of freedom and equality are implicitly built into these procedures from the beginning. In such cases, it is unsurprising that the same values of freedom and equality become aspects of the norms that are agreed to.[27]

I have instead proposed an explicitly normative basis for human rights, understanding it as having two interrelated elements – (equal) agency and its elaboration or development, the first referring to a capacity serving as a condition for the second. While agency as a basic existential capacity or power is implicitly recognized in ordinary interaction, it does not merely exist to the degree that it is recognized. As a capacity for change and self-transformation, it is manifest in the intentionality of human action and in our concrete ways of being in the world. Yet, as inseparable from ongoing processes of human life activity, such agency is partly constituted by previous social relations, and by ongoing contexts of shared meanings and practices, which are appropriated and elaborated subsequently in new ways, through concrete responsive and collective relations with others. This agency-in-relations, moreover, develops over time, both in the life of an individual and of a collectivity or cultural group. As a capacity for freedom-in-interdependence with others, such agency may also come to be explicitly recognized in its normative importance in the course of historical development. Its more concrete elaboration in processes of capacity formation, realization of long-term projects, and the cultivation of relationships can also come to be acknowledged as important aspects of really effective freedom.

The proposed approach, then, has a quasi-transcendental or indeed quasi-foundationalist aspect in its reliance on a norm of equal agency (or more fully equal positive freedom). But the analysis also gives considerable weight to specific social relations as they emerge historically, and particularly the overcoming of relations of domination and exploitation, which in turn enable the fuller and more inclusive recognition of agency. The account thus differs from traditional liberal or transcendental ones

---

[27] See also Gould, *Globalizing Democracy*, chapter 1.

human rights as non-natural, post-metaphysical.

in not supposing that agency even as a capacity or mode of being is complete *ab initio*. With historical accounts, it acknowledges the relevance of the method of rational reconstruction of the conditions of emergence of these broader and more universalistic capacities. But I suggest that it is not helpful to construe this in terms of what people would counterfactually agree to under ideal circumstances, since the latter does not in my view carry sufficient normative weight, or else it simply tacitly presupposes these very norms of freedom and equality. Such counterfactual approaches are in one sense, then, not normative enough, while in another sense they are too normative. They are not normative enough if they are limited to making a kind of prediction about what people would agree to, or else they are too normative in tacitly appealing to the very norms that are supposed to emerge through the relevant processes of dialogue and discourse. The account given here can, I think, more adequately explain why people should agree to recognize the agency of others and correlatively their human rights, without simply embedding this recognition in processes of interaction or of historical development. Nonetheless, this should also not be taken as traditionally deontological, but is instead based on what I have characterized as an experientially based normative social ontology.

In this perspective, human rights are emergent in regard to their explicit normative status but should not be reduced to, or seen as merely relative to, existing forms of social life, or to particular stages of social and historical development. The approach attempts to go beyond the abstract universalism of liberalism (or indeed of natural rights conceptions) while avoiding an excessive historicization by making use of the additional notion of *concrete universality*.[28] This conception sees particular forms of social relations as not merely accidental to individuals as human agents. Instead, it sees individuals as, in part, constituted by these relations, whether egalitarian ones of reciprocal recognition, or else one-sided relations of oppression, domination, or misrecognition. This concrete universality can be usefully tied to what Marx characterized as a historical process of cultivating a many-sided individuality, one that is multiply related to others within particular structurally important forms of relationships and institutions (particularly economic ones).[29] For Marx in

---

[28] I introduced this concept, drawing on a notion of it in Hegel, in Carol C. Gould, "The Woman Question: Philosophy of Liberation and the Liberation of Philosophy," in *Women and Philosophy: Toward a Theory of Liberation*, ed. Carol C. Gould and Marx W. Wartofsky (New York: G. P. Putnam's Sons, 1976, Originally published in *The Philosophical Forum* 5, nos. 1–2 (fall–winter, 1973–74): 5–44). I subsequently discussed it at some length in Gould, *Globalizing Democracy*, chapter 2.
[29] Gould, *Marx's Social Ontology*, particularly chapter 1.

the *Grundrisse*, this is a matter of the emergence of a multidimensional personality, which is universal in the sense of being open to multiple and wide interactions and constituted by a plethora of such diverse interactions, which Marx sees as, for the most part, supplanting abstractly universal notions of the human. But while Marx at times conceives of the person simply as the node of a set of relations, in a way comparable to contemporary intersectional analyses, I think it is important to recognize that individuals have the power of agency, whether individually or more often jointly with others, such that they can (at least sometimes) change the conditions of their action, as well as in some ways their agency itself.

Thus, my own view departs from Marx's own in attempting to articulate more fully than his does the relation between an open conception of agency as characteristic of each individual and this universalizing multisidedness of persons and their relations, which develops over time. In Marx's trenchant analysis, such elaboration is facilitated by the emergence of a world market along with extensive trading relations, and by an economy that breaks down barriers, in the first instance through capitalist processes themselves. More generally, I think it useful to clarify the role of abstractly universal norms in the context of these constitutive social relations and to more fully consider how such concrete universality is related to those abstract norms. Clearly, the abstractly universal norms have an important critical dimension of their own in positing the equality and universality of individuals as a basis for assessing as deficient the one-sided relations of domination that prevent people from realizing their freedom. But the necessary supplement is a notion of the many-sidedness of the relations that makes it possible for people to become fully aware of these norms and to articulate their ramifications over time. (This many-sidedness can also be seen as part of the notion of positive freedom itself, to the extent that it is understood as a process of the development or flourishing of agency over time.)

The implication for understanding human rights is that they too need to be taken in their concrete elaborations and interpretations across cultures and contexts, and not only as abstractly universal norms. This elaboration involves not only discursive processes of articulating and agreeing to the norms but also concrete constructions of fuller realizations of it, on the ground as it were. This occurs through the cultivation of specific (many-sided) relationships, for example, of solidarity both within nations and across borders and also through institutional innovation and development. Thus the relevant universality of agency is recognized in germ but only implicitly in basic social practices of reciprocity and it comes to be explicitly acknowledged only as a result of a process of development that can take more inclusive forms over time (though there is no necessity to this). Wider interactions in practice actually serve to construct the conditions for these norms to come to be recognized as fully universal. So the process of this concrete and differentiated universalizing presupposes the form of agency and the implicit reciprocity which support the abstractly universal norm, but practical processes are also conditions for its coming to be recognized more fully as a norm. It is the openness and multi-sidedness of the agency itself and its differentiation that makes possible such norm recognition.

The notion of concrete universality also ties in with the account of sociality as discussed earlier in this chapter. The suggestion was that human rights have a double basis:

(1) in agency, understood as a creative power of self-transformation, taken both in individualistic and social forms;
(2) in interdependence as constitutive of this agency, in that the choices and intentions operate in and through a set of given social conditions and relations.

Thus, people are not understood as *using* social cooperation in order to meet independently identified goals and aims, but instead their action presupposes cooperative contexts, and their self-understandings are already informed by interdependent relations with others. Power is still identified with agency – whether individual or collective – but the context and the form of the agency, as well as the conditions needed to realize projects and develop capacities, are all social. So the idea of human rights as claims potentially on everyone for supporting institutions that can fulfill them can be understood as an expression and generalization of this fundamental interdependence and of the basic claims that we make on each other for the realization of our needs. This is clear in the case of our early claims on those close to us, especially members of our own families, but there is no principled restriction of such social claims to that context. Yet, it would be impractical for all others, including those at a distance, to have to realize our particular needs (and we theirs) and it seems clear that no one can be expected to do so without the intermediation of institutions. Rather, I suggest that human rights are valid claims on others to work to create the institutions that will enable us and others to fulfill human rights. It is in the first place a claim on each other to create relevant structures that will function effectively to fulfill these rights, basic and (eventually) nonbasic.

Human rights and the conditions for agency

I have suggested that human rights are justified in terms of their connection to (positive) freedom as a norm ingredient in agency and are understood as specifying the most salient conditions for such agency, including basic and nonbasic conditions. As previously noted, these conditions include both negative ones that require freedom from interference, as well as positive or enabling ones. In these ways, these rights are responsive to both embodiment and sociality, and also presuppose some form of political community with others.

Inasmuch as the agents in question are understood to exist substantially in nature and need to interact with it for their continued existence, economic human rights and especially the right to means of subsistence and to security of the person take on major importance. (Needless to say, to recognize the relevance of material needs in this way does not mean that these very needs are not also socially interpreted and constructed.) Other salient conditions for agency are given in the traditional liberal rights that protect individuals from interference by the government or other authorities. But the view here goes beyond such an emphasis on negative liberty or freedom from interference to call attention to the requirement of freedom from domination or exploitation, omitted from these traditional accounts. It also goes beyond all those negative freedoms to propose the importance of enabling conditions for effective freedom, for example, education, health care, welfare, rights to work, and so on, themselves specified in other human rights.

To understand such rights as specifying the necessary conditions for both basic and developed forms of agency is distinct from emphasizing the provision of primary goods or even of resources for goal fulfillment. In a way similar to capabilities approaches, the notion of conditions for action is understood in terms of a conception of development or effective freedom. But unlike some capabilities approaches, the relevant notion of equal positive freedom eschews any lists of essential functionings. Instead, it makes room only for lists of human rights themselves, and even there it sees them as provisional. Although rights specify necessary conditions of agency, they nonetheless can be variably used and need to be understood in a way consistent with the open conception of freedom advocated earlier. Moreover, the list of human rights can be thought of as somewhat variable for different social and historical contexts, though the basic rights, as conditions for any human life activity whatever, are likely to be relatively stable through time, although subject to different interpretations and elaborations.

Since such lists of basic and nonbasic (though still important) human rights pertain to conditions rather than actual functionings or even exclusively to capabilities, they avoid essentialism as well as the potentially ideological aspect of lists. And although lists of capabilities have certainly proved helpful for assessing a country's (or society's) development, it is implausible to suggest that such lists are definitive for all human development through time. Lists of human rights, by contrast, somewhat more modestly address not agency itself but its conditions, which can be variably used or appropriated. Thus, the role of ideological bias or one-sidedness is minimized, though probably not eliminated. Further, such lists of human rights are best understood as provisional and as articulated through cross-cultural dialogue. This does not undermine their fundamental character, however, since they are rooted in the features of agency, interdependence, and embodiment. Yet, as conditions, they go beyond abstract goods and resources, in gaining their significance from the uses that people can make of them (a feature also emphasized in capabilities and other positive freedom approaches). In this way, such human rights should be understood as speaking to our shared needs and our potentials for cultivating fuller freedom, both individually and collectively.

3 Interpreting freedom dynamically: beyond liberty and autonomy to positive freedom

Introduction

In this chapter, I analyze the concept of positive freedom more fully, retrieving it from critics like Berlin and defending its importance. I indicate how it differs from liberal conceptions of choice and autonomy, and indeed goes beyond even feminist reconceptions of autonomy in more social terms as "relational autonomy." I want to explicate the ways in which positive freedom is a more open and dynamic conception than traditional understandings of liberty or freedom, and suggest that it is better able to take into account the interdependence of persons. When viewed in an intercultural context, moreover, the proposed understanding of freedom has implications for how we understand universality, and requires a norm of concrete universality.

The first part of this chapter takes off from Isaiah Berlin's critique of positive liberty, which has resonated through decades of liberal theory. Building on criticisms already advanced by C. B. Macpherson, I first indicate how – contrary to Berlin's allegations – positive freedom does not in fact entail the mastery of the state or of a collectivity over the individuals within it. I then move to further explicate the conception of positive freedom, understanding it as self-developing or self-transformative activity, in a sense that requires the availability of a set of conditions, material and social. The positive freedom conception also presupposes the important notion of negative liberty, but in an interpretation that includes *freedom from* oppression, domination, or exploitation, as well as the traditional liberties. Yet, the notion of positive freedom points to the importance of economic and social human rights, in addition to civil and political ones (along with the significance of institutional design for fulfilling these human rights). It also gives rise to rights of democratic participation in a range of joint activities and institutional contexts, as discussed in Chapter 4. I focus here on the comparison of positive freedom with the ideas of autonomy and relational autonomy, and consider the

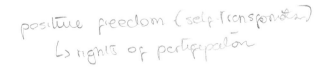

implications of these various interpretations of freedom for the possibility of universal or fully global norms.

Beyond Berlin: From negative liberty to positive freedom

The cold war intellectual context in which Berlin presented his influential account of freedom in "Two Concepts of Liberty" was one in which the defense of negative liberty in the face of authoritarianism was of paramount importance. This defense continues to be relevant today, especially in view of new forms of governmental power and surveillance. Yet, in his justifiable concern to criticize then-existing forms of "socialist" societies, Berlin somehow came to misinterpret the notion of positive freedom, and also to defend a narrowly individualistic notion of liberty. Beyond critique, however, my interest here is more to further analyze the alternative account of positive freedom and its integral relation to negative freedom, following my own analysis of these norms in my 1988 book *Rethinking Democracy*.[1] Since equal positive freedom is the core principle of justice, in my view, there is much at stake for me in retrieving this fuller notion of freedom from Berlin's critique. While arguing for more attention to social and political institutions that enable our choices, we need to do so in a way that avoids the authoritarianism or the centralization of power over individuals that so exercised Berlin.

I do not intend to revisit here the great variety of critiques of Berlin's essay. These are nicely surveyed by George Crowder in his book *Isaiah Berlin: Liberty and Pluralism*.[2] I want to focus on a few criticisms that I believe show the need for an alternative reading of the conception of positive freedom, and to a degree of negative freedom as well.

For Berlin, in the case of negative freedom, "I am normally said to be free to the degree to which no man or body of men interferes with my activity. Political liberty in this sense is simply the area within which a man can act unobstructed by others . . . Coercion implies the deliberate interference of other human beings within the area in which I could otherwise act. You lack political liberty or freedom only if you are prevented from attaining a goal by human beings."[3] Although he recognizes that people can be prevented by economic arrangements from attaining their goals, Berlin dismisses this fact as too dependent on a particular

---

[1] Gould, *Rethinking Democracy*.

[2] George Crowder, *Isaiah Berlin: Liberty and Pluralism* (Cambridge: Polity, 2004), especially chapter 4.

[3] Berlin, "Two Concepts of Liberty," 122.

Gutes Berlin To rash.

"theory" – unlike his own view, which he seems to regard as common sense or as simply evident in experience. Of course, Berlin's own view implies a broader theory too. He famously sharply separates freedom from its conditions, which is something I will come back to, as I believe it is a fundamental problem with his approach.

Berlin's account of positive freedom raises even more questions than does his conception of negative liberty inasmuch as it incorporates several notions that do not necessarily harmonize with each other. Unlike negative freedom, which Berlin says concerns "What am I free to do or be?" positive freedom supposedly concerns "'By whom am I ruled?' or 'Who is to say what I am, and what I am not, to be or do?'"[4] In fact, simply going with ordinary language as Berlin tended to do, it would seem more natural to say that positive freedom in fact poses the question of "What am I free to do or be?" Berlin instead chooses to build into the definition of positive liberty (in a somewhat question-begging way?) the concern with rule against which he wishes to argue. Moreover, he focuses on the notion of self-mastery here (why not self-determination or other possible variants? we might wonder), and famously claims that it turns, or has turned, into the domination of the state over the individual. Somehow, the division of the self into a rational higher part and a lower desiring part is supposed to lead to the real higher self being identified with a social whole that can impose its will on the members to help them achieve their freedom. Macpherson in his 1973 book *Democratic Theory: Essays in Retrieval* effectively shows not only the illogicality of the slide, which Berlin hints at (the reasoning proceeds "not always by logically reputable steps" he notes),[5] but also its inaccuracy as a historical model.[6]

Feminist philosophers have criticized the radical separation of reason from desire, as did a host of other twentieth-century figures, and their criticisms are important. But why a notion of self-determination or autonomy or even "self-mastery" can be indicted as leading to holism in politics and then to authoritarianism remains mysterious. Perhaps some of the figures that Berlin criticizes may have thought that the collective embodies reason, but even Hegel cannot simply be interpreted as advocating authoritarian dominion over individuals,[7] and, in any case,

---

[4] *Ibid.*, 177–8.   [5] *Ibid.*, 179.   [6] Macpherson, *Democratic Theory*, chapter 5.
[7] See, for example, Shlomo Avineri, *Hegel's Theory of the Modern State* (Cambridge: Cambridge University Press, 1972); Allen Wood, *Hegel's Ethical Thought* (Cambridge: Cambridge University Press, 1990); Michael O. Hardimon, *Hegel's Social Philosophy: The Project of Reconciliation* (Cambridge: Cambridge University Press, 1994); and Frederick Neuhouser, *Foundations of Hegel's Social Theory: Actualizing Freedom* (Cambridge, MA: Harvard University Press, 2000).

Hegel was critical of Kant's approach to self-determination.[8] Certainly the indictment is incorrect for Marx,[9] whom Berlin apparently implicitly blames in part for the authoritarianism of the first half of the twentieth century, namely the degradation and oppression perpetuated by Stalin. (One wonders whether if Berlin had access to Marx's deeply philosophical work *Grundrisse* that he would have been so likely to accuse Marx in this way.)

The issue of this slide from self-mastery to authoritarianism raises the deeper question of the extent to which ideas can be blamed for political events and structures (or credited with producing them). Even granting for the sake of argument that self-mastery is a wrong-headed idea, to say that Kant or the notion of self-mastery more generally is responsible for authoritarianism would seem to be similar to blaming Berlin for the financial crisis of 2009! One might ask, why isn't the idea of freedom from interference just as much the root of the absence of regulation that has led to our present dismal economic predicament? Or perhaps it's like saying that American ideals are wrongheaded because they led to George Bush's misuse of them in going to war in Iraq. Rather, I see Berlin's polemic on this point to be excessively ideological, even though it is presented in the guise of a critique of ideology.

Moreover, it requires adopting the perspective of a thoroughgoing idealism to credit ideas in political theory with a direct relation to practice and to history. One can recognize the power of, and important role of, ideas without supposing this sort of cause–effect connection. By contrast, I suggest that good political philosophy reflects on contemporary practices (in historical context) and attempts to clarify progressive and helpful notions that practice itself throws up for us. This clarification can be helpful for political actors and for the populace more generally but it is up to people themselves in their concrete social and political relations to implement these notions if they so choose and this is itself a contextual enterprise, dependent on specific social and historical circumstances and on people's own interpretations of the ideas.

We now get to the crucial issue of whether Berlin was right to separate negative and positive freedom and to dismiss positive freedom. I do not mean to point to MacCallum's observation that all freedom is always a triadic relation involving both "freedom from" and "freedom to." Though helpful, this is fundamentally a point about how the concept

---

[8] See, for example, the discussion in Jürgen Habermas, "Morality and Ethical Life: Does Hegel's Critique of Kant Apply to Discourse Ethics?" *Northwestern University Law Review* 83 (1988).
[9] See Gould, *Marx's Social Ontology.*

A One role of political phil. vis-a-vis
political actors

is used, or more precisely, the conditions for the intelligibility of our use of it.[10] Rather, I think that there is an intrinsic connection between negative and positive freedom of a more substantive nature that Berlin fails to see, where this connection, and positive freedom on a certain interpretation, is important for understanding a range of central social and political questions. This conception brings freedom together with its conditions, as already suggested in previous chapters. In the course of this analysis, it will be seen that Berlin's interpretation of negative freedom is too narrow, because it is asocial if not antisocial and because it cannot take into account the importance of being free from domination and exploitation.[11]

I propose by way of explanation that because Berlin placed such overriding emphasis on the dangers of authoritarian regimes and holistic understandings of social and political organization, he insisted on the priority of the individual's freedom from interference, taking the individual quite narrowly, almost atomistically, despite his acknowledgement in other contexts of the importance of social relations and interdependence. And because Berlin was critical of socialist societies and of the theories to which they appealed, he relegated freedom from exploitation and the existence of poverty to the domain of mere "conditions of freedom," rather than understanding them as constraining, or even coercive, human arrangements that contribute to the creation or perpetuation of such exploitation or poverty. In addition, he requires that any constraint be "deliberate," in a sense that apparently excludes their being the foreseeable result of human choices, but his view on these matters is also presented without much argument.

Choice, conditions, and self-transformation over time

I take the positive freedom tradition to be at least partly about the notion of *effective freedom*. That is, for the exercise of choice to be more than empty intention it requires that agents have access to a range of

---

[10] Gerald C. MacCallum, Jr., "Negative and Positive Freedom," *The Philosophical Review* 76, no. 3 (1967).

[11] Philip Pettit has given a well-known critique of negative liberty in terms of the significance of nondomination as protection not from interference per se but from arbitrary interference (especially in Phillip Pettit, *Republicanism: A Theory of Freedom and Government* [Oxford: Oxford University Press, 1997]). It can be seen in this chapter and later ones that my own account advances a somewhat different interpretation of domination, and more importantly goes beyond negative liberty to a notion of positive freedom as the freedom of self-transformation, understood in terms of a notion of effective freedom. Clearly, too, the conception of positive freedom at stake in my approach differs from understandings of it as requiring political participation or forms of civic republicanism.

effective freedom . i.e choice + means .
or, in more philosophical language, the absence of
constraining conditions to the availability of enabling

conditions through which they can make their choices effective. To illustrate with a crude example, I am not free to go to China without the money and the means of transportation to get there; the choice to go is insignificant without the availability of means. Or, again, even if no legal or discriminatory barriers prevent me from entering a desired profession or trade, I cannot make the choice effectively if there are no jobs available.

As elaborated previously, the conditions for making effective choices include the absence of constraining conditions and the availability of a set of enabling conditions.[12] Berlin's notion of negative liberty focuses only on freedom from constraint or interference and indeed only on one sort of constraint, albeit an important one – interference by other individuals or by the state with one's actions. Another important type of constraint escapes Berlin's analysis – freedom from domination, oppression, or exploitation. Domination can be external or internal, and it often proceeds not through direct coercion or control by one person or group over another, but by way of controlling the conditions that these others need for their actions.[13] Feminist philosophy has brought to the fore the critique of domination in several of these senses, focusing on psychological factors as well as more direct forms of oppression and abuse, while Marxist philosophy has focused on the critique of economic exploitation within capitalist political economies. In my view, these are important senses of "freedom from" that supplement the civil liberties and political rights that remain essential for protecting freedom of choice (although Berlin does not give much attention to the political rights).

Beyond these forms of freedom from constraint, I have suggested that free action also has enabling social conditions – recognition of people by others, as well as forms of socialization and of social and cultural practices – and material conditions. The satisfaction of basic material needs – means of subsistence and indeed an adequate level of well-being – are clearly required if people are to be able to effectively choose. (As clarified in Chapter 1, this does not imply that these means should be directly provided to people but that economic institutions should be set up so as to enable them to be met.) Some philosophers have tried to subsume even the enabling social and material conditions under the head of negative freedom but in my view that involves tortuous reasoning, since these conditions would have to be construed as what one is free from the

---

[12] My initial discussion of positive freedom and the notion of enabling and constraining conditions is in Gould, *Marx's Social Ontology*, especially chapter 4 ("The Ontology of Freedom"). A fuller discussion is in Gould, *Rethinking Democracy*, especially chapters 1 and 7.

[13] Gould, *Marx's Social Ontology*, especially chapters 4 and 5.

absence or lack of. It is more straightforward to recognize this idea of effective choice as appealing to a notion of positive freedom. But that notion remains to be further explicated.

With Berlin, I think that choice is indeed a central feature of human action, though I understand it to be often embedded in actions rather than separate from them and prior to them. We often engage in intentional activities, which embody conscious purposes, and do not always deliberate and choose prior to action. Freedom of choice in these various senses should be protected by negative liberties. Yet choice or purposive, intentional activity can itself be viewed as the fundamental capacity that enables people's further self-transformation or self-development as a process over time. Through this process, people develop various capacities, including some general or socially necessary ones that are shared with others and also individualized ones like talents or special skills that are unique to them.[14] They also attempt to realize projects or goals and engage in relationships (including widening them or deepening them). These three parameters – capacities, goals, and relationships – are central aspects of freedom as self-development, which is not to say that they are the only aspects.

Positive freedom thus goes beyond engaging in isolated actions and, instead, involves a *biographical* or *historical* dimension. Moreover, it can be understood as practical self-transformation, insofar as it is ingredient in people's actions, interactions, and social practices, rather than always or even mainly a matter of conscious self-reflection. In this way, as argued later in this chapter, the notion of positive freedom differs from traditional conceptions of autonomy, and has a broader range of applicability. I have further suggested that such self-development or self-transformation is a normative imperative posited in free activity itself.[15] Freedom as a process of intentional activity has a teleological aspect involving capacity development, goal realization, and relationship building, through which people and groups differentiate themselves. But a full explication of this social ontological feature of it goes beyond what we need to discuss here, which concerns freedom as a social and political ideal.

In this account, choice or intentionality as a general feature of action[16] can be recognized as an abstract capacity of human beings as a class, and

---

[14] The conception of capacities that I introduced is thus broader than the notion of capabilities, associated with the work of Sen and Nussbaum (See Chapter 1, fn. 11). Other notable differences are discussed in Chapter 2 (concerning the status of lists of functionings and capabilities), and in the comparison with Sen on well-being and agency later in this chapter. See also Gould, *Globalizing Democracy*, chapter 2.

[15] For an analysis, see Gould, *Rethinking Democracy*, esp. chapters 1 and 3.

[16] I am using intentionality here in its ordinary usage as connoting intentional action, rather than in its philosophical usage, as the directedness or "aboutness" of consciousness. There are some connections between the philosophical use and the ordinary one,

one that is exercised individually or jointly with others, while processes of self-development and self-transformation necessarily differ among various individuals and groups, and range widely over goals, capacities, and relationships (of both discursive and nondiscursive sorts). Choice and its protection are thus necessary for this sort of flourishing but are not sufficient, since effective freedom requires access to positive or enabling conditions as well.

This notion of self-development or self-transformation is not perfectionist, since it looks to a wide and open range of modes of instantiation, and to the recognition of persons as differentiated beings. It remains a very general notion of self-directed change and, as noted, does not necessarily involve conscious self-improvement or self-realization taken as a personal goal. This conception also specifically rules out that individuals can choose for each other their modes of self-development, or enforce or impose freedom. Nonetheless, as a normative conception, it does not admit of every possible course of action and interaction. Self-transformation is constrained by the requirement that it does not undercut its own possibility through choices that would wholly bar further self-transformative activity as well as by the normative limitation posed by the fundamental equality of people's agency or freedom, which sets limits on what any given individual can rightly do.

Self-transformative beings in this analysis are understood as social individuals, or what I call "individuals-in-relations." Although the power of choice or creative, conscious activity is to be found in individuals, these individuals are fundamentally interdependent, such that their activity depends on the care and nurturance of others, on solidarity with others, and on a set of social, economic, and political institutions that frame their choices. People are historically and socially situated, and they appropriate and learn from the ideas, capacities, and realized purposes of others. In these respects, the view here presents what could be called a *networking* conception of people's freedom and identity. Moreover, their intentional activity is embodied and operates within a natural world, though one already transformed by human beings in purposive ways. Especially in view of the social emphasis of this account, it is clear that recognition by others is crucial for people's freedom, where this recognition can take both interpersonal and institutional forms (e.g., legal ones). Importantly, many forms of action are themselves collective, and involve the pursuit of joint goals or purposes by groups, or else involve shared care, or discursive or dialogic interactions, and the cultivation of cultural practices and meanings.

especially in the work of some phenomenological philosophers such as Sartre. But in analytic work, the two usages have parted company for the most part.

self-transformation can only be achieved with others, r not in isolation.

Besides these features of sociality, equality plays an important role in such an account, inasmuch as choice or intentionality, which also serves as a capacity for self-transformation over time, is characteristic of human activity. Some degree of freedom or agency is generally characteristic of people from infancy through the course of their lives, but at every stage requires access to conditions for its effectiveness. While it is true that people may be variously accomplished in making use of these conditions, and in rare cases seem to lack the capacity for self-transformative activity altogether, on this view their potentials can only be definitely assessed in retrospect, given the provision of adequate care and education, as well as the other basic conditions of life. People's status as agential beings and as possessing fundamental dignity constitute a basis for equal regard and treatment, which I have suggested is often recognized in elementary ways in experience, and which needs to be recognized and provided for more fully as required by the principle of equal positive freedom.

In virtue of the connection of choice to its exercise in various forms of self-transformative activity, then, the recognition of basic human equality by each of all others requires also the recognition of the equal validity of the claims of all individuals to the conditions necessary for self-transformation or self-development. And inasmuch as a valid claim can be understood as a right, I have argued that people have (prima facie) equal rights to the conditions of self-development, that is, equal positive freedom (as a principle of justice).[17]

The sociality and equality of individuals serve to qualify self-transformation or self-development by requiring that not only negative liberty but also positive freedom in this sense should be compatible with a like right on the part of others. However, this delimitation concerns the normative concept of positive freedom and does not support repressive legislation of the sort Berlin feared. Indeed, the priority of protecting choice on this view and the openness of the notion of self-transformation require a minimization of coercion, as Berlin advocated. A strength of the view I argue for here is its insistence on strong civil liberties protections while also requiring other protections and provisions. The importance of a broader understanding of the requirements of action than Berlin acknowledged implies that efforts be made to reduce oppression and exploitation, as well as to positively provide for the enabling conditions of free activity. It is a mistake to see this provision as exclusively, or perhaps even mainly, a matter of government provision at the national level. Rather, the fulfillment of people's human rights (which express the various requirements for these necessary conditions of action) calls for the

---

[17] See also the discussion in Gould, *Rethinking Democracy*, chapter 1.

design of a range of economic, social, and political institutions at various levels, from local to transnational. For people to have access to means of subsistence and meaningful work requires an economy that enables decent jobs and that operates without exploitation (leaving aside for now precisely how exploitation is to be interpreted). In the current period, this requires attention to regional or global factors beyond the nation-state, as explicated later in this book.

Crucially, too, if joint or common forms of activity are among the central arenas for self-transformation, and if people are to be equally agential in these activities, then they have to be able to codetermine these activities, that is, participate in controlling or directing them (as discussed in Chapter 4). If they are not to be dominated or controlled by others in these shared activities, they must have some role in defining or redefining the goals and in determining the means for carrying them out. In my view, this supports requirements for democratic participation in a wide range of institutions in society, and not only in politics (in my view extending also to democratic management in firms, as argued in Chapter 14). We can add that mutuality or reciprocity in non-institutionalized forms of common or joint activity (e.g., in families) equally follows from this approach. The latter requirements are of course only normative and not legal, though this view more clearly than Berlin's rules out abusive relations within the private sphere and lends support to the extension of human rights to prohibit domestic violence.

Berlin himself occasionally points to a broader conception of freedom that touches on certain aspects of the notion of self-transformation.[18] However, in that case, I would suggest that Berlin should have drawn the above conclusions with respect to the intrinsic connection of freedom to its conditions, and should thus have given greater weight to positive freedom. I would add that Berlin also seems to have erred in not taking more seriously his own stated belief in people's interdependence and sociality.

Positive freedom and intercultural connections

We can now briefly turn to the challenge to this conception of positive freedom posed by the awareness of the plurality of cultures and the increasing degree of global interconnectedness that marks contemporary life. As is frequently observed, both of these factors raise difficulties for liberalism, and seemingly for any sort of normative view that tries to

---

[18] In "Two Concepts of Liberty," this is clearest in his discussion of "the extent of my freedom" (177, fn. 1).

the concern for +ve freedom means (co control) room for participation in more spheres, e-g workplace.

incorporate universal or cosmopolitan dimensions. They pose the question of whether a conception of freedom can avoid a narrow appeal to the traditional liberal individualism characteristic of political societies of the global north.

Although the term *self-development* still has something of an individualistic ring (though less so than the term *self-realization*, which is not only individualistic but implies a notion of an authentic self), the notion of self-transformation can be taken to characterize forms of cultural change as well as individual ones, and in this way, would appear to be relevant not only to liberal but also to communally oriented societies. Likewise, this conception recognizes that although the power of agency begins with individuals, as social beings people often exercise their agency in joint forms of cultural and social practice. The approach additionally emphasizes that institutions are human arrangements that are subject to change over time. Indeed, while many leading cultures worldwide may not share our own preference for constant, even frenetic, innovation, they are certainly internally differentiated and transformative, both internally and by virtue of their external interactions. Moreover, the creativity and contributions of individuals – for example, artists, rulers, scholars – in processes of social and cultural transformation are widely recognized worldwide. Yet, it must be acknowledged that the contributions of women in particular often continue to be demeaned or ignored.

Despite the persistence of forms of oppression and discrimination, I have suggested that a certain elementary equality of agency is more widely recognized than many philosophers and politicians may believe. That is, a sort of "proto-equality" is already recognized in many interactions in ordinary life (note the previously mentioned examples of greetings or "vehicular interactions," as well as basic modes of dialogue and communication). It is, of course, a long and historical struggle to overcome those forms of domination and oppression that have limited the recognition of equality in law, politics, and economics, as well as in everyday life, in and across different forms of society, including "Western" ones. But we can suggest that the basis for this recognition is already anticipated in certain everyday forms of action and interaction.

Certain other commonalities across cultures arise from the preconditions required for individual or collective agency, especially those that designate human needs of material or social types, as specified in human rights. And where there are disagreements on the range and scope of these rights, we can expect that intercultural dialogue has potential for interpreting human rights and the modes of protecting and fulfilling them, though such dialogue is itself a difficult enterprise, conceptually and in practice. I consider this form of dialogue (including in newer online forms) in later chapters.

An obvious point can perhaps be reiterated in concluding this part: an emphasis on freedom of this sort requires that we eschew the imposition of forms of government, even of liberal democratic ones, on others. As has been demonstrated in recent contemporary practice, this sort of imposition is specifically inimical to freedom. Nonetheless, from this recognition it does not follow that it is out of place to criticize cultural practices that violate human rights or that fail to recognize people's equal freedom. Action in solidarity with others struggling to fulfill their human rights is in order (discussed in Chapter 5), as are efforts to help set up transnational democratic institutions (preferably regional ones in the first instance), which are discussed in Part III of this book. Clearly, both solidarity actions and efforts at institutional design have to be guided by those whose freedom is at stake and should aid their struggles in the ways that they determine to be most beneficial. I believe that when freedom is taken in this open and non-coercive way, and interpreted in more social terms than on traditional liberal approaches, it can be seen to retain much of its global reach.

Universalizing the concept of freedom: Liberal autonomy and cultural critique

We can now consider how the conception of freedom presented above goes beyond standard views of "autonomy" and even beyond the notion of "relational autonomy," a conception to which it may seem similar. We also need to confront the claim that only a notion of liberal autonomy will enable us to criticize cultural practices that violate human rights. Anthony Langlois has argued along these lines and has objected to the conception of concrete universality that I presented in *Globalizing Democracy and Human Rights*, which I claimed importantly supplements an understanding of freedom in the abstractly universal sense characteristic of liberalism.[19] A consideration of Langlois's critique will enable us to address the relation of norms of equal agency to historical and social contexts of their emergence. I argue that attention to cultural differences and interactions, to the social and historical context for the emergence of norms, along with the use of a critical methodology and the critique of oppression in practice – as required by a norm of concrete universality – is essential to an adequate account of agency, even of the traditional sort that liberals like Langlois favor.

In his article "Liberal Autonomy and Global Democracy," Anthony Langlois takes up the question of which norms can provide an adequate

[19] Anthony Langlois, "Liberal Autonomy and Global Democracy," in *Global Democracy and Its Difficulties*, ed. A. Langlois and K. Soltan (London: Routledge, 2009).

basis for universal human rights (and undergird increasingly global forms of democracy). Langlois favors a reliance on what he calls "liberal autonomy," which he acknowledges is a distinctively "Western" notion, as the indispensable normative basis for criticizing cultural practices and modes of social and political organization that violate human rights, as well as for constructing a positive account of new transnational institutions of democracy. He further proposes that I, like other critics of liberal individualism, in fact have to fall back on just such liberal conceptions in order to give any normative bite to our recommendations for extending freedom, democracy, and human rights in the present globalizing context.[20]

In passing, I would note that Langlois presents something of a "straw man argument" in criticizing my earlier account, by incorrectly taking the analysis I give of concrete universality out of its relation to the norm of equal positive freedom and social ontology. I explicitly focus on norms of equal agency, which I, like Langlois, believe are essential for effective critique. I agree that the features of human agency that support claims to equality cannot be deduced from merely historical observations about changing social relations. I think it is incorrect to regard these norms as emerging only in modern times, for that would require us to be able to say, for example, that some centuries ago there was no basis for claiming that slaves should be free. I characterized my account as "quasi-foundationalist" in this respect.

Yet, it can be seen that the social ontological conception of freedom and of the equal agency of individuals differs from traditional liberal conceptions of autonomy in some important ways. In broad terms, although it retains the idea of self-determination (in a certain interpretation), the account emphasizes the integral role of freedom from oppression and domination in its understanding of equal agency. It highlights the social relatedness of individuals, including their participation in common activities, and recognizes the significance of culturally and socially diverse forms of agency. The dynamic aspect of the transformation of people over time, in a sense that requires access to material and social conditions of agency, is another feature of agency that tends to be omitted in traditional liberalism.

When freedom and individuality are reinterpreted in these ways, it becomes clear that we need a notion of concrete universality to supplement the abstract one. As I discuss further in the concluding section of this chapter ('Interpreting universality concretely'), this notion cannot be understood as a simple historicist, empirical, or "sociological" account

---

[20] *Ibid.*

of the generation of norms, to which Langlois relegates it. Rather, it brings to our attention the perspectival and potentially ideological nature of social and political views, including contemporary ones, and a concurrent need for social critique and self-criticism in generating an adequate normative framework for transnational democracy and global ethics, and indeed for realizing the norms inherent in traditional liberalism. In a more material mode, it calls for non-oppressive and solidaristic social relations and theorizes the interconnection of individuals within newly transnational communities. The emphasis placed on difference and relationality makes a difference, so to speak, especially in establishing wider frames of human rights and transnational democracy.

Autonomy, relational autonomy, and positive freedom

It would be helpful to consider more fully how positive freedom is related to liberal autonomy and to the newer notion of relational autonomy. In recent years, theorists of the notion of autonomy have elaborated conceptions that not only distinguish it from the notion of liberty, but that sometimes bring it close to the notion of positive freedom discussed here. For example, John Christman writes that, "Generally, one can distinguish autonomy from freedom in that the latter concerns the ability to act, without external or internal constraints and also (on some conceptions) with sufficient resources and power to make one's desires effective."[21] He continues: "Autonomy concerns the independence and authenticity of the desires (values, emotions, etc.) that move one to act in the first place."[22] Yet, in another place Christman notes that positive freedom conceptions can overlap with those of autonomy. He writes that "personal (or individual) autonomy should also be distinguished from 'freedom', although again, there are many renderings of these concepts, and certainly some conceptions of positive freedom will be equivalent to what is often meant by autonomy."[23]

Christman further distinguishes between basic autonomy and autonomy as an ideal. The former bears some relation to my own emphasis on choice as a fundamental characteristic of agency (although in my view choice is often ingredient in actions), while "ideal autonomy" for him is "an achievement that serves as a goal to which we might aspire and

---

[21] John Christman, "Autonomy in Moral and Political Philosophy," in *The Stanford Encyclopedia of Philosophy*, ed. Edward N. Zalta (2011), citing Berlin, "Two Concepts of Liberty"; Larry Crocker, *Positive Liberty* (The Hague: Martinus Nijhoff, 1980); and MacCallum, "Negative and Positive Freedom."
[22] Christman, "Autonomy in Moral and Political Philosophy."   [23] *Ibid.*

according to which a person is maximally authentic and free of manipulative, self-distorting influences."[24] Yet, the latter is distinct from the conception of the development of capacities, projects, and relationships over time that to me constitutes the core notion of positive freedom.[25] Focusing on the authenticity and independence of the individual's actions, however worthwhile, does not capture the developmental or social aspects of freedom as discussed here.

Relational autonomy views advanced by feminist theorists helpfully reflect on the role of systems of gender (and other forms of) oppression and the constraints they pose for autonomy. Feminists additionally tend to emphasize social conditioning and social relationality. In those respects, their account has similarities to a positive freedom approach. Yet it remains a question whether the notions of either autonomy or relative autonomy sufficiently capture what is needed for an adequate account of freedom as a political ideal. A positive freedom approach covers some of the same ground as autonomy views, in particular in protecting individual choices, and also giving a role to an important political concept of self-determination, of both individuals and groups. And like relational autonomy, it focuses on the critique of forms of domination and oppression, and privileges a relational understanding of individuals, along with an emphasis on interdependence within and across complex societies, and the cultivation of caring and solidaristic relations as aspects of people's freedom.

Yet, the positive freedom view can avoid some of the problems that beset autonomy approaches and, I think, is able to capture a more open and less culturally biased notion of freedom. The idea of autonomy was early subjected to criticisms by feminist, Marxist, and communitarian philosophers for its seemingly narrow focus on the individual apart from his or her social relations.[26] Subsequent notions of second-order

---

[24] *Ibid.*   [25] Gould, *Rethinking Democracy*, 35–60.

[26] The critique of autonomy has been part of the critique of liberal individualism more generally. Markers of the broader critique include discussions by Marx himself, and in the past several decades by Macpherson, *Democratic Theory*, and C. B. Macpherson, *The Life and Times of Liberal Democracy* (Oxford: Oxford University Press, 1977); Michael Sandel, *Liberalism and the Limits of Justice* (Cambridge: Cambridge University Press, 1981); and Charles Taylor, "Atomism," in *Philosophy and the Human Sciences: Philosophical Papers, Volume 2*, ed. Charles Taylor (Cambridge: Cambridge University Press, 1985). Feminist theorists have been critical of liberalism from the standpoint of the critique of domination, for example, Iris Marion Young, *Justice and the Politics of Difference* (Princeton, NJ: Princeton University Press, 1990), or from a care perspective, including Carol Gilligan, *In a Different Voice* (Cambridge, MA: Harvard University Press, 1982), Virginia Held, "Non-Contractual Society: A Feminist View," in *Science, Morality and Feminist Theory*, ed. M. Hanen and K. Nielsen (Calgary, Canada: University of Calgary Press, 1987), and subsequent writing, and Sara Ruddick, *Maternal*

endorsement by an individual of first-order desires, needs, or motivations are important from an ethical standpoint. But such views may intensify the emphasis on the inward rational reflectiveness of individuals, in ways that seem narrowly liberal and not always fully cross-cultural as political ideals. Although relational autonomy variants have gone on to helpfully emphasize sociality and the damaging effects of oppression, they encounter the difficulty of either having to advocate minimal conceptions of autonomy, which protect and respect individual choices, or else judging women (and men) to be non-autonomous when they are oppressed in various ways, thereby denying people's basic choices the requisite respect and protection.[27]

The advantages of a positive freedom account over the autonomy versions, at least for social and political philosophy, are several. In analytically separating basic agency as choice or intentional activity from its development over time as aspects of a full account of freedom, it allows us to see the importance of protecting these choices both in regard to individuals' own concerns and in such overtly political forms of code-termination as democratic decision-making. Yet it regards bare choice as formal and insufficient without access to a range of conditions that social and political organization should provide, including the important liberties and rights emphasized by liberal political theory (though these do not entail unlimited private property rights, on my view),[28] the elimination of oppression and exploitation that feminist, critical race, and Marxist theorists have incisively criticized, and a set of enabling material and social requirements.

Importantly, the notion of positive freedom in its open, dynamic, and social aspects allows for an interpretation of freedom as not only dependent on rational reflection, but as including responsiveness and emotional factors, to be explicated later. Unlike autonomy views, we do not have to judge people as autonomous or not in order to be critical of systems of oppression. The intentionality manifest in human life activity supports requirements of mutual recognition of this basic capacity of each

Thinking (Boston, MA: Beacon Press, 1989). My own work from the mid-1970s to the present has also been based on a critique related to several of these: Gould, "The Woman Question"; Gould, *Marx's Social Ontology*; Gould, *Rethinking Democracy*; Gould, *Globalizing Democracy*, chapter 2. Prominent criticisms of autonomy per se include those by Alison Jaggar, *Feminist Politics and Human Nature* (Totowa, NJ: Rowman & Allanheld, 1985), and Lorraine Code, *What Can She Know?* (Ithaca, NY: Cornell University Press, 1991).

27 Cf. Natalie Stoljar, "Feminist Perspectives on Autonomy," in *The Stanford Encyclopedia of Philosophy*, ed. Edward N. Zalta (http://plato.stanford.edu/archives/sum2013/entries/feminism-autonomy/: 2013).

28 See the arguments for this claim in Gould, *Rethinking Democracy*, chapter 6 ("Contemporary Legal Conceptions of Property and their Implications for Democracy").

by others, while people's full freedom in forms of self-development, can be present in quite various manifestations. Their development of capacities, building of relationships, and fulfillment of long-term goals depends both on their own choices, individual or joint, and on the availability of the means for their freedom to become effective, where several of these means are specified in human rights. We can rightly be critical when these prerequisites are not provided through social and political organization, which instead should aim to fulfill them.

Across cultures, the various dimensions of capacity formation, relationships, and goal realization are open to multiple and diverse emphases and interpretations. And indeed, the approach sees self-transformative activity as applying to cultures and societies in addition to individuals (though it understands such collectivities or groups as entities constituted by individuals-in-relations).[29] Although this perspective does not require us to judge others' development as autonomous or not, it does require us to be critical of systems of oppression and exploitation. Choice and self-determination (or basic autonomy) should be protected, but fuller forms of freedom must be supported by transformations in the forms of social and political organization.

Before returning to the norm of concrete universality, which helps to explicate the openness and inclusiveness of the positive freedom view and its intercultural dimensions, we can note that the conception of capacities used here (along with related conceptions of agency and development) differs in various ways from the well-known capabilities approach of Amartya Sen,[30] although in my view both theories can be said to emerge from the positive freedom tradition, broadly speaking. In Chapter 2, I suggested that the conception of agency and self-transformative activity aims to avoid the essentialism that can sometimes mark lists of functionings, and even of capabilities.[31] In contrast to fixed human nature views, which provide a set of unchanging characteristics held to be constitutive of humans, the account offered here posits the central feature of agency to be change and self-transformation itself. It specifically aims to deny the fixity or unchangeability of human beings and finds their commonality in this capacity for change itself, understood in terms of social or individual modes of self-transformation over time. I believe that

[29] See chapter 5, "Cultural Identity, Group Rights, and Social Ontology," in Gould, *Globalizing Democracy*.

[30] Sen, "Well-Being, Agency, and Freedom"; Amartya Sen, *Inequality Re-examined* (Oxford: The Clarendon Press, 1992), among other works.

[31] I argued in Gould, *Globalizing Democracy*, chapter 2, that this problem can be seen in some of Martha Nussbaum's formulations of the capabilities approach (though generally not in Sen's version).

such self-transformation is widely characteristic of people across various cultures and cannot be dismissed as a "Western" notion. Recognizing the capacities that people have for such self-generated transformative activity provides a basis for their fundamental equality. Another crucial shared component is the fact of interdependence in meeting needs and in realizing projects, whether individual or collective.

In much of his work, Sen sharply distinguished between agency and well-being. My conception of agency, in contrast, attempts to hold these two features together, reflecting what I take to be their interconnection in practice. In more recent work, Sen seems to put forward a conception of agency that is closer to the one advocated here. But in earlier work, at least, he distinguished well-being freedom from agency freedom, where this well-being freedom is a matter of capabilities or real opportunities.[32] My own view is more directly influenced by Macpherson and by Marx, who himself harked back to some degree to Aristotle, in operating with a conception of agency as a process of transformation over time and in tying well-being to this activity (in the case of Aristotle, in the concept of *eudaimonia*). Following Marx, the account here sees agency as largely embodied in interaction and as operating in interrelation with nature (though the latter aspect does not receive the full attention it deserves in this work). Like Marx, too, it interprets human activity as free life activity, such that it includes elements of well-being within it. It seems misleading, then, to separate out as two dimensions rational choice and the state of a person.

The notion of capabilities, in Sen's account, helpfully points to the importance of people having real opportunities and being able to make use of them in activity. I think that this is similar to the positive freedom emphasis on effective freedom. I have analyzed positive freedom as involving the development of capacities (beyond the liberal notion of the realization of goals or even a plan of life); moreover, following feminist care theory, I suggest that the cultivation of relationships is another crucial parameter. But the conception of capacities here differs from that of capabilities in highlighting unique capacities that are distinctive to an individual as aspects of their full freedom, in addition to a range of social or communal capacities, and moreover, it does not tie capacities to functionings. Besides having opportunities and capabilities, which are no doubt significant, particularly as measures of development,

---

[32] See the discussion of the evolution of Sen's conception of agency and its relation to capabilities and well-being in David A. Crocker and Ingrid Robeyns, "Capability and Agency," in *Amartya Sen*, ed. Christopher W. Morris (Cambridge: Cambridge University Press, 2010).

difference with Sen.

my view emphasizes the availability of the various means or conditions for self-transformative activity, many of which are specified in human rights. These conditions include more than resources and extend to such requirements as freedom from oppression. Many of these conditions of agency should be understood as available for use or to be worked on. In this way, they are relative to or dependent on the various purposes of individuals and groups, and in turn help to structure those goals and the possible modes of their realization.

Interpreting universality concretely

Although differing sharply from liberal individualist conceptions of agency and freedom in the ways indicated, we have seen that a positive freedom account preserves an element of what could be called abstract universality in its recognition of equal agency as a crucial part of the normative basis for human rights. Yet, I suggest that a concretely universal interpretation of freedom as a norm is an important supplement. Contrary to Langlois's interpretation and critique, an emphasis on concrete universality not only explains how universal norms come to emerge, but does some important normative work of its own. (Indeed, even the process of attending to the emergence of norms is of more significance than critics like Langlois grant.)

It is perhaps worth noting that the term *concrete universality*, though drawn from Hegel in his *Logic*[33] (and used fairly extensively by the British Idealists) is not employed here in Hegel's sense, but rather in a distinctive way. The account bears, at most, only a certain resemblance to Hegel's own usage, which is itself quite complex,[34] having primary significance as an epistemological and metaphysical conception for him, and only secondarily as a socio-political and normative one.[35] Even the term

---

[33] According to Hegel, "As negativity in general or in accordance with the first, immediate negation, the universal contains determinateness generally as particularity; as the second negation, that is, as negation of the negation, it is absolute determinateness or individuality and concreteness. The universal is thus the totality of the Notion; it is concrete, and far from being empty, it has through its Notion a content, and a content in which it not only maintains itself but one which is its own and immanent in it. We can, indeed, abstract from the content: but in that case we do not obtain a universal of the Notion but only the abstract universal, which is an isolated, imperfect moment of the Notion and has no truth." G. W. F. Hegel, *Science of Logic*, trans. A. V. Miller (London: Allen & Unwin, 1969), 603–4.

[34] An impressive and helpful attempt at explication of Hegel's view and the readings of it by Anglo-American Idealists like F. H. Bradley and Josiah Royce is given by Robert Stern, "Hegel, British Idealism, and the Curious Case of the Concrete Universal," *British Journal for the History of Philosophy* 15, no. 1 (2007).

[35] The question of whether Hegel and the British idealists themselves can be considered as social holists is discussed in *ibid*.

abstract universality is used distinctively here. Unlike the use of the notion of the abstract in Marx, for example, the idea of choice or intentionality as a capacity for freedom is not to be understood as simply abstracted from across all concrete differences in a conceptual process; it is not a bare abstraction, so to speak. Although it is a formal notion relative to positive freedom and as a capacity for full freedom is ineffective without the conditions for its exercise, in my own account it points to an actual feature of human beings in their activity, evident experientially or phenomenologically, which in turn supports the requirement that it be mutually recognized. That is, the capacity for freedom in this sense is manifest in our concrete action and more generally in our way of being, although it is insufficient in itself and moves towards more differentiated modes of development.

Concrete universality goes beyond the various abstractly universal characterizations of the human that have been offered historically, and can be seen to function as a corrective to the one-sidedness of many of them. This sort of one-sidedness is especially evident in fixed human nature views that characterize the human in terms of a favored and historically delimited conception, most often derived from the activities of the powerful in a given society.[36] Along these lines, I have suggested that lists of human characteristics (even the progressive ones offered in recent years by Martha Nussbaum, for example) inevitably end up favoring the dominant characteristics of the age or of a particular culture (e.g., in her case, "strong separateness" in an early list).[37] Such lists in turn can easily omit or downplay other characteristics that are associated with marginalized or oppressed groups or that are of considerable importance in other cultures (even where the authors in question claim to do otherwise).

A more interactive and ideologically sensitive account of the genesis of norms, which the notion of concrete universality aspires to, can play an important role in countering one-sidedness. It requires us to be self-critical and to focus explicitly on potentially distorting and narrowly self-interested features of our own and other perspectives when advancing claims to universality, as well as in giving an account of the development of universal norms. It counsels recognition of the biases in theories that can be introduced in virtue of people's particular background or position within broader groups or societies, and it advises the use not only of self-criticism but also of dialogue with these other groups as useful correctives to overcoming such one-sidedness.

---

[36] This was also a central thesis of my early essay, Gould, "The Woman Question."
[37] Martha Nussbaum, "Human Capabilities, Female Human Beings," in *Women, Culture and Development*, ed. M. Nussbaum and Jonathan Glover (New York: Oxford University Press, 1995).

In progressive interpretations of this concrete universal approach, special attention can be given to marginalized groups who can call attention to previously unnoticed or unincorporated normative considerations, in virtue of the distinctive experiences they bring, including experiences of relative disadvantage or oppression. In present forms of society, it requires that critical attention be given to the economic class interests or political power concerns of dominant groups. Moreover, when a norm is placed in a concretely universal perspective, it is not primarily a matter of "applying" a pre-given norm to a non-normative subject matter but rather clarifying the norms themselves and their import through reflecting on the specific practices and modalities in which these norms have gained significance over time. We can then aim to create more inclusive interpretations that may result from intercultural, if sometimes conflictual, dialogue about them.

A process of correction of norms by the contribution of hitherto marginalized or oppressed groups contributes to an understanding of how the gradual universalization of communications and interactions within regional and global contexts can expand normative structures and make them more solidly grounded. One-sided interpretations are displaced over time by encounters with others who bring new perspectives and potentially reveal how norms have been narrowly drawn in the interests of the powerful and the ways these norms may be distorted by oppressive or discriminatory social structures. A classic case is the process of interpretation of civil rights norms in the United States – with the gradual inclusion of more groups within the prevailing understanding – but many such examples can be found elsewhere. In such processes, we can observe the contribution that more universal or "many-sided" relationships (to use Marx's phrase in the *Grundrisse*)[38] can make to the development and fuller understanding of the norms themselves.

Such concrete processes of universalization point to the importance of open discourses and dialogue among conflicting views in developing normative understandings and enlarging their scope, as considered later in this work, for example, in Chapter 11. One implication for Western philosophers is the need to keep interpretations of basic normative understandings open to interactive contributions from others outside the given framework.[39]

---

[38] Karl Marx, *Grundrisse: Foundations of the Critique of Political Economy*, trans. M. Nicolaus (New York: Vintage, 1973), 409. On his conception of the development of more universal relations under capitalism, see also p. 162 of that work. For a discussion, see Gould, *Marx's Social Ontology*, chapter 1.

[39] See John Dryzek, *Deliberative Democracy and Beyond* (Oxford: Oxford University Press, 2002), and John Dryzek, *Deliberative Global Politics* (Cambridge: Polity, 2006);

Besides the epistemic importance of criticism and self-criticism in regard to universal norms, I proposed in *Globalizing Democracy and Human Rights* that increasing universalization in regard to common projects, care and solidarity, and discursive processes can affect the constitutive features of the norms themselves. I suggested that in each of these areas of interaction, universality functions as a horizon or limit notion that grows out of our encounter with others – whether individuals or groups – and expresses our interdependence with them.[40]

We can see how, on such a view, the abstract and concrete norms complement and correct each other. In the abstract norm, all should be recognized as equals and treated with respect. This can helpfully serve as an inclusive principle, in its universal application to all human beings. Concretely, such recognition necessarily has to attend to differences as well as commonalities, in regard to needs and in the facilitation of common and individual projects, capacities, and relationships. Thus, the norm concretely requires the elimination of the specific disadvantages brought about by systemic injustice or oppression. In this sense, what the norms of equal agency and human rights actually require when taken in this concrete way is different from purely liberal interpretations of their demands. What are called for are not only abstract recognition of agency, and its protection by civil and political rights, but also recognition of relevant differences and especially the elimination of disadvantage and of oppression that different social and economic positions may entail. Moreover, the concrete norm requires specificity in institutional design to meet local conditions, whether economic, environmental, or cultural. Concrete universality thus connotes just such attention to the specific contexts for action and the various differentiated social interrelations that support people's equal freedom. Of course, since on this view it is not only individual activity but also common or joint activity that requires access to conditions, enabling substantial opportunities for cooperation and for participation in directing the course of such joint activity is important as well. These last requirements are discussed in Chapter 4.

Yet it is important to note here that, besides serving as an inclusive principle, the recognition of abstract equality (of agents and of their human rights) usefully serves as a corrective on just this multiplicity of interrelations. It does so by positing limits set by human rights on what are acceptable cultural practices, as discussed in Chapters 8 and 11.

Seyla Benhabib, *The Claims of Culture* (Princeton, NJ: Princeton University Press, 2002), and Seyla Benhabib, *The Rights of Others* (Cambridge: Cambridge University Press, 2004).

[40] Gould, *Globalizing Democracy*, chapter 2.

Conversely, the multiplicity of interrelations in practice over time can itself benefit self-transformative agency and individual flourishing, since individuals can draw on and appropriate an enriched stock of capacities and modes of expression. Granted, several of these practices generate conflicts as well, but sometimes (though certainly not always) the process of overcoming the obstacles and conflicts can itself contribute to flourishing. As Karl Marx aptly puts this point in his *Grundrisse*: "The overcoming of obstacles is itself a liberating activity."[41]

It is clear, then, that processes of constructing more universalistic interconnections have an important place in this normative account. I have suggested that this has to be accomplished in practice through designing effective institutional models, as well as by supporting solidaristic movements oriented to mutual aid among people, even in transnational contexts (as analyzed in Chapters 5 and 6). Solidarity practices along these lines can help to motivate and further the fulfillment of human rights and instantiate social forms of recognition.[42] In this way, they give concrete embodiment to the abstract norms that require such recognition.

---

[41] Marx, *Grundrisse*, 611, discussed in Gould, *Marx's Social Ontology*, 105–6.
[42] Carol C. Gould, "Recognition, Care, and Solidarity," in *Socialité Et Reconnaissance. Grammaires De L'Humain*, ed. G. W. Bertram *et al.* (Paris: Editions L'Harmattan, 2006).

4   Is there a human right to democracy?

Introduction

A human right to democracy is controversial, at least among political philosophers, if not on the streets of Tunisia, Egypt, Syria, and even Iran. Although the UDHR specifies a right to take part in the government of one's country – including free elections with universal suffrage – in an Article sometimes referred to as specifying a right to democracy, the term *democracy* is not explicitly mentioned,[1] perhaps because of political concerns at the time of its drafting. Indeed, some philosophers have advanced influential arguments against recognizing such a human right, generally proceeding from within a Rawlsian framework of justice. In this chapter, I begin by considering – and putting aside – some of the objections that have been lodged against recognizing democracy as a human right. Among these objections are:

(1) that if democracy were recognized as a human right, that would enable forcible intervention to impose it on countries that lack it, which would in turn involve interference with the internal affairs of the country involved;

(2) that requiring democracy would also violate the premier human right of self-determination and would additionally not show an appropriate level of toleration for societies that are not fully liberal though presumably respectful of human rights (what Rawls calls "decent societies");

(3) and relatedly, that it would involve a Western or liberal imposition on societies organized around a common good or social harmony conception; and

(4) perhaps most problematically, that democracy requires equality, which is too demanding for some societies, and is not required by a minimal or less demanding list of human rights.

---

[1] Note that Article 29 does refer to the role of law in "meeting the just requirements of morality, public order and the general welfare in a democratic society."

I am unable to consider all these objections in depth in this chapter, but will focus primarily on the last one, which has been advanced by Joshua Cohen.[2] I then go on to indicate what is involved in the claim that democracy is a human right and provide some arguments to support that proposition, drawing on my own earlier writings on the justification of democracy, as well as on the theoretical framework presented thus far in this book. It will be seen that the conception of democracy advocated here goes considerably beyond its rather bare understanding in the recognized international human rights as a matter simply of the free and universal election of representatives (however important that may be) and sees it as taking more participatory and deliberative forms. Moreover, in this view, democracy can pertain to institutional contexts beyond the political, that is, in economic and social life. And the scope of democratic decision-making can extend beyond the governments of nation-states to certain transnational contexts. After providing grounds for thinking that democracy should be recognized as a human right, we will therefore be faced with an additional question: What are the implications of such a human right for global governance? Should we be supporting global democracy writ large or more modest forms of democracy across borders?

In the discussion that follows, I appeal to two criteria for justifying democratic participation and deliberation and for determining their appropriate scope. These criteria have importantly different spheres of application. I call them the *common activities* criterion and the *all-affected* (or *affectedness*) criterion.[3] Both of these grounds for justifying democratic participation in turn raise interesting philosophical conundrums, which I can only point to here, and I address these with some brief clarifications and arguments. The first criterion, which appeals to rights of democratic participation among the members of a political community (broadly construed) raises the problem of what I previously called the *constitutional circle*, in which rights agreed to in a democratic process of constitution making would already have to be constrained by rights (in my view, these are human rights).[4]

The new case of global governance and the concomitant need for input into global policies by a broader public for which I argue also raises an interesting conundrum. While being affected can likely be interpreted to support democratic rights of input (though not full participation) by

---

[2] Joshua Cohen, "Is There a Human Right to Democracy?," in *The Egalitarian Conscience: Essays in Honour of G. A. Cohen*, ed. Christine Sypnowich (Oxford: Oxford University Press, 2006).

[3] I discussed the first of these at some length in Gould, *Rethinking Democracy*, esp. chapter 1, and the second in Gould, *Globalizing Democracy*, chapters 7 and 9.

[4] Gould, *Globalizing Democracy*, chapter 1, esp. 39–46.

distant publics in global governance, is this sort of democratic input also something that people can claim as a human right? If we choose to demarcate those affected by the degree to which their human rights are impacted by these decisions (as I in fact have previously suggested),[5] we run the danger of a different kind of potential circularity, in which human rights fulfillment serves both as a criterion for being affected and as a ground for participation by those so affected. Moreover, to further complicate matters, some level of democratic or quasi-democratic participation may be required (or at least desirable) in the process of interpreting human rights themselves and certainly for giving them effect. But this could take us in the direction of a possibly vicious circle, in which some sort of democratic participation is required for interpreting and specifying the human rights, while at the same time these very rights serve to justify democratic participation. I suggest that these issues raise theoretical questions about a human right to democracy that have not been adequately explored by political philosophers, while the practical import of such a right for global governance contexts also needs to receive much more attention from political and social theorists.

Objections to a human right to democracy – are they viable?

The most sustained and prominent set of criticisms regarding democracy as a human right has been advanced by Joshua Cohen in his article "Is There a Human Right to Democracy?"[6] Without reviewing his entire argument, we can note that – in large measure in accord with Rawls's approach – Cohen proposes that democracy is required by justice and entails a "demanding conception of equality," a conception that is more demanding than what human rights entail. Human rights, on his view, are a subset of what justice requires, and are "entitlements that establish the bases of membership" in a political society. Further, human rights are "part of an ideal of global public reason," serving as "a shared basis for political argument" among "adherents of conflicting religious and philosophical and ethical traditions."[7]

Before considering these various claims, we can note that Cohen helpfully does not endorse one of the leading objections to democracy as a human right, namely, that recognizing it would support forcible intervention in other nation-states. A consideration of this sort seems partly to have motivated Rawls's rather short list of human rights, which Rawls seems to believe would support such intervention in case they were

[5] *Ibid.*, chapter 9.   [6] *Ibid.*   [7] *Ibid.*, 226.

violated. In somewhat analogous fashion, Michael Walzer thinks of human rights in terms of a minimal list – he mentions life and liberty – that constitutes a condition for international legitimacy, and where only severe infringement would justify intervention. Clearly, for Walzer too, democracy is not one of these rights.[8]

In my view, in contrast, there need be no direct connection between recognizing or criticizing human rights violations and intervening to stop such violations. What, if anything, should be done to help people recover their human rights, or what would be involved in putting institutions in place to fulfill them is a separate question. Therefore, recognizing democratic participation as a human right would not entail that the United States or other powerful countries or alliances, or even the UN, would have the right or the duty to establish democracy in other nation-states through the use of force or other forms of intervention. The question of what duties the international community has in regard to protecting various human rights is an important question but it does not settle the issue of what rights should properly be included among the list of human rights. Although a right's being a human right surely establishes its significance, human rights also serve as goals for the development of institutions that can fulfill them, and as a basis for critique and for social and political changes short of intervention.[9] Of course, none of this implies that intervention is never justified, and it may indeed be called for in cases where basic rights are abrogated; rather, it implies only that intervention is not entailed in the recognition of something as a human right.

Accordingly, it should also be clear that human rights are not taken here as limited to the legally recognized list of international human rights. Rather, as indicated in Chapters 1 and 2, in the first place they are central normative or moral claims that call for the establishment of political (and economic and social institutions) that would realize them, along with legal instruments to assure their recognition and protection. I have interpreted their scope as fundamentally cosmopolitan in nature, though instrumentally their fulfillment may be best assured through primary institutionalization within nation-states, and secondarily at regional and more global levels.

Before proceeding to consider some of Cohen's own views regarding the meaning of democracy and human rights, I should perhaps clarify that I am operating with a broader conception of democracy than is common in the literature, broader even than electoral democracy and

---

[8] Michael Walzer, *Arguing About War* (New Haven, CT: Yale University Press, 2004), 184.
[9] Charles Beitz, "Human Rights as a Common Concern," *American Political Science Review* 95, no. 2 (2001).

certainly not requiring a particular structure of government. (I discuss this broader significance later.) Cohen himself recognizes that democracy can – and indeed should – be used to refer to a democratic form of society (in addition to its political meaning), and in this sense involves a general notion of equal respect for persons (or alternatively, in a different tradition, of equal consideration of their interests). It is therefore odd that Cohen takes democracy's commitment to equality to militate against recognizing democracy as a human right. Surprisingly, he seems not to fully acknowledge that human rights also entail a strong commitment to equality. This consists in the recognition that human rights can be claimed (equally!) by all humans. Indeed, the equality of these fundamental rights is one of their main normative features, and speaks to the power they have in contemporary discourses. Although Cohen mentions in passing that some of the human rights clearly pertain to humans as such, he chooses instead to interpret them more narrowly as bases for membership in particular political societies, seemingly modeling his view on those rights that specifically apply to modern forms of political and social life. But this interpretation does not take seriously enough the notion that human rights are those that people have simply in virtue of their humanity, an understanding that pervades the human rights documents and people's own understanding of these rights. A social or relational account of the human such as I have argued for here can also recognize the relevance of social and political organization as informing several of these rights (as recognized in the human rights documents) without losing their cosmopolitan force.

Given the reliance of human rights on notions of the fundamental freedom and equality of persons worldwide, Cohen's central objection to democracy as too egalitarian to be a human right is mystifying, since it too follows from such freedom and equality (as he acknowledges). Moreover, once the egalitarian dimension of human rights is acknowledged, it becomes impossible to accept the inequality of women or of other groups within a society as consistent with human rights, contrary to what seems implied by Cohen's (and Rawls's) view.

We can also question Cohen's underlying conception of human rights as entitlements that articulate the requirements of membership in a political society. One of the strengths of human rights, which in fact served as a ground for introducing them into global politics, is that they apply to all humans everywhere, even to stateless persons, and to immigrants and refugees seeking membership in a given political society. Although nation-states were given the role of implementing them in the first place and these rights hold primarily against the members of one's own political society, the significance of human rights transcends state boundaries, as is increasingly evident in the contemporary world. Cohen takes the social and economic human rights (e.g., in regard to welfare) to show that such rights necessarily elaborate conditions of membership in a political society. But as the recent global justice literature has revealed, it is possible to see economic human rights as showing the need for more transnational forms of transfer or redistribution.

Finally, with regard to Cohen's claims regarding global public reason and toleration supporting a limited scope for democracy around the world, we can recognize the importance of intercultural dialogue concerning the meaning of human rights without going along with the idea that it is acceptable for societies to allow systematic or structural forms of domination of some groups over others. The more cosmopolitan perspective of human rights counsels respect for the freedom and dignity of each person[10] and respect for groups that are genuinely self-determining. Such self-determination requires that all members of a society be able to participate in these dialogues and cultural interpretations, and that we not take the word of the powerful for what the people as a whole want. This would seem to require democratic forms of dialogue and interpretation, with full participation by all involved, rather than only consultative hierarchies. Indeed, it is not clear how one can ascertain that people actually endorse their own system of government unless all members have an opportunity to express this endorsement in some way. But this amounts to a requirement for forms of expression that are essentially democratic or representative. In practice too, the Arab Spring uprising of 2011 (whatever its ultimate outcome) seems clearly to have put to rest the idea that only the Global North is interested in human rights and democracy. And such groups as Women Living under Muslim Laws and various other progressive women's groups around the world have shown that it is essential to hear from historically oppressed and

---

[10] Cohen suggests that Confucian and Islamic perspectives may possibly recognize human rights in his sense but not universal human equality, and he presents this as a consideration against the more robust sort of perspective I give as being suitable for global public reason. See Cohen, "Is There a Human Right to Democracy?," 244. However, several theorists have given alternative interpretations of these and other traditions that find bases within them for important dimensions of universal equality. See, for example, Abdullahi An-Naim, "Human Rights in the Muslim World: Socio-Political Conditions and Scriptural Imperatives," *Harvard Human Rights Law Journal* 3 (1990): 13–52; Joseph Chan, "A Confucian Perspective on Human Rights for Contemporary China," in *The East Asian Challenge for Human Rights*, ed. Joanne R. Bauer and Daniel A. Bell (Cambridge: Cambridge University Press, 1999), 212–37; and Kwasi Wiredu, "An Akan Perspective on Human Rights," in *Cultural Universals and Particulars: An African Perspective* (Bloomington: Indiana University Press, 1996), 157–91. For an Islamic approach to democracy, see Azizah Al-Hibri, "Islamic Constitutionalism and the Concept of Democracy," *Case Western Reserve Journal of International Law* 24, no. 1 (1992): 7–9.

marginalized groups before accepting the notion – normally promulgated by elites – that people are satisfied living in conditions of unfreedom and inequality.

However, this sort of ringing endorsement of freedom and equality, and of democracy as a human right, should not be understood as a proclamation of simple liberal democracy, as Cohen would see it. Indeed, I have already suggested that the notions of freedom, human rights, and democracy need to be taken in more social and relational ways than they usually are and are susceptible to a certain range of cultural interpretations. I am unable to elaborate this claim in depth in this chapter, but I hope it will be evident that this social conception informs the justification of democracy as a human right.

Democracy as a human right

On the view presented in this work, human rights specify the material, social, and political conditions needed for the development of people's agency, where this agency is taken in the first place as human life activity and in a fuller sense as the development of capacities and relationships, and the realization of long-term projects over time. Human rights are part of this broader account of positive or effective freedom, which understands people to be equally agents. Given that individuals realize their projects or develop capacities in interaction with others, various forms of *common or joint activity* play a major role in this conception, and this is especially important for the case of democracy.

I have argued that the full recognition of human rights is supported by a normative conception of justice as equal positive freedom, as equal rights to the conditions of self-transformation (whether the latter are individual or social). This argument proceeds from the equal (basic) agency of all to the requirement of access to conditions for people to develop capacities and realize projects. Since their basic agency is equal, and requires conditions for its development, no one of them has more of a claim to these conditions than do others. This asserts that they have prima facie equally valid claims of access – that is, in Feinberg's terms, equal rights – to these fundamental conditions of action. Various democratic rights (e.g., freedom of expression and association) evidently play an important role in protecting people's basic liberty and also their further flourishing.

Beyond this, we can see the argument for democracy as itself is a human right. Inasmuch as people are social beings, or "individuals-in-relations," engaging in common or joint activities with others can be seen as itself one of the prime conditions for their freedom. Common activities are here broadly understood to be activities oriented to shared goals. If none are to dominate others in these joint activities, they must have equal rights to participate in determining their course. This is a very general principle that pertains to joint activities of diverse sizes. In my view, when such common activities are institutionalized, they serve as arenas for democratic decision-making in a formal sense, and no longer remain merely casual or ad hoc. Democracy is thus a form of decision-making involving equal rights of participation among the members of a given community or institution. It is therefore broader in application than only to political societies, although the latter have been its prime context and certainly remains the main sphere in which it is taken to apply. Beyond this broader scope, democracy as a form of deliberation and decision-making needs to be understood more flexibly than simply as a political system defined by elections and majority rule (although there is much to commend those procedures). Accordingly, the approach here does not take a stand between parliamentary or winner-take-all systems of representation or between different sets of voting rules. Democracy can include consensus decision-making and even certain consultative methods, providing the procedures respect equality among the participants.

It is evident that this represents a quite expansive conception of democracy, one that supports the extension of democratic forms of decision to institutions beyond the political and also sees it as applying to all intensionally defined communities, that is, where people take themselves to be part of a community, or engaged in "common activities" defined by shared goals. The global import of this is that democratic participation is required not only within nation-states, but also in the newer transnational or cross-border communities that are emerging with economic, technological, and ecological globalization. This approach would also support democratic participation at the global level to the degree that the world came to be understood as a single political community.

However, it is also clear that this justification for democracy, however wide-ranging, does not yet address what are perhaps the most important forms of democratic participation that are lacking globally and seem very much to be needed. The need for such new forms grows out of the impacts that decisions or policies by the institutions of global governance or by other powerful actors like nation-states and corporations have on people who are distantly situated and not part of these institutions or communities. This problem, of exogenous impacts on distant others and of the democratic deficit involved in global governance, needs to be addressed with a different criterion for democratic participation, though one that has some deep connections to the first. I have previously proposed the relevance of the "all-affected" or affectedness criterion for

If I choose not to participate, am I giving up a human right?

such contexts, and have argued that this criterion needs to be further specified in order to avoid the implication that since everyone may be distantly affected by many global policies therefore everyone would need to be able to participate in every decision and policy – clearly an unsupportable consequence. I have suggested instead that it is possible to demarcate those who are *importantly affected* in terms of a notion of the *fulfillment of basic human rights,* and to propose that when people are thus affected in their ability to realize these basic rights, they should have significant input into the decision or policy in question, though not necessarily fully equal rights of participation. This contrasts with the case of the "common activities" criterion discussed previously, where equal opportunities for participation among the members of a given community are always required.[11]

We now have the question whether "affectedness" serves to support a claim to a human right to democracy in this sense of having a say, or significant input, in cases where people at a distance are importantly impacted by a given policy or decision. That is, does the human right to democratic participation pertain not only to the robust sense of equal rights of participation within communities (the "common activities" criterion) but also to rights of participation in decisions or policies of powerful institutions on the part of nonmembers (in accordance with the "affectedness" criterion)? On the one hand, one could argue that this latter sort of participation in decisions that affect human rights fulfillment is in fact mandated, because of the importance of these human rights conditions for their agency, and because their individual self-determination must be respected. Insofar as human rights specify central conditions that people require for self-transformative activity – that is, are conditions for their positive freedom – democratic participation by those so affected would indeed be needed to avoid domination or control by outsiders, whether this domination takes structural and institutional form or is exercised more directly. On the other hand, in regard to many global policies, at least at present, people tend to be *differentially* affected, so that they would lack *equal* rights of participation, which seem to be required by the earlier argument for a human right to democracy. In the case of the necessary contribution to decisions by distant others, I think it makes sense to limit the democratic participation to what can be called significant input or "having a say," to distinguish it from the equal membership case, which requires fully equal rights of robust participation. However, it should be remembered that many of those affected at a distance are

---

[11] Carol C. Gould, *Globalizing Democracy,* chapters 7 and 9; and Gould, "Structuring Global Democracy," included in revised form as Chapter 12 of this book.

in fact more seriously impacted by the decisions or policies in question than are the current powerful decision makers themselves. For example, if Shell Oil decides on actions in Nigeria, it may in fact have more of an effect on Nigerians than on the policy makers. So, given this affectedness criterion, there is no necessary conclusion that they should have fewer opportunities to take part in the decision-making or to influence the outcome than do those currently holding the power to decide or to make policy.

I believe it is possible to argue for a human right to democracy in both the cases I have discussed – that of equal rights of participation for members of existing communities and institutions (whether national or transnational), and rights of democratic input into decisions that importantly affect one's fulfillment of basic human rights, even when one is not a member of the polity or community in question. In fact, both of the criteria – common activities and all-affected – as applied here can be interpreted as deriving from a conception of positive freedom. The first one does so by virtue of the fact that participation in common activities is a condition for such freedom and from the recognition that there should be equal rights of codetermination of these activities. The second case, of participation by those at a distance but importantly affected by decisions, also appeals to people's rights to have some control over their own activity and the conditions for it. If others are determining the fundamental possibilities for the agency of distantly situated groups of people by affecting their basic human rights, then these latter should have some say about it.[12] The forms of appropriate input will vary from consultation to some representation within the decision procedures themselves. Nonetheless, to the degree that these distant others are exogenously affected by policies rather than being equal members of a community (political or otherwise), their participation is presumably not subject to the robust requirements of the common activities criterion.

Interestingly, some recent theorists have sought to reinterpret rights of participation even in communal or standard democratic cases in differential ways depending on the various and differential impacts that

---

[12] Note that being affected here need not always be negative. For example, even if the impact of a transnational corporation is held to benefit the affected people and the people are disposed to make the required transition, for example, an agrarian society gaining important access to means of subsistence but in a way that impacts their traditional way of life, the argument here is that others ought not to make these decisions – including any tradeoffs between basic rights – on behalf of those affected without their input and consent. Those affected would have a right to participate in the decision or policy in question and appropriate institutional arrangements are needed to facilitate this input. It is thus a matter of who makes the decision rather than which decision is the better one; the claim here is that those people affected in their basic rights need to be an essential part of the process.

policies have on people within the community, and have accordingly argued for proportional rights of input or participation.[13] My own inclination is instead to retain the emphasis on equal participation for communities or for the members of institutions, and to add the possibility of differential participation for nonmembers whose interests and human rights fulfillment are foreseeably seriously affected by the decisions and policies of these communities and institutions. As we will see, this is particularly important in regard to global governance institutions. However, it should be remembered that it may not always be the powerful decision makers who have the most at stake in these various policies and plans.

Theoretical problems in the relation of democracy and human rights at the global level

In *Globalizing Democracy and Human Rights*, I articulated a problem that I called the 'constitutional circle,' in which democratic or consensual processes of determining constitutional rights in a democracy themselves have to be constrained by rights.[14] My proposal for avoiding that circle was to suggest that the rights that are recognized in this process are not in fact constituted by democratic choice but are those that are already ingredient in social life and that also give rise to the requirement of democracy in collective decision-making. I identify these fundamental rights with the valid claims that each makes on others for the conditions of self-transformation and see this sort of claiming as based on social processes of reciprocity and of care. Whereas reciprocal recognition may often take an instrumental or tit-for-tat form, more developed versions may come to involve mutual respect and explicitly shared aims. When the interdependence of persons is most fully realized, reciprocity can take the form of what I earlier called mutuality, which involves not only a recognition of equal agency but relational forms oriented to enhancement of the other.[15] This latter is, of course, more common in interpersonal relations, rather than in politics or economics or in institutional forms more generally.

When we move to the global level, however, new problems of potential circularity emerge, especially if we take impact on (or being affected in)

---

[13] See Eric Cavallero, "Federative Global Democracy," *in Special Issue on Global Democracy and Exclusion, ed. Ronald Tinnevelt and Helder de Schutter, Metaphilosophy* 40, no. 1 (2009), 42–64.

[14] Gould, *Globalizing Democracy*, 39–46.

[15] See also Gould, "Beyond Causality"; and Carol C. Gould, "Feminism and Democratic Community Revisited," in *Democratic Community: NOMOS XXXV*, ed. J. Chapman and I. Shapiro (New York: New York University Press, 1993), 396–413.

one's possibilities for fulfilling human rights as a criterion for requiring democratic input into a given decision. This might seem problematic if it is also recognized that democracy is one of the human rights. And it would indeed be awkward (at best) to propose that what justifies democratic input is the effect of decisions on the possibilities of exercising democratic decision-making. Explaining why the approach I propose for input from distant others is not in fact circular in this way can also help clarify the significance of "affectedness" as a justification for democratic participation and its connection to the first criterion of codetermination of common activities.

If we examine the significance of "being affected" (in the specified sense of being importantly affected), we can see that it is in fact grounded in positive freedom, as are the human rights themselves, which in my view specify the conditions required if freedom is to be effective. Likewise, the requirement of democratic participation in determining common activities (the first criterion given above) has roots in this same norm of positive or effective freedom, on my account. This suggests that the two criteria I have proposed – common activities and impact on distant others' human rights – share much of the same basis. In the affectedness case, the requirement for people to have a say follows from their need to have some control over the conditions of their life activity. The impact on human rights thus only provides a determinate, and in some cases a measurable, way of gauging whether decisions will significantly affect people's freedom. It is what triggers the need for democratic input, where these human rights are valuable by contributing to the more basic value of positive freedom. Thus I suggest that there is no circle at the level of justification.

Still, some might suggest that a circularity remains (though a less troubling one), if we claim that the human rights to be considered as affected by a given decision or policy include democracy among others. One way around this would be to clarify that impact only on the basic human rights of subsistence, security, and fundamental liberty is what triggers the need for democratic input. In this case, democratic input would be instrumental to realizing these basic human rights (as distinct from impacting those conditions needed for its fuller flourishing as specified in the nonbasic, though still essential, human rights). An alternative way of dismissing the circularity would be to distinguish between the two senses of democratic human rights characterized earlier, with the robust requirement of equal participation in common decisions characterized as Democracy1, and the input sense articulated in the second case as Democracy2. Even if the argument were made that impact of decisions or policies on the possibilities of fulfilling the human right to democracy

EPF "triggers the need for democratic input"

(as Democracy1) is sufficient to trigger the requirement for input into these decisions, circularity would be avoided since the claim would then be that Democracy2 is required for the fulfillment of Democracy1.

Moreover, regarding the further potential circularity that there is a need for some (quasi-) democratic deliberation regarding the meaning of the various human rights themselves, we can observe that this is not a serious problem for my approach, since this sort of deliberation is not constitutive of the rights themselves and does not itself serve to justify them (as would be the case on some deliberativist views of democratic justification). Finally, it is worth emphasizing that despite the close connections I have indicated between the common activities criterion and the democratic input one, a difference between them remains with regard to whether strictly equal decision-making is required (at least in principle). The first criterion requires equal rights of participation. The second criterion – namely, affectedness – may admit of some differentiation, recognizing again that people at a distance may in fact be more affected by decisions than are the decision makers. In that case, they should have a greater say, even though they are distantly situated in space. It is clear, then, that the "affectedness" principle cannot be satisfied by simply hearing from broader publics in a superficial or random way. It requires the development of procedures for systematically involving the affected people in the decisions or policies taken by powerful transnational actors or institutions of global governance. Thus, when taken in its relation to human rights and ultimately to people's positive freedom, this criterion can also be a highly demanding one, even though it does not necessarily incorporate the requirement for equal rights of participation by equal members as the more familiar communal criterion does.

Democratic input into global governance institutions

We can finally sketch some possible applications of this analysis to the difficult issue of how more democracy can be introduced into the various forms of transnational decision-making. I propose that there are four possible directions for moving toward democratic participation in those contexts, which I briefly take note of in this final part and only in general terms. It is important to acknowledge that none of these are likely to be developed in the short term and also that their development will require considerable institutional innovation.

The fourfold strategy is as follows:

(1) Democratic procedures need to be introduced into all (self-understood) communities and institutions, which are increasingly

non-deliberative.

by whom?

cross-border or transnational, whether regional or global. This requirement follows from the common activities criterion discussed above, in view of the principle of equal positive freedom. I have suggested that members of these communities have equal rights to codetermine these institutionalized contexts, whether in politics, economics (e.g., in firms), or social life, and whether the relevant institutions are within or across borders. Indeed, as we see in Chapter 14, democratic participation in economic institutions, especially in the form of worker management in firms, is an especially important step in making these institutions more responsive to people's needs. To the degree that large companies and wealthy donors have come to dominate over democratic politics in the United States and elsewhere, this change may also help to mitigate those deleterious tendencies to a degree. An additional, more general benefit of proliferating contexts of democracy is that widespread opportunities for democratic procedures (formal or informal) – if they were genuine and made use of – would likely contribute to a democratic culture and to the evolution of what I earlier called the democratic personality.[16] The democratic procedures involved here would include not only equal opportunities for participation and deliberation where possible, but also forms of representation coupled with online and offline input and deliberation, which are discussed in Chapter 12. A relevant principle for the organization of decision-making in these various contexts is provided by the idea of subsidiarity, with decisions to be taken at the most local levels possible, but where the local is taken to apply to geographical localities like cities,[17] and can also extend to new forms of cross-border or transnational communities organized around ecological, economic, or communicative shared goals or interests.[18]

(2) Proposals for a global democratic parliament, or Global People's Assembly, within the UN should be implemented. However, such a parliament would only be significant if it had real authority. Moreover, a people's assembly does not yet amount to some sort of ultimate plan in my view, primarily because it leaves the "great powers"

---

[16] Gould, *Rethinking Democracy*, 283–306.

[17] There is a growing literature on urban democracy, which would helpfully supplement the analysis here. See, for example, David Harvey, *Rebel Cities: From the Right to the City to the Urban Revolution* (London: Verso, 2012); Neil Brenner, *New State Spaces: Urban Governance and the Rescaling of Statehood* (Oxford: Oxford University Press, 2004).

[18] For a discussion of this new conception of the local, see Carol C. Gould, "Negotiating the Global and the Local: Situating Transnational Democracy and Human Rights," in *Democracy in a Global World: Human Rights and Political Participation in the 21st Century*, ed. Deen K. Chatterjee (Lanham, MD: Rowman & Littlefield, 2007).

in place as they are currently. Nonetheless, to the degree that a set of global shared ends are emerging and coming to be recognized, this sort of global parliament could also be seen to follow from the common activities criterion, as enunciated here. A full discussion of global vs. regional democracy is undertaken in the final chapter of this book.

(3) As already suggested in Chapter 1, there is a need to devise new forms of public input and new modes of transnational representation within the institutions of global governance. This representation would have to go beyond giving INGOs a seat at the table; and the NGOs themselves must in any case become more representative. As with the first proposal, the public input called for can be increasingly enabled by the use of deliberative software and other forms of online interaction (e.g., in forums), and I have elsewhere suggested how these new formats can contribute to influence in decisions and policies by a dispersed transnational public.[19] Representative deliberative polling is also a possible direction for innovation at the global level. However, such polling would need to go beyond sampling or merely soliciting opinions. If polling is to be effective, politicians would have to commit to taking the results of these deliberations as binding. But we can see how these suggested directions could help to concretize the second criterion's requirement for gaining input on the part of those significantly affected by the policies of global governance institutions. These options for increasing transnational participation and representation are taken up in Part III of this book.

(4) Finally, the least likely new direction in the short run, but worth considering for the longer term would be the development of a system of delegate assemblies, based on principles of subsidiarity, with real power to determine global policies, for example, concerning regulatory matters and labor policies. These assemblies could be geographically based or for some issues could be functionally oriented, and would need to involve the election of delegates at higher levels. This alternate approach to representation (including in transnational contexts) would be designed to give ordinary and distantly situated people a say in accordance with the affectedness criterion, and if successful could serve as something of an antidote to the currently unresponsive and very powerful institutions of global governance. Delegate assemblies or people's assemblies have been used in southern Europe and in Latin America. Perhaps they could take different forms in other regions of the world. In any case, it may well be

---

[19] Gould, "Global Democratic Transformation and the Internet."

who is going to build them?

helpful to think about constructing some of these alternate sources of democratic power, in addition to finding ways to make existing political communities and economic institutions, whether domestic or transnational, more deeply democratic and more responsive to the needs and the participation of distant others.

Part II

The social roots of global justice

5   Transnational solidarities

Introduction

It should be clear from the foregoing chapters that the fulfillment of global justice and human rights, as well as increases in democracy, cannot be accomplished through political changes alone, or by means of individual acts of humanitarianism or charity. In this part of the book, I want to investigate some of the key social roots of global justice and related norms, and to consider the social dispositions and transformations that their fulfillment requires. In this investigation, the notion of solidarity and the related concept of mutual aid loom large. Later in this part, I take up care and recognition, gender equality in diverse cultures and the issue of interpreting human rights, expression in cross-cultural perspective, and new cooperative notions of power that may help to deal with contemporary violence and the problems it poses for extending democracy and justice transnationally.

This chapter attempts to re-envision solidarity from its primary historical meaning as a relationship binding all the members of a single cohesive group or society toward a conception more suitable for the new forms of transnational interrelationships that mark contemporary globalization. It considers the supportive relations we can come to develop with people at a distance, given the interconnections that are being established through work or other economic ties, through participation in Internet forums and especially through social media, or indirectly through environmental impacts. Solidarity relations are reconceptualized here as potentially contributing to the emergence of more democratic forms of transnational interaction within regional or more fully global frameworks of human rights, for which I have argued earlier in this book and in previous work.[1] Beyond this, I propose that affective relations of solidarity are an essential complement to the recognition of these human rights themselves. This new notion of solidarity is understood here as one of *overlapping*

---

[1] Gould, *Globalizing Democracy*.

overlapping solidarity networks

solidarity networks. It will be seen that this conception also engages the idea of justice, and indeed of global justice, in an important way.

This analysis builds on previous attempts by feminist theorists to articulate a notion of care suitable for globalization, including Fiona Robinson on women's care work and human security, Joan Tronto on public care in a national context, and Virginia Held on the impact of care ethics for the consideration of moral relations among nations.[2] I propose that solidarity is a more helpful notion than care for these contexts because it is more suitable for describing the relations of social and political groups and associations to each other, while care is most fully applicable to interpersonal relationships (though care work is a significant factor in our understanding of international political economy). Further, while care has sometimes been seen as a replacement for rights talk, I see both care and solidarity as supplementing and motivating a commitment to equal rights (especially as human rights).

Feminist theorists have also articulated a role for *empathy* in order to illuminate certain features of moral reflection in international affairs. This signifies an imaginative understanding of the perspective, situation, and needs of others as a basis for moral action in response to them, and I have previously given an argument along these lines.[3] Such approaches have sought in different ways to introduce elements of sentiment or emotional understanding in order to explain the ties that bind people to distant others in this period of greater global integration and that can provide a basis for conceptualizing moral responsibilities toward them, or at least an account of our motivations for taking these seriously. In this chapter, I suggest that solidarity, as a form of *social empathy*, is an even more useful concept than simple care or empathy for these new transnational contexts.

Yet, any effort to theorize global care, empathy, or solidarity immediately comes up against what seems to be an impossibility theorem, namely, that it violates the stricture that "ought implies can." How can people possibly feel care, empathy, or solidarity with everyone else? To the degree that these normative notions are in fact based in sentiment, which is inevitably particularistic and limited, they would seem inapplicable to our relations to distant others in any universalistic sense. Even applying them to a subset of strangers seems exhausting and hopeless.

---

[2] Fiona Robinson, *Globalizing Care* (Boulder, CO: Westview, 1999); Fiona Robinson, *The Ethics of Care: A Feminist Approach to Human Security* (Philadelphia, PA: Temple University Press, 2011); Joan Tronto, *Caring Democracy* (New York: New York University Press, 2013); Virginia Held, "Care and Justice in the Global Context," *Ratio Juris* 17, no. 2 (2004).

[3] See Gould, *Globalizing Democracy*, chapter 12.

Indeed, the specific concept that concerns us here, solidarity, has in fact had its proper home, sociologically speaking, in *intra*group relations, as the solidarity among the members of a particular group, which has, at most, been extended to understanding the relations among individuals within a particular nation. Here, I highlight another, rather different, use of the concept of solidarity, in which it can reasonably apply to relations to others at a distance. This move is only possible if we take solidarity to denote a relationship to individuals or groups smaller than the universe of human beings generally. Thus it will become clear that my concept does not fall prey to Richard Rorty's criticism of any purely abstract concept of human solidarity;[4] however, I later go on to demarcate a certain sense of it that is nonetheless universalistic.

I do not simply propose a revision of solidarity that takes it in a wholly new direction, diverging from any of its existing meanings. We can see how the historic dialectic of the concept itself (so to speak) requires, or better, enables the move to a notion of transnational networked solidarities. This becomes evident if we analyze the treatment of solidarity by its great theoretician in sociology, Durkheim. So, in what follows, I begin by outlining and evaluating some of the existing analyses and categorizations of solidarity. I then consider certain of its constructive features, taking off from the accounts of mutual feeling and mutual aid offered by Sandra Bartky, Andrew Mason, Tommie Shelby, and Klaus Rippe, and go on to sketch the way that I envision norms of solidarity applying to cross-border or transnational relationships.

A methodological point is worth making here: In both the review and the positive account, solidarity is treated both descriptively and normatively. The analysis does not, I think, confuse these uses, although it sees the norm as, in part, emerging from practical social and historical solidaristic activities and movements, and as capable of being formulated on the basis of these actual phenomena. The discussion seeks to foreground key features of solidarity relations that are normatively desirable by reflecting on facets of certain actually existing relationships. The suggestion is that it would be good to see them become more widely adopted, and the philosophical conceptualization here is intended to make a contribution, however small, to that process.

After laying out a conception of transnational solidarity, the chapter concludes with a consideration of some of the philosophical issues that remain problematic in this account. These difficulties arise with the new conception of solidarity proposed here, insofar as it functions as a moral

---

[4] Richard Rorty, *Contingency, Irony, and Solidarity* (Cambridge: Cambridge University Press, 1989).

notion within global ethics and as an important social aspect of transnational democratic interrelationships between people.

Conceptions of solidarity – social, political, human

The concept of solidarity came to prominence in sociology in the analysis of Emile Durkheim, who distinguished between mechanical and organic solidarity. Surprisingly, perhaps, "mechanical" does not apply to post-industrial-revolution societies, but, on the contrary, characterizes the relation among members of traditional communities where each member is similarly characterized in terms of identities and perspectives, and stands in the same relation as others to the community as a whole. This holistic interpretation is contrasted with the more modern "organic" solidarity, where people are linked in interdependent relations with others through an extended division of labor. Here their ties to each other occur almost behind their backs, especially proceeding via their economic interrelations, in which they function as differentiated parts of a large organism.[5]

Even this brief account of organic solidarity – in which relations are mediated by the division of labor – already sharply suggests the need for an expanded understanding of solidarity within a global context. For it is evident that economic integration has in fact extended the division of labor beyond the borders of a given society. And the interdependencies that contribute to this sort of solidarity are thus increasingly transnational rather than only local or national. This lends support to the move I am proposing here, which is to envision a conception of solidarity beyond the two that Durkheim describes, one that takes the concept past the idea of a certain unity within a group or within a society, although it retains the notion of differentiation characteristic of Durkheim's second sense. We can name this new significance *network solidarity*, or better, the plural *solidarities*, and I characterize it later in the chapter. For now, we can briefly take note of some contemporary attempts to offer typologies of solidarity that go beyond the initial Durkheimian conception in various ways.

Kurt Bayertz begins his important account by distinguishing between the descriptive and normative uses of the term *solidarity*, where both refer to a form of mutual attachment between individuals, and where

---

[5] Emile Durkheim, *The Division of Labor in Society*, trans. George Simpson (New York: The Free Press, 1964), especially 63–4 and 127–9. See also the discussion in David Heyd, "Justice and Solidarity: The Contractarian Case against Global Justice," *Journal of Social Philosophy*, Special Issue on Solidarity, co-edited by Carol C. Gould and Sally Scholz, 38, no. 1 (2007).

the normative use requires mutual obligations to aid each other when necessary. He characterizes solidarity as designating positive obligations to act, which are particularistic, and pertain to other members of the community to which one belongs.[6] He distinguishes four uses of the term:

(1) The first refers to a relation among humans, conceived as "one big moral community," or as universal solidarity, in other words, as a fraternity among human beings generally. Yet, the conflict and competition between people counts against the viability of this interpretation, in his view, as does the inevitably particularistic nature of solidaristic feelings.

(2) This recognition is reflected in the second usage, where solidarity designates the "inner cement" holding a society together. A further distinction here is between the sort of friendship possible within a community, such as Bayertz finds in Aristotle's idea of civic friendship,[7] and the more anonymous forms of interconnection characteristic of modern societies. In this regard, he holds that Durkheim's distinction between the ideal types of mechanical and organic solidarity is helpful.

(3) Another sense of solidarity occurs when people form a group to stand up for common interests. Descriptively, for Bayertz, this can include negative manifestations like a band of criminals or more positive ones like social movements (e.g., labor, women, ecology, etc.). Normatively, this use involves a reference to justice and the achievement of rights, and "involves a commitment against an opponent, from whom positive goals must be wrung."[8] Labor movement solidarity falls within this type.

(4) Finally, there is the use of the concept prevalent especially in Europe, as the solidarity of the welfare state. Here it designates the responsibility of compatriots to help the needy among them, not out of charity but in virtue of the ties that bind fellow citizens to each other, and in recognition of the role of luck and other extrinsic factors in contributing to such neediness. These requirements are often transferred to a bureaucratic apparatus, which leads to a dilution of the solidarity involved.

---

[6] Kurt Bayertz, "Four Uses of 'Solidarity.'" in *Solidarity*, ed. Kurt Bayertz (Dordrecht: Kluwer, 1999).

[7] On civic friendship, see Sibyl Schwarzenbach, "Civic Friendship," *Ethics* 107 (1998); and Sibyl Schwarzenbach, *On Civic Friendship: Including Women in the State* (New York: Columbia University Press, 2009).

[8] Bayertz, "Four Uses of 'Solidarity,'" 17.

In some contrast with Bayertz's account, Jodi Dean has advanced a tripartite division among types of solidarity. She distinguishes between affectional solidarity, conventional solidarity, which "grows out of common interests and concerns," and finally the type she advocates, "reflective solidarity," which emerges from discourse in situations of dissent and difference.[9]

This cursory review of typologies of solidarity already suggests how difficult it is to find within them a space for the new sorts of transnational solidarity that I am attempting to conceptualize here. Most existing usages pertain to the relations among individuals within a single group, usually thought of as a community. Where theorists discuss transnational applications at all, it involves conceiving solidarity as involving a (rather haphazard) relationship of an individual to others at a distance or to dialogical relations with others. I believe that we need to develop the norm of solidarity beyond these characterizations and suggest that it can characterize both relations among individuals and among associations. In this way, it takes on a more dispersed but also more social aspect.

Of course, Bayertz and others do take brief note of labor movement solidarity, where this idea has been developed in its international import by Karl Marx and some subsequent writers in the Marxist tradition, as well as by more recent labor movement theorists.[10] But we can say that the labor movement represents only one rather limited model for transnational solidarity, though it is an especially important one. A more general and potentially transnational account is suggested by Chandra Mohanty, who focuses on something like Bayertz's third sense, but highlights its conflictual aspects and departs from Bayertz's interest-based account. Thus, Mohanty interprets solidarity as involving an "inherently oppositional nature and a mutually shared vision."[11] In her terms, "it is the common context of struggles against specific exploitative structures and systems that determines our potential political alliances."[12]

Before moving to a fuller positive account of transnational solidarity as a contemporary phenomenon and norm, we should make mention of Craig Calhoun's interesting discussion of social solidarity constructed through a public sphere of discourse and cultural interpretation,

---

[9] Jodi Dean, *Solidarity of Strangers* (Berkeley: University of California Press, 1996), chapter 1.

[10] Henry J. Frundt, "Movement Theory and International Labor Solidarity," *Labor Studies Journal* 1, no. 2 (2005).

[11] Chandra Talpade Mohanty, *Feminism without Borders: Decolonizing Theory, Practicing Solidarity* (Durham, NC: Duke University Press, 2003), 49.

[12] *Ibid.*

especially through the participation of civil society associations.[13] Although this can be potentially transnational, as in the EU, Calhoun sees solidarity as a matter of the construction of a people, or a single democratic polity. Moreover, with Dean, solidarity in this reading is understood as taking place through discourse and not also through shared activities, though it is helpfully understood as constructed.

A conception of solidarities as constituted in this way is useful for transnational contexts in one important sense: it suggests how new cross-border communities and associations, whether in Internet forums, or worldwide professional associations, or local cross-border ecological or economic groupings, can develop some degree of social solidarity (in its traditional sense) among themselves. This older idea of solidarity within groups has a place in globalization, not only in its application to the still robust political communities that make up nation-states on an ongoing basis, but also in application to emerging cross-border communities or associations, whether local or regional.

Feeling-with, mutual concern, and mutual aid

In order to lay the ground for analyzing a newer sense of solidarity as an ethical and social norm suitable for the emerging transnational situation, we can examine more closely some central notions that have been regarded as constitutive of the idea by philosophers – first of all, fellow feeling or mutual concern, and second, mutual aid, or at least a disposition to mutual aid. An obvious question to keep in mind here is to what degree mutuality in either sense can be regarded as a plausible dimension of cross-border interactions with people one most often does not know personally.

Sandra Bartky has given a useful analysis of the idea of solidarity by way of a return to Scheler's original notion of "Mitgefuhl," or feeling-with.[14] Drawing on his account of what she reluctantly translates as "fellow-feeling," Bartky emphasizes the affective aspects of solidarity. She rightly stresses the role of imagination as a basis for the intuition of the feelings and situation of the other, while also showing how one need not presuppose that one has already experienced those feelings oneself. Bartky also helpfully calls attention to the importance of having a certain cognitive understanding of the concrete specifics of the other's context.

[13] Craig Calhoun, "Imagining Solidarity: Cosmopolitanism, Constitutional Patriotism, and the Public Sphere," *Public Culture* 14, no. 1 (2002).
[14] Sandra Lee Bartky, *Sympathy and Solidarity* (Lanham, MD: Rowman & Littlefield, 2002), chapter 4.

However, Bartky's characterization of solidarity would seem to apply just as well to empathy, and although she recognizes the importance of socializing the notion of solidarity, it remains for her primarily a relation of one individual to another. By contrast, I propose that we understand solidarity as in part the social counterpart to empathy, and see it as applying also to relations of an individual to the members of a different group, and to the relations among groups.

Andrew Mason identifies "mutual concern" as a key feature of solidarity, used in a normative sense to characterize the relation among members of what he terms a moral community.[15] He writes that "minimally, this means that members must give each other's interests some non-instrumental weight in their practical reasoning."[16] He adds an additional requirement – that there be no exploitation or systematic injustice. This latter condition importantly ties normative solidarity to justice. And although Mason considers mutual concern among the members of a single – presumably given – community, this is certainly a feature that can be extended more widely. The problem, however, is whether or not we can speak of mutual concern among strangers, and particularly when others may not even be aware of the people standing in solidarity with them.

Beyond mutual concern, several authors have identified mutual aid as a feature of descriptive solidarity among members of a given community or political state, and duties of mutual aid as the normative counterpart. Of course, as we have seen, solidarity owes much to Durkheim's account of its modern form, in which there is not simply common feeling but a cooperative relation between individuals established through the division of labor. In this way, solidarity diverges from the earlier emphasis on *fraternity*. Solidarity in principle makes room for the diversity of individuals who are concerned for each other and either do aid each other or recognize obligations to do so when necessary. It is this latter use that I find especially interesting for theorizing transnational solidarity.[17]

As requiring such positive duties of aid, solidarity may be thought to go beyond justice, though it is its partner. Thus Habermas treats solidarity

---

[15] Andrew Mason, *Community, Solidarity and Belonging* (Cambridge: Cambridge University Press, 2000), 27.

[16] *Ibid.*

[17] It is perhaps misleading to say that descriptive solidarity even within a given community involves mutual aid. It would be more precise to say that it is characterized by a disposition to provide mutual aid, since some members of a solidaristic community may not need this aid. Yet, perhaps the idea is that cooperative relations within a community necessarily entail mutual aid. But this would be a rather strange use of the idea of mutual aid to signify any sort of cooperation. Normatively, the case seems clearer – it involves duties or obligations (without settling which of these terms is more apt at this point) to aid others in need.

as the other side of justice.[18] Some theorists, for example, Andreas Wildt, in his helpful historical account of the term, hold that solidarity requires that "the agent does not believe that the recipient has a legal or moral right to his help,"[19] and that it is thus supererogatory. In this sense, solidaristic action cannot be demanded, but only appealed for. Nonetheless, a reading that separates solidarity from justice would make it difficult to see feelings of human solidarity as a ground for the universal respect for human rights, which we have seen are centrally important constituents of a normative framework for contemporary globalization. Further, such a division would diminish the role of solidarity in situations of perceived exploitation, where it is called on to help rectify injustice. These interconnections between solidarity, rights, and justice are considered further at various points in what follows. We may note here, however, that in some uses, solidarity may apply more broadly, even to cases where people are impacted by natural disasters, in addition to these socially caused situations.

If mutual aid is an important aspect of the concept of solidarity, then this implies that it is connected to the concept of reciprocity. In this sense, the people involved in solidaristic relations are not only reciprocally concerned about each other, but are also mutually disposed to aid each other when required. Even if one of them is better off than the other, there is an expectation of a reciprocal readiness to aid the first if the need were to develop. However, the category of mutual aid is presumably larger than that of solidarity, since the former includes various sorts of aid offered as "tit for tat," by way of exchanges or instrumental relations between people. Solidarity specifies the more general category of mutual aid to cases where there is some degree of fellow feeling and a positive moral obligation to act, presumably along with an altruistic motivation to provide such aid. There is normally the desire to help the recipient and, furthermore, a desire to help in rectifying a perceived injustice that the recipient suffers. If this is so, then while solidarity goes beyond respect for rights, it can be concerned with action to help realize rights, including the range of human rights, both positive and negative. However, it is not yet clear that reciprocity can be operative in most cases of solidarity with distant others, since these others may not be aware of one's actions in solidarity with them. So this poses yet another difficulty for the transnational application to be addressed in the next part.

---

[18] Jürgen Habermas, "Justice and Solidarity: On the Discussion Concerning Stage 6," in *The Moral Domain: Essays in the Ongoing Discussion between Philosophy and the Social Sciences*, ed. Thomas E. Wren (Cambridge, MA: MIT Press, 1990).
[19] Andreas Wildt, "Solidarity: Its History and Contemporary Definition," in *Solidarity*, ed. Kurt Bayertz (Dordrecht: Kluwer, 1999), 217.

Before proceeding to that application, some further insight into the construction of an adequate theory of solidarity can be gleaned from the work of Tommie Shelby on black solidarity. Abstracting from his complex and nuanced account, I wish to emphasize the connection that he draws between solidarity and resistance to oppression, as well as his disjoining of a solidarity group from the idea of collective identity. Rejecting the view that such a group is constituted by blackness as an identity or as a culturally self-determining community or group, Shelby instead places the emphasis on shared oppression and action to eliminate it as the key factors in the constitution of such a group.[20]

A final contribution to our understanding of solidarity can be found in the work of Klaus Peter Rippe. This contribution can be found in his interesting articulation of what he calls "project-related solidarity." Although he regards this phenomenon as relatively trivial from a moral point of view, I think it is of some importance, and partly captures what is involved in transnational solidarity. Rippe cites Bayertz in understanding solidarity "as a term used to describe acts carried out in order to support others, or at the very least to describe a disposition to help and assist."[21] In its positive sense for Rippe, it is characterized not by interpersonal relationships among people who know each other, but by such phenomena as solidarity movements or appeals to solidarity. He gives as examples "the solidarity with the leftists in Chile, with the Sandinistas in Nicaragua, with transport workers on strike in Paris, with children afflicted by cancer . . . with Salman Rushdie, or with the hunger strikers in Bischoferrode in Thuringia."[22] In these cases, he says, solidarity is a matter of special problems, where "individuals, groups or nations requiring special assistance arouse real acts of solidarity."[23] He asserts – unhelpfully – that the assisted and those giving assistance are not fundamentally equal, but argues correctly that "one person makes the concerns of another person or group, which faces a special plight, her own."[24] He limits this concern to a very temporary effort to assist with a particular problem or to find a remedy for the plight, narrowly construed. He therefore sees solidarity as "target-oriented." Unlike charity, solidarity for Rippe must fit in with one's own concerns and meet one's own interests or goals. Since the

---

[20] Tommie Shelby, "Foundations of Black Solidarity: Collective Identity or Common Oppression?," *Ethics* 112 (2002).

[21] Klaus Peter Rippe, "Diminishing Solidarity," *Ethical Theory and Moral Practice* 1, no. 3 (1998): 256, citing Kurt Bayertz, "Staat und Solidarität," in *Politik Und Ethik*, ed. Kurt Bayertz (Stuttgart: Reclam, 1996), 308. For an elaboration of this sense of solidarity and a helpful comparison of its various meanings – political, social, civic, and human, see Sally J. Scholz, *Political Solidarity* (University Park, PA: Penn State University Press, 2008).

[22] Rippe, "Diminishing Solidarity," 357.   [23] *Ibid.*   [24] *Ibid.*

addressee of solidarity in this sense does not even have to know about it, it can be directed to fictitious beings or animals (he gives the example of solidarity with whales).

Transnational solidarity

We can put aside the idea that a norm of transnational solidarity[25] would require that one feel and act supportively toward all individual human beings worldwide, or even toward all those who need help in fulfilling their human rights. A norm that required people to feel, express, or stand in solidarity with every other human being would be impossible to apply, if not also utterly vague. This would be especially the case if the norm were understood to include positive duties or responsibilities, rather than simply negative duties to refrain from interfering with people or respecting their rights. Such an overbroad interpretation has struck some theorists as revealing an inevitable limitation of the concept in transnational applications. Yet, the objection lodged by Richard Rorty to such a notion of general human solidarity goes beyond such considerations of its impracticability. Rather, his concern is whether the objects of such a disposition make sense at all, at least philosophically. Oversimplifying, we could say that Rorty denies the possibilities of universal human solidarity because he thinks there are no humans.[26]

In contrast, I would suggest that it is useful to retain a concept of general human solidarity as a limit notion, or what might be called a horizon of possibility, where it refers to a disposition that each can have to act in solidarity with some others. Additionally, it could plausibly designate a willingness to acknowledge need in everyone else and to act in general ways to support their human rights, especially by working toward the construction of transnational institutions that can allow for their fulfillment worldwide, or by participating in social movements that take such egalitarian rights fulfillment as a goal.

Yet, in the account I am proposing here, the norm of solidarity is in the first instance understood as one that holds among particulars; however, it necessarily demarcates a distinctive subset of the relations among these particulars. Thus, we can wonder about some uses of the term in politics. For example, in the summer of 2005, following the terrorist attacks on the London Underground trains and a bus, President Bush expressed

---

[25] This section develops a conception of solidarity that I initially presented in earlier work, including Gould, *Globalizing Democracy*, especially chapters 2, 9, and 12; Gould, "Self-Determination," especially 57–9; and Gould, "Recognition, Care, and Solidarity."

[26] Admittedly, this is something of a caricature of his view. Rorty, *Contingency, Irony, and Solidarity*, especially 191–2.

solidarity on behalf of the American people with the people of Great Britain. In a different perspective, during the war with Iraq, progressives in the United States expressed their solidarity with the Iraqi people. Clearly, the first was no more than an expression of sympathy with the Brits, particularly since it involved few or no actual measures of support for them. The second, too, seems mostly expressive in a political and emotional sense, though of course the options for solidaristic actions on behalf of the Iraqi people at the time were, unfortunately, quite limited.

What can we say about the particulars that are understood as the object of acts of transnational solidarity or of solidaristic dispositions? In the first place, there is no good reason to limit our conception of these particulars to individuals, as most theoretical accounts have proposed. Solidarity can extend also to relations among groups or associations, where these are increasingly cross-border or transnational. The entities standing in this sort of solidarity with each other are thus conceived of as relatively autonomous individuals or associations, who link up through networks of interrelations with other individuals or associations. We can say further that when people or associations stand in solidarity with others at a distance, they identify with these others in their efforts to overcome oppression or to eliminate suffering, and they take action to aid these others or stand ready to do so if called upon. Clearly, such identification with the others does not commit us to an account of solidarity as a matter of identity. We are here focusing on identification with the lived situation of others and with an appreciation of the injustices to which they may be subject.

The shared values that characterize these solidarity relationships consist, then, in a shared commitment to justice, or perhaps also, in more consequentialist terms, to the elimination of suffering. Note that this formulation posits a shared commitment and not necessarily a shared conception of justice. The latter seems too demanding in requiring a high standard of theoretical agreement at the level of the meanings of terms. Nonetheless, some reasonably egalitarian or nondominating significances of justice would seem to be necessary in order to rule out solidarity in support of inhumane, dominating, or pernicious projects. Where some theorists, particularly those who emphasize the descriptive use of solidarity, would accept a wholly uncritical interpretation of all manifestations of it, this explicitly normative account seeks to relate it to norms of equal freedom and human rights, delimiting its meaning in certain ways. The account also acknowledges a broad range of potentially solidaristic stances and actions, in order to avoid imposing an overly demanding normative requirement.

The solidarity conceptualized here centrally involves an *affective* element, combined with an effort to understand the specifics of others' concrete situation, and to imaginatively construct for oneself their feelings and needs. If possible, listening to people's own accounts of these is important. Solidarity in this reading centrally makes reference to what has been called the social standpoint and social context of the others, which are often dissimilar to one's own. Thus solidarity in this sense is a disposition to act toward others who are recognized as *different from* oneself, by way of being differently situated. It is evident from this how transnational solidarity is not properly subject to Rorty's restriction to recognizing others who are "one of us."[27]

However, solidarity cannot be limited to either cognitive understanding or empathy, but moves beyond this to a readiness to take action in support of the others.[28] And crucial here is a requirement to allow the others to determine the forms of aid or support most beneficial to them. This requirement, which I have called 'deference,' is thus a way to avoid the imposition on the others of the customary expectations and practices of those offering aid. It recognizes that it is the people in the oppressive or needy situation who are usually best able to say what support they wish and expect to benefit from.

It is evident that in contrast to previous interpretations solidarity not only presupposes some degree of empathy but also goes beyond it in various ways. For while it is possible to empathize with people with whom one is acquainted only at a distance, such empathizing is certainly easier to accomplish in face-to-face contexts, as a felt understanding with another. Solidarity, especially in its transnational variants, crucially adds to empathy an emphasis on understanding the social perspective of others, and on constructing ties in action among multiple individuals or associations. Accordingly, solidarity may exist among civil society associations, as well as among individuals operating within them and the people the organizations serve; yet, it applies as well to social movements, where these are understood as involving (loosely) shared goals and overlapping networks of people and groups.

As for the difficult category of reciprocity, we can say that solidarity entails a certain reciprocal expectation of aid from the others were this to turn out to be necessary. This expectation is, most often, only implicit, especially where the solidarity relation is between a well-off person or group and less advantaged ones. Solidarity thus differs from charity, in part because of its connection to eliminating an oppressive situation and its appeal to a shared struggle, in which the aim or project predominates. On the international scene, it can also be said to largely differ from

---

[27] *Ibid.*, 189–98.

[28] See also the discussion in Steiner Stjerno, *Solidarity in Europe: The History of an Idea* (Cambridge: Cambridge University Press, 2004), especially 326.

humanitarian aid, though many of those who give such aid feel solidarity with those they serve. Humanitarian aid, at least as presently understood, entails no requirement or even expectation of reciprocity.

What, then, are the domains of the concrete manifestation of solidaristic relations in transnational contexts and the sources for their emergence? Such relationships can in the first place be motivated by affective ties of care or concern, perhaps enabled through media coverage of victimized or needy people situated elsewhere. Many of these cases give rise to charity or humanitarian aid, as is often appropriate, for example in the tsunami of 2004 or the Katrina hurricane in the fall of 2005. Nonetheless, associations of those who are suffering or oppressed, together with those who recognize the plight of these others, can also emerge in such contexts, as it did in the aftermath of Katrina. Another example of this on the international stage is the growing social movement regarding the trafficking of women and girls.

Solidaristic interrelations can also occur through *common* or *cooperative projects*, for example, economic ones, as in the recovered factories movement in Argentina, which involved reciprocal forms of solidarity and a substantial degree of mutual aid among the workers in various factories and also with some workers' groups elsewhere. The concept of horizontality, advanced in connection with the democratic relations of grassroots associations and individuals, blends well with this notion of solidarity. Theorists attempting to articulate the forms of interrelations involved in the Global Justice Movement or the World Social Forum also advanced conceptions along these lines, and I have discussed a related conception of *intersociative democracy* in my book *Globalizing Democracy and Human Rights*.[29]

Transnational common projects can also be found among professional associations of people or groups working to achieve particular ends, for example, among scientists working on climate change or nuclear proliferation. These manifest a solidaristic readiness to provide mutual aid, and may in fact involve a struggle for justice, at least on a certain interpretation. But the condition of being oppressed or suffering is not apparently met except in a broad and prospective sense of the term.

In addition to common projects, the basis for solidarity can be more purely discursive. An example might be found in the relations among feminist groups in North America and Africa to counter female genital cutting. Although this does not exemplify the reciprocity characteristic of more traditional forms of social solidarity, it can become more reciprocal to the degree that interlocutors are ready to learn

---

[29] Gould, *Globalizing Democracy*.

from the others (e.g., in regard to new modes of conflict resolution that have been effective in African cultures and can perhaps be applied elsewhere).

It is clear that solidarity as conceptualized here is not only a moral disposition but also requires social critique and attention to institutional structures, as well as to the opportunities that changes in such structures might afford for improving the lot of others. If people are to be helpful to others and act to support them, it is useful for those involved in the solidarity relationships to have some idea of the causes of the oppression or suffering. But this socially critical perspective need not be understood as a highly theoretical one, which would again be overly demanding. It is clear that, in its emphasis on social critique, this conception goes beyond identity theories of groups. However, the subjective and affective identification with the situation of the others emphasized in those theories and the establishing of commonalities across differences remains important in this analysis as well.

In these various concrete cases, we can speak of *overlapping solidarities* or of a new *network notion of solidarity*. This is admittedly a weaker notion than the traditional accounts of intragroup social solidarity (e.g., within a nation). Although these new solidarities are implicitly reciprocal, this feature is not a salient aspect of its meaning when it pertains to better situated groups helping those worse off. In this context, we can suggest that perhaps solidarity relations function socially in some ways as gifts do, that is, without the requirement of a return in kind, and with only a weak expectation of reciprocity.

There may be a suggestive analogy here to certain features of Marcel Mauss's treatment of the gift, although there are also important differences. On Mauss's view, exchanges of gifts through a society set the basis for the development of reciprocal practices and social trust, and likewise perhaps so do contemporary forms of solidarity. Although not extended in expectation of mutual aid, the interconnections and hence the further disposition to reciprocity are strengthened through these overlapping solidarities. Of course, there are also sharp differences from an account like Mauss's, primarily in virtue of the linkage of solidarity as conceptualized here to the achievement of justice, in place of the exchange of gifts functioning to perpetuate traditional statuses within a society. Further, although Mauss suggested that gift giving can establish trust throughout a society and this feature is shared in cross-border contexts by transnational solidarity, nonetheless, gifts have the sense of being gratuitous or, at least, supererogatory (at least in contemporary contexts), whereas the connection of solidarity relations to overcoming oppression makes them seem more fully necessary.

Although I have suggested that most current forms of solidarity remain particularistic in involving connections with specific other individuals or groups, these forms can be normatively understood in a new way that takes them beyond mere particularity or partiality. I propose that the idea of *openness* ought to characterize these relations; and, this importantly transforms particularity, without moving it completely to a universality of principles. Whereas the related concepts of care or empathy have been thought to be ineluctably limited to specific others, particularly to the degree that they apply to relations between individuals, solidarity as understood here entails a readiness to establish broader interrelations with a range of others who share in a situation of being oppressed or exploited or who, more generally, are suffering through no fault of their own. This is shown in the emergence of solidarity movements, where associations or groups attempt to interact in mutually supportive ways to achieve greater degrees of justice or related goals. In this way, we can see a role for the norm of *inclusiveness*, heretofore primarily theorized as pertaining to a political community or to rights of participation in political discourses or deliberations. Although the transnational solidarity relations theorized here remain particularistic in scope, they can be normatively open and inclusive in regard to other individuals and associations within a justice project or social movement. In this way, these transnational solidarity relations differ from the older highly exclusionary forms that characterized identity-based solidarity groups.

Since solidarities as described here are seen as constructed through the interactions and understandings of groups or individuals over time, the sort of universality that is possible here is what I have previously called a *concrete* one, in contrast to the abstract universality of traditional moral principles. Solidarities are established in practice among those who are actually oppressed or suffering or by those who support these others without having a current need for reciprocal aid. It therefore is universalistic in certain additional senses – for one thing, as noted, the disposition to solidarity can be general, though the particular others to whom it is actually extended are a limited subset of humanity. In addition, to the extent that everyone can find themselves at some time or other in a situation of oppression or suffering, the need for support from others and expressions or actions of solidarity from them is a standing possibility for every individual and association (though in some cases a rather abstract one). Finally, as I suggested earlier, there is some utility to retaining the notion of general human solidarity, at least as a limit notion. The feelings that this evokes can undergird people's commitment to working to fulfill the human rights of others, and doing so in a way that is relatively equal for all people. I return to the connection of transnational solidarity to a cosmopolitan conception of human rights in the final section.

A notion of solidarity of the sort theorized in this chapter, then, sees it as centrally requiring openness and receptivity to the situation of other individuals and groups. In this way, it characterizes an ethical disposition and importantly supplements a theory giving a central role to democracy and human rights. In more political contexts, solidarity suggests the importance of supporting others in their own efforts at democratization. It is obvious, too, that this concept stands in opposition to efforts to impose democracy abroad, or even, in labor contexts, to projects of organizing workers in just the precise ways that have proven to work elsewhere. In the latter case, it is rather a matter of sharing resources and methods and engaging in joint projects or activities. In respecting the modalities of various associations and communities, this norm of solidarity can be regarded as one of *democratic solidarity*.

Hard questions for global ethics

There remain some difficult philosophical issues for such a conceptualization in global ethics to address, and I touch on three of them in this final section. The first two questions are practical, one concerning the motivation for solidarity itself, and the other the often idiosyncratic character of the choice of its objects. The third question concerns the difficult theoretical issue, already broached earlier, of clarifying the relation of this extensive but still particularistic conception of solidarity to the more fully universalistic norms of human rights, a question that engages the idea of democratic solidarity introduced above. I point to some directions for the further consideration of these hard questions.

The first of these problems begins from the observation that although solidarity helps to provide a motivation for taking the human rights of others seriously and for respecting their rights, it poses a motivational question of its own. Doesn't it require altruistic behavior? And how can this be expected of people? In fact, what is the motivation for engaging in solidarity behavior itself? Is this yet another moralistic expectation of unreasonable altruism, whether of individuals or projected onto the level of the group? And although rational choice theorists have shown the utility of solidarity for group integration and collective action within social groups,[30] the conception of network solidarities in transnational contexts does not seem to function in that way, so is it reasonable to

---

[30] For a classic analysis, see Michael Hechter, *Principles of Group Solidarity* (Berkeley: University of California Press, 1987).

expect people to establish solidaristic relations of this sort? Isn't it in any case too demanding a notion from the moral point of view?

Without answering these difficult questions directly here, we can make a few points that frame their further consideration. First of all, we have to acknowledge that solidarity does call for a certain sort of altruism, but one that is evoked morally in two different, but related, ways. These hark back to the twofold approach proposed in the analysis in this chapter, in terms of human rights on one hand and empathy on the other. In terms of human rights, we can recognize that their fulfillment is ultimately a claim of each of us on all others. This fulfillment is best organized through a particular set of economic and political institutions short of universal ones. Yet, when these institutions fail to provide for fulfillment of basic human rights, solidarity with others within the interdependent contexts of modern life requires that we step in and attempt to help the affected others gain the conditions they need for rights fulfillment. In addition, to the degree that we are participants in economic and political systems that may have contributed to rendering human rights fulfillment difficult for these people, or even blocked it, we ought to help to provide these conditions in the ways that we presently can.[31]

Considered from the side of empathy, the desire to help is a matter of feeling for the other along with a shared understanding of the importance for all of us of meeting basic needs and alleviating suffering. Where this goes beyond requirements of aid or charity is partly in solidarity's counsel to work to overcome whatever systematic factors are contributing to the problem. In this way, the ethical requirement of empathy is blended with a requirement for social critique in order to make action effective. In addition, as I have noted, solidarity puts the affected other in the lead position for dealing with the situation and determining relevant forms of aid. I believe that the two factors cited here – the recognition of the equal claims to human rights fulfillment of others, and the role of empathy in social contexts – go at least part of the way to accounting for the motivation we have to stand in solidarity with others, keeping in mind that this norm does not require that a person act in solidarity with all individual others.

The second problem, which I can only mention, is how to avoid the episodic and haphazard aspects of contemporary transnational solidarity. That is, at least where such solidarity stems from empathy for and caring about those in need, it is highly dependent on the selective attention

---

[31] This approach can be found in different ways in the work of Thomas Pogge and Iris Young. See Pogge, *World Poverty and Human Rights*, and Iris Marion Young, *Responsibility for Justice* (New York: Oxford University Press, 2011).

of the media. There is not only an incompleteness to this process, but a serious unfairness as well, owing to the chance element concerning which particular cases are singled out for such attention. We can say that, if the disposition to solidarity were to become widespread, even this problem could be ameliorated to a degree, in that there would be greater readiness to notice and attend to the people needing assistance wherever they existed. Needless to say, too, greater openness of the media to uses by ordinary people (rather than their contemporary dominance by corporations) would help in promulgating requests for assistance and for sharing in these struggles. But while social networking has provided some opportunities in this regard, greater openness and inclusiveness by mainstream media would require substantial social changes, in addition to ethical and educational ones.

The third problem is the more fully theoretical one concerning the connection of the particularity of solidarity relationships to the universalist norms of human rights and global justice. Here, I want simply to add some further suggestions to those introduced in the previous section and I consider the problem further in Chapter 6.

In light of the preeminence of the universal norms, there may well be a temptation to regard dispositions toward solidarity as simply explaining the feasibility of the principles or theories of cosmopolitan justice or human rights, which are often regarded as arrived at independently through reasoning or discursive processes. On such an account, solidarity would be useful primarily in explaining why people might be inclined to follow these principles.[32] However, while the contribution made by solidaristic dispositions to the feasibility of these norms is certainly important, this contribution does not encompass the full significance of solidarity relations in regard to justice and human rights. For these principles do not emerge from a pure rationality; rather, as discussed earlier, the proliferation of solidarity relations that establish commonalities across differences, along with the linkages that develop among individuals and groups within solidarity movements, help to construct more universalistic conceptions of our obligations to each other. To recognize this surely does not imply that there is no place for an idea of universal human rights, which rightly serves as a constraint on certain social and political practices that may violate it. Moreover, on my view, human rights also express universalistic claims that we can make on each other for the positive fulfillment of the basic conditions of human activity. Although human rights

---

[32] This suggestion is made in a helpful critical discussion of my book *Globalizing Democracy and Human Rights* by Pablo Gilabert, "Global Justice, Democracy, and Solidarity," *Res Publica* 13, no. 1 (2007).

may well be most effectively realized within delimited political societies, they are in principle claims that each can make on all others, in view of our fundamental interdependence as social beings. In this context, the social empathy involved in solidarity relations helps to explain why we come to take the rights of others seriously and beyond this, these relations can contribute to making these rights more extensively realized.[33]

Framed in terms of the norm of justice, we have seen how transnational solidarity relations are aimed at supporting people in overcoming oppression and in that sense involve a commitment to establishing justice. In this way, the features of empathy and imaginative reconstruction of the situation of others that characterize solidarity relations help to explain people's motivation to take norms of justice seriously, as well as why justice may come to be established in more cosmopolitan ways in practice, as people engage more fully with others across borders and over time. Needless to say, a process of rational reflection on these universalizing phenomena is also essential in order that conceptions of human rights and justice can be adequately articulated as norms that can guide social and political practice. But such rational reflection does not operate in a theoretical vacuum nor is it wholly separated from our affective attachments; rather, reasoning and affect can work symbiotically in the case of solidarity relations. We can say, then, that solidarity mediates between the more fully particular relations evident on an interpersonal level and the abstract universal principles incorporated in norms of human rights and justice. And solidarity does so, I have suggested, by contributing to more supportive and open, indeed democratic, relationships between people and groups in increasingly transnational contexts.

[33] See the discussion on this point in *Ibid.*

6   Does global justice presuppose global solidarity?

Introduction

The preceding analysis of transnational solidarities enables us to confront here a troubling objection frequently posed to the very possibility of global justice. The objection is that global justice is impossible because it would require global solidarity among everyone worldwide in order to support obligations to redistribute resources and wealth at that scale, or at least to motivate people to care about something like alleviating or mitigating extreme poverty. But since solidarity cannot have global or universalistic applicability, the objection proceeds, global justice itself is an impossible goal.[1] The global irrelevance of solidarity has been posited on several grounds: First, because solidarity is taken in its older sense as applying primarily among people within a delimited national community, involving a shared national identity and a reciprocity of benefits and burdens; or because solidarity is thought to have an inherently particularistic meaning that entails an antagonistic relation to others against whom the solidarity group acts;[2] or finally, because notions of general human solidarity are by their very nature held to be inherently vague and empty.[3]

I begin this chapter by analyzing and evaluating these various grounds for dismissing the applicability of solidarity globally and then go on to address the question presented in the title – whether global justice presupposes global solidarity. Perhaps predictably, the answer to our question will be seen to partly depend on the interpretations given to the various terms included in it – global justice and global solidarity. Nonetheless, in an important sense that I attempt to delineate, this answer is seen to be "yes." This analysis attempts to concretize claims made in Chapter 5. Specifically, I show how the transnational solidarities discussed there play an important role not only in motivating people's commitment to the

---

[1] See, for example, Heyd, "Justice and Solidarity."
[2] Chantal Mouffe, *The Democratic Paradox* (London: Verso, 2000).
[3] Rorty, *Contingency, Irony, and Solidarity.*

realization of global justice but contribute to its construction or constitution as well.

Alternative conceptions of solidarity and of global justice

We have already seen the range of significations of the term *solidarity*, which is perhaps even wider than that of justice itself. Three modern uses of the concept were discussed and are relevant to answering the current question:

(1) as denoting a sense of collective identity and mutual sympathy among members of a single community, most often thought to be national in scope;

(2) as a network notion made up of overlapping relationships among particular individuals and groups feeling empathy with each other and standing ready to give mutual aid to each other to counter oppression or relieve suffering;

and less often:

(3) as the interconnectedness of people in groups oriented to shared purposes primarily within institutional contexts (e.g., corporations or markets), where the connections among the people may at least initially operate behind their backs (and thus the extent of their shared goals and purposes may not always be evident to them).

The second and third senses here rather obviously can extend in transnational ways beyond the borders of nation-states. In Chapter 5, I argued primarily for the second interpretation. Even the first sense, as solidarity within a community, can apply transnationally, to the degree that it may characterize the new intensionally defined communities arising through cross-border interactions or through processes of globalization. Such new communities often arise through people's mobilization around common interests – for example, ecologically based cross-border concerns – or in voluntary associations in the forms of transnational NGOs, or they may arise as communication-oriented groups, for example, in online forums, social networks, or similar discursive communities.

Each of these three meanings poses for us a different sense of the problem of the relation of global solidarity to global justice. But we can observe that the concept of global justice too is highly variable. As shown in Chapter 1, many theorists seek to separate the question of the requirements and justification of economic distributive justice in the global sphere from the importance of respecting human rights or meeting basic needs, or from a basic ("natural") duty of assistance. These theorists may focus on forms of global egalitarianism that require global distribution or redistribution (and possibly the production) of goods and services within an increasingly interconnected political economy. They may differ regarding whether cosmopolitan equality of persons requires full redistribution to reduce the impact of bad luck in the original allocation of resources, or perhaps requires a global original position, or requires equalizing people's welfare or capabilities. Various approaches have more narrowly urged respecting people's human rights, extending to means of subsistence, or to meeting basic needs, but they often couple that recognition with the claim that justice permits giving priority to one's own fellow co-nationals in redistributive processes. This priority can in turn be justified on associative grounds,[4] contractarian ones,[5] or on the basis of the reciprocity involved in participation in cooperative political processes,[6] which moreover, may involve coercion[7] (in a sense that some theorists regard as decisive).

As laid out in Part I of this book, I argue for a broadly egalitarian approach to global justice, based on equal positive freedom, bearing on both economic production and distribution processes and requiring democratic decision-making in those matters, coupled with basic requirements for equal recognition and liberty, and for freedom from oppression and exploitation. The approach advocates a focus on human rights as a way of achieving more egalitarian distributions globally, inasmuch as these rights are taken to include not only basic rights necessary for any human activity whatever – among these, rights to means of subsistence – but also a richer range of nonbasic rights to the conditions for fuller flourishing. I argue that it is plausible to prioritize the basic rights in practice, at least for the foreseeable future, since fulfilling these is a very large task. Yet, this view posits the need to realize the full range of human rights as an ideal to guide practice.

This relatively strong interpretation of human rights brings the view closer to global economic egalitarianism in a way that more minimalist interpretations of human rights do not. In prioritizing the achievement of basic human rights, I have suggested that it constitutes a more practicable approach for moving ahead on global justice than more demanding ones that advocate a fully egalitarian distribution in the first instance. Yet, it can be granted that even fulfilling a wide range of human rights will not yield full global equality. But when coupled with the requirements for

---

[4] See Samuel Scheffler, *Boundaries and Allegiances: Problems of Justice and Responsibility in Liberal Thought* (Oxford: Oxford University Press, 2001).
[5] See Heyd, "Justice and Solidarity."
[6] See Andrea Sangiovanni, "Global Justice, Reciprocity, and the State," *Philosophy and Public Affairs* 35, no. 1 (2007).
[7] See Michael Blake, "Distributive Justice, State Coercion, and Autonomy," *Philosophy and Public Affairs* 30, no. 3 (2001); and Nagel, "The Problem of Global Justice."

recognition, and the protection from domination along with the extension of democracy that it proposes (as described further in Part III), it becomes more egalitarian still. Beyond this, we can say that equal positive freedom as requiring equal rights to the conditions of self-development constitutes a regulative ideal for global distribution, provided it is taken as a prima facie principle, which would enable it to take account of other relevant desiderata that may sometimes qualify it. I have proposed that it is a principle that should be seen to have important implications for the organization of production processes, and not only for distribution and redistribution; moreover, it sees distribution as often relevantly connected to the organization of the production process (including its structuring through laws of property).[8]

Before going on to explicate my own view of how global solidarity is related to global justice within this approach, it would be useful to further clarify where the problems are thought to reside in applying solidarity beyond local or national contexts, or even beyond the delimited transnational communities or solidarity groups that are emerging with contemporary globalization. That is, we need to understand why so many theorists have thought that solidarity cannot be global (or even significantly transnational beyond some exceptional groups that may mobilize around specific issues).[9]

Arguments against the possibility of global solidarity

The impossibility of global solidarity, or perhaps even of importantly transnational forms of solidarity – is held to arise in the first place from the necessary restriction of solidarity to national contexts. This is supplemented with the claim that distributive justice is only possible on the basis of feelings of solidarity with co-nationals. Thus only pre-given solidarity communities where people already care about fellow citizens, at least in the limited sense of feeling at one with them, are thought to be capable

---

[8] The interpretation of equal positive freedom and its import for production and distribution, as also for democratic organization of political, economic, and social life, is discussed in Gould, *Rethinking Democracy*, especially chapters 1, 5, and 9.

[9] In developing these apparent inconsistencies between solidarity and the global level, including its applicability to global justice, we can use not only the analyses that have been given of solidarity itself, but also draw on those that have been given of cognate notions like associative groups and perhaps also communities, both of which are held to be inevitably particularistic. Thus the discussion of global justice and solidarity in some aspects seems to replicate the older concerns about the relation of cosmopolitanism and communitarianism. Yet, though solidarity lacks an altogether established meaning at present, it would be a mistake to simply assimilate it to these other notions of associations and communities, although all these forms of social interaction may exemplify mutual concern and common interests.

of motivating people to redistribute wealth toward less well-off citizens or to support other challenging tax policies. In this case, then, justice presupposes solidarity, but both are held to be limited to nation-states and impossible at the global level.

A related objection to global solidarity emphasizes the agonistic nature of solidarity groups, in which they necessarily define themselves against an Other. While not necessarily restricting feelings of solidarity to fellow citizens (although it tends to), this approach, like the first, regards global solidarity as a pipe dream because there is no Other as far as humanity as a whole is concerned (barring an alien invasion!). This view has, in turn, been subjected to critical analysis by Arash Abizadeh, who identifies this approach with the work of Carl Schmitt and to a degree also Chantal Mouffe.[10] Abizadeh argues that this approach makes a mistaken use of the Hegelian struggle for recognition by applying it to collective identities and taking them to require an Other, rather than understanding recognition simply as required among people understood as individuals who differ from each other, where this would indeed be possible at the global level, and consistent with a global sense of solidarity.[11]

A further objection to global solidarity applies broadly to conceptions of solidarity generally, including some versions of network or social movement-oriented ones, such as the one I laid out in the Chapter 5. The problem with solidarity, it is claimed, is that it is necessarily particularistic, denoting delimited relations among members of a group. How, it is asked, could these particularistic and partial relations ever succeed in becoming universal, and thus fully cosmopolitan or global? Note that this objection also pertains to the national identity reading of solidarity, as well as in large measure to the variety of solidarity groups conceived in a Marxian way, in which they can apply to associations of labor unions or members of working-class collectives who are mutually supportive of each other's strikes or related activities. It may be granted that on such views solidarity contributes *motivation* to achieving justice (however the latter is defined), but even so, these solidarity groups remain fundamentally particularistic and perspectival rather than universalist or global.[12] We

---

[10] Arash Abizadeh, "Does Collective Identity Presuppose an Other?," *American Political Science Review* 99, no. 1 (2005).

[11] *Ibid.*

[12] It should be noted that Marx believed that the proletariat was a universal class in that it represented general human interests and aims at eliminating oppression in a universal sense (achievable, on his view, in a communal society of the future), although under capitalism it remains particularistic and stands in antagonistic relations with capital. See, for example, Karl Marx, "Contribution to the Critique of Hegel's Philosophy of Right," in *The Marx-Engels Reader*, 2nd edn, ed. Robert Tucker (New York: Norton, 1978), 64, 174, 92–3.

can add that this particularist characterization would also seem to apply to the Durkheimian notion of organic solidarity established through the division of labor, since the interconnections within modern enterprises and the common interests established through the division of labor have not become fully global (and perhaps may never become so) although these interconnections extend much more widely than heretofore.

A final objection raised against the notion of global solidarity consists in the familiar claim that it is too demanding, in requiring shared empathy or another sentiment held by everyone for and with everyone else, which appears to be empirically impossible. Indeed, the notion can be regarded as simply empty and deeply vague. Thus it is not even clear what it would mean to feel empathy with everyone else, and even if we can make conceptual sense of this, it seems to be beyond human capacities to actually accomplish this in view of the sheer numbers of people involved and the limits of our imaginations (however strong they may be).

In case global solidarity is really impossible in this and other ways, then the question addressed in this chapter would appear to have no application (if it is not completely meaningless). And in Chapter 5 I argued that as a particularistic relationship, solidarity cannot simply apply globally, though we can make out some attenuated meanings even in the global context. Yet, I will delineate several senses in which the notion of transnational solidarity is in fact highly significant, relying in part on that earlier analysis. On the basis of those understandings, we will finally be able to squarely address the question posed in the title of this chapter.

Solidarity and the construction of global justice

I previously argued that although traditional nation-state solidarities have become a little less relevant with globalization, new forms of transnational solidarities conceived in terms of networks of solidarity groups gain importance. As we have seen, this conception draws on the Marxist analysis of solidarity but extends it beyond the context of labor movement solidarity. In terms of more recent authors, this sense is related to Rippe's notion of project-related solidarity,[13] though it attempts to retain the Marxian emphasis on overcoming oppression and struggling for social justice. We can distinguish a range of cases here: At the least demanding extreme are those that remain close to the established form of the provision of aid to those in need and at the other extreme are those

---

[13] Rippe, "Diminishing Solidarity." See also Scholz, *Political Solidarity*, chapter 7, for a nuanced account of several senses of global solidarity.

pertaining to groups and movements that are self-consciously oriented to maintaining and enhancing solidarity, where this is marked by mutual concern and a readiness to give mutual aid when needed. In these developed forms of explicit solidarity movements or interrelationships, we can speak of "standing in solidarity" with others and being ready to help them when called upon, where this readiness is reciprocal, at least in principle. In this normative elaboration of the conception, solidarity groups can be seen to act with a commitment to equality and to achieving justice, at least in the form of overcoming oppression. They therefore normally do not include groups that are defined mainly in ethnic terms that exclude others, nor can they include hate groups of various sorts that are aimed at elevating one set of people over others.

Examples of transnational solidarity movements can be found among certain progressive movements in Latin America and among consensus-oriented communities, such as those that characterized the World Social Forum or Indymedia. Classic examples can also be found among some labor unions, while more informal networks of women around the world can also constitute solidarity groupings, and these can even occur online and not only through face-to-face interaction (e.g., WLUML).[14] Additionally, various INGOs can exemplify solidarity networks in this sense, for example, the activity of Partners in Health in Haiti and elsewhere.[15]

In fact, if we consider the case provided by the responses to the 2010 Haitian earthquake, we can illustrate this range of possibilities for solidarity, from weak to strong. Thus in the weak sense, it was possible for people to act in solidarity with the Haitian people by simply providing aid to them to help relieve the medical and other aspects of the humanitarian crisis there. In this sense, solidarity would differ little or not at all from the standard cases of humanitarian aid. But this case would lack the reciprocity of mutual aid or even the mutual concern that can exist within a solidarity group in the stronger manifestations of this phenomenon. Moreover, the solidarity involved in aid remained with the alleviation of suffering and did not include a concern with eliminating oppression or positively achieving justice. In order for those dimensions to be added, groups would need to become socially critical concerning the various ways in which exploitation, colonialism, and the Haitian government itself contributed to the wide-scale misery that the earthquake brought about, greatly exacerbating its effects as a devastating natural phenomenon. And, indeed, these complicating factors of structural oppression over the longer term have been the focus of

[14] See www.wluml.org/   [15] See www.pih.org/

some of the solidarity groups that developed in response to the Haitian catastrophe.[16]

We can use this analysis of what could be called *critical transnational solidarity* to address our central question of the relation between global solidarity and global justice. Insofar as this sort of solidarity involves a disposition to act in support of others at a distance who are oppressed or impoverished, where this action is undertaken in the interests of justice, it can be said to exemplify a particularist and emergent phenomenon with a universalist intent. It is universalistic not only in aiming at justice but also in being open to aiding others who may be oppressed or suffering in an inclusive way. Although such solidarity groups are necessarily particular, since it is impossible to link up with and help everyone at once, there is no barrier in principle to helping others who are similarly situated and no barrier to others joining in. Moreover, it is best to look at these solidarity groups as related to each other within networks rather than as a single, unified phenomenon. Whatever universality is involved here, then, is constituted or constructed rather than pre-given. Nonetheless, egalitarian notions of global justice play a role as regulative ideals and as goals of the various groups that compose the network.

In this interpretation, solidarity, like the related notion of care or concern, provides part of the motivational account that is needed for a full account of global justice. That is, the empathy with the plight of others that gives rise to solidarity groups and networks helps to account for why people can be expected to work toward the fulfillment of the human rights of others, along with the other achievements involved in bringing about more global forms of justice. Likewise, in my view, solidarity networks of this sort directly help to constitute or construct global justice by linking particular individuals and groups in these networks of mutual concern and aid. In this way, solidarity not only provides the "glue" for many social relationships, but also does so in a positive, constructive way. Some of these solidarity networks, moreover, instantiate just and democratic forms of social relations in the very way they function, thereby preparing the ground for further instantiations of global justice, at least to the degree that the solidarity is based on the recognition of people's fundamental equality. While it must be granted that many contemporary cases involve better-off people helping those less well off, there is an implicit reciprocity involved in the normative application of

---

[16] Among these groups are Partners in Health (see n. 20 above); Haiti Action Committee (www.HaitiSolidarity.net); Haitian Women for Haitian Refugees (http://haitianwomen.wordpress.com); and Grassroots International (www.grassrootsonline.org/where-we-work/haiti).

solidarity such that if the well off were to need similar help in the future, they would have grounds for expecting it. So, in this sense of networked transnational solidarities, we can say that global justice presupposes this sort of transnational, if not fully global, solidarity.

Another sense in which global justice presupposes solidarity can be found in the more objective notions of solidarity that arise from a Durkheimian perspective. This involves a different sense of "presuppose." In the case of transnational solidarity networks, we have seen that justice presupposes solidarity as a motivation for taking seriously the human rights of others or about achieving egalitarian justice and also presupposes it as a means for the construction of justice itself, that is, of concretely working toward it in practice. In the different case of solidarity achieved through the division of labor, "presuppose" signifies that the various cooperative activities that bring people together and the new social interconnections that are established through such activities are presuppositions of the new forms of associations and communities, as well as the common interests, that link them. On the basis of these solidarities established in practice, people can eventually come to see themselves as participating in one world or at least a broad interconnected net of relations. This, in turn, supports global justice in one of two ways: it can give rise to an awareness of their shared needs and common interests as human beings in a way that underlies global justice notions, or it can establish their unity within a broad transnational association within which redistribution can now be seen to be justified, in view of their interconnections with each other. The former account of shared human needs and universal human interests gives rise to human rights theories, as in Gewirth's or my own theories,[17] or to notions of basic needs, as in Gillian Brock,[18] or to fundamental human interests, as in Simon Caney.[19] The latter account is elaborated, for example, by Iris Marion Young in her social connections model of responsibility,[20] or in a different way by Pogge in his account of Western responsibilities for imposing, and for alleviating, global poverty.[21]

A final respect in which global justice presupposes global solidarity is the relatively abstract one in which people may feel solidarity with all other human beings in two senses – first, drawing on the transnational

[17] Gewirth, *Reason and Morality*; Alan Gewirth, *Human Rights* (Chicago, IL: University of Chicago Press, 1982), and Gould, *Globalizing Democracy*, esp. chapters 1, 8, and 9.
[18] Gillian Brock, *Global Justice* (Oxford: Oxford University Press, 2009).
[19] Caney, *Justice Beyond Borders*.
[20] Young, "Responsibility and Global Labor Justice," and Young, "Responsibility and Global Justice: A Social Connections Model."
[21] Pogge, *World Poverty and Human Rights*.

sense of solidarity discussed above, in that they can be disposed to feel solidarity with any other human being who needs it, which is not to say that they have to feel it collectively with all others. This qualification makes the notion realizable. That is, they are ready to feel empathy with anyone else and to understand oppression wherever it may occur. The second sense corresponds to the usual notion of general human solidarity, or solidarity with all of humankind. My own inclination is to explicate that as a limit notion, or a horizon of imaginative possibilities. Here, too, we can discern two possible meanings: an identification with what is human in everyone, focusing on the common needs, potentialities, and constraints that mark human life; or an identification with human beings collectively, for example, as a form of life on earth increasingly threatened by climate change. In the first of these uses – the distributive one – the presupposition for global justice consists in the solidaristic focus on each individual's life situation as requiring protection and fulfillment through human rights or through the provision of the conditions for a minimally decent life (as several recent philosophers would see it). In the second sense of global solidarity as a limit, namely, the focus on human beings collectively, the presupposition for global justice consists more in the sense of shared responsibility that solidarity engenders with regard to previous actions that have produced the current problematic situation for humankind, as well as a shared responsibility for dealing with and obviating the problems for present and future generations that these previous negative actions have engendered.

It may be observed finally that all these senses of solidarity as well as their relations to global justice are apparently consistent with each other, although they may each draw on somewhat different philosophical roots. That is, there is no inconsistency in seeing that the solidaristic recognition of general human needs, interests, and rights is importantly facilitated by empathic openness to the particular needs and oppression that characterize individuals and groups denied justice and around which solidarity movements may form. Likewise, the organic solidarity interconnections established through economic and technological globalization can usefully generate feelings of shared responsibility and efforts to jointly address human problems in effective ways. Moreover, I have suggested how solidarity in these various transnational and global forms is importantly related to the fulfillment of global justice, whether the latter is understood in negative terms as avoiding depriving people of their rights or eliminating oppression, or more positively as the fulfillment of basic human rights or fundamental human interests or else as the achievement of a greater degree of equality worldwide. This is not to say, however, that more work isn't needed on the philosophical interconnections of these various notions. On the contrary, it will be important for future work to articulate more clearly the ways that emerging and particular solidarity relations can work to fulfill global justice in a general sense.

Is solidarity required beyond justice?

The question may arise whether solidarity with others is needed or desirable in politics for its own sake, and not only because of its role in motivating and helping to construct justice, nationally and transnationally. Especially given the social ontology I have presented, which gives an important role to group membership and joint action with others, it seems plausible to say that solidarity is valuable as an important expression of our social being. In the forms of mutual aid that I have described, it reflects an awareness of our interdependence, our neediness and vulnerabilities, and our mutual claims on each other. A qualification on the value of solidarity groups, however, is that they need to respect human rights and follow the requirements for equal recognition and nondomination, as required by the broad conception of justice as equal positive freedom. Otherwise, we would have to equally endorse gangs or hate groups in view of the solidarity they display, just as much as groups that are oriented to the achievement of justice and are inclusive in the ways previously discussed.

In his work on Kohlberg and moral development, Habermas has interpreted solidarity as the other side of justice, so to speak.[22] He sees it as addressing the affective bonds and empathic dispositions that characterize our affiliations within the life-world and that undergird the application of norms of justice within a given community.[23] In somewhat related fashion, I take solidarity as contributing to the motivation for fulfilling justice (though I interpret this differently and see it as actually helping to construct justice in practice, when it takes the form of actions

---

[22] Habermas, "Justice and Solidarity."

[23] Habermas writes, "Thus, the perspective complementing that of equal treatment of individuals is not benevolence but solidarity. This principle is rooted in the realization that each person must take responsibility for the other because as consociates all must have an interest in the integrity of their shared life context in the same way. Justice conceived deontologically requires solidarity as its reverse side. It is a question not so much of two moments that supplement each other as of two aspects of the same thing. Every autonomous morality has to serve two purposes at once: it brings to bear the inviolability of socialized individuals by requiring equal treatment and thereby equal respect for the dignity of each one; and it protects intersubjective relationships of mutual recognition requiring solidarity of individual members of a community, in which they have been socialized." *Ibid.*, 244–5.

in solidarity with others). Perhaps more fully than Habermas, I think that the social empathy and the desire to aid others that is characteristic of solidarity can extend beyond a given community. His account is also distinctive in giving a leading role to discourse ethics, which he sees as required to break through ethnocentrism and the other limits of solidaristic associations.[24] Like him, though, I see a need for the correction of one-sided affiliations by more universalistic understandings, relying on both solidaristic social connections in practice and on notions of human rights, based on a conception of justice as equal positive freedom. For Habermas, the main avenue for the required universalization is discourse, and specifically discursive will formation. Despite this contrast, intercultural dialogue will also be seen to play a part in the theory presented in this book, as discussed in Chapter 11.

What can be said, then, about the value of solidarity beyond justice in the view I have proposed? Solidarity can be seen as an expression of our freedom as social beings and the correlative importance of common or joint activities and of our interdependence, which constitute basic conditions for the fulfillment of individuals' freedom. Solidarity can potentially express freedom along all three of the basic parameters I laid out earlier, namely, realization of long-term goals, cultivation of relationships, and the development of capacities. In regard to the first parameter, many of these goals are common or collective, often arising from our participation in institutions or communities. (Some of these goals can be said to be implicit in the practices and rules definitive of these institutions and others can be explicitly reflected on and adopted through collective decision procedures.) Solidarity within the group or institution is often instrumental to the achievement of these goals or it can express people's participation in common tasks and the importance to them of mutual aid. Likewise, solidarity can itself be valuable as an end within processes of cultivating relationships as an expression of our freedom (and thus not only instrumental to the success of these relationships), and it can contribute to relationships not only in political contexts but in personal ones as well. Finally, the disposition to solidarity (along with associated forms of empathy with others) is an important capacity for people to develop, one increasingly required in transnational or global contexts. Indeed, the development of this capacity and disposition should be an aim of the more cosmopolitan forms of education needed in contemporary life.

---

[24] *Ibid.*, 245. Habermas writes, "The ideas of justice and solidarity are present above all in the mutual recognition of responsible subjects who orient their actions to validity claims. But of themselves these normative obligations do not extend beyond the boundaries of a concrete lifeworld of family, tribe, city, or nation. These limits can be broken through only in discourse, to the extent that the latter is institutionalized in modern societies."

In Chapter 7 I take up a distinctive form of recognition of others that I call 'solidaristic recognition' (or 'generous recognition'). This type is argued to be an important addition to the theory of recognition advanced by Axel Honneth and others. It also represents part of an effort to introduce features of care and empathy into the account of the bases for global justice. Yet, the theory advanced here does not reduce politics to ethics or our sociality to forms of interaction only between individuals. Rather, it sees requirements of reciprocal recognition as both an aspect of democratic social and political institutions and also as speaking to elements of personal character that form the essentials of the democratic personality (as I have previously called it).[25] Moreover, given the continuities between our public and private lives, I suggest that the elaboration of caring, solidaristic, and empathic dispositions in informal contexts of interaction, including in family life, friendships, and associations, is an important aspect of a broad account of justice as equal positive freedom, one that is conducive to the fulfillment of central social and political norms. Conversely, it seems apparent that the achievement of formal reciprocal recognition and justice within political, economic, and social institutions would contribute to supporting the flourishing of recognition, solidarity, and forms of freedom in informal contexts of social and personal life.[26]

---

[25] Gould, *Rethinking Democracy*, chapter 11.

[26] For a discussion of some of the interactions between public politics and private care, and other forms of interaction between these domains, see especially Gould, "Feminism and Democratic Community Revisited"; and Gould, *Globalizing Democracy*, chapters 1 and 6.

Introduction

Two features of social interaction that have been proposed as fundamental bases for the achievement of global justice are the recognition of others (including in their differences) and care for the vulnerable. How do these features function within a political theory of transnational democracy, human rights, and justice across borders? Although some attention has been given to care as a relevant disposition or way of acting, care work in international political economy has most often been neglected by current global justice theories. Caring for others and the labor of care pose for us the question of whether changes are required in our political and social norms to support these forms of relationships and to address any oppressive modes that may attach to them. This chapter considers both the question of the types of recognition required for the extension of equal positive freedom, and the place of care in an account that seeks to highlight network solidarities, along with a social – as well as political – interpretation of human rights.

Recognition and care are not entirely separate phenomena; they are interconnected in various ways, especially in distributive justice contexts. Several theorists have called for the recognition of groups, particularly cultural minorities, within a broad justice framework, while care theorists have argued that we need to go beyond that to attend to individuals' particular needs and vulnerabilities, counting these vulnerabilities among the relevant differences that should be recognized and supported within contemporary societies. In order to bring care into an account of global justice in this way, however, its political rather than purely interpersonal aspects will need to be analyzed.[1] While I have thus far focused on solidarity, including networks among groups, as relevant for transnational

---

[1] For the importance of a political interpretation of care, see Joan Tronto, *Moral Boundaries: A Political Argument for an Ethic of Care* (New York: Routledge, 1993); and Joan Tronto, "Human Rights, Democracy and Care: Comments on Carol C. Gould, Globalizing Democracy and Human Rights," *The Good Society* 16, no. 2 (2007).

politics, it will be seen that care and recognition have import for dealing with differences in those contexts. Care work too requires analysis, along with the development of new policies for facilitating it and for carrying out the responsibilities it entails. Beyond these issues, the question can be posed whether care itself should be recognized as a human right, in addition to the ones currently acknowledged in morality and law.

In order to address the complex interrelations between recognition, redistribution, care, and the role of differences within a theory of justice on the global scale, it will be helpful to begin by considering the exchange between Axel Honneth and Nancy Fraser in the late 1990s, in which Fraser argues against Honneth's privileging of recognition, holding that it needs to be paired with a concomitant consideration of redistribution.[2] Fraser argues for coupling the recognition of identities – racial, gender, cultural, and so on – with attention to the need for economic redistribution. In reply, Axel Honneth suggests instead that recognition itself is at the root of the theory of justice.[3] However divergent their approaches, both theorists discussed this issue in the context of a nation-state or political society, leaving open the question of the global applicability of these notions. Although Fraser has turned to considering norms for this transnational domain,[4] the question remains not only how to conceive the interrelation of these two concepts of recognition and redistribution, but also specifically which sorts of differences should be recognized as playing a significant role within redistributive principles themselves or in their practical applications. This problem becomes acute in the context of global justice and transnational recognition, where a multitude of differences comes into play – not only between the Global South and North, but also in terms of culture, nationality, and gender, among others. I make some suggestions for addressing this issue and consider the phenomenon of care, along with the related notions of empathy and solidarity, in regard to the contributions they can make to transnational recognition and redistribution.

Besides its role in thematizing a mode of attending to difference, care has been connected to globalization in other significant ways, particularly in feminist analyses such as those of Fiona Robinson. In a series of articles and a recent book, Robinson criticizes theories of global justice and human rights for omitting the crucial role of caregiving within the ethics of globalization, and proposes care ethics as an alternative

---

[2] Nancy Fraser and Axel Honneth, *Redistribution or Recognition? A Political-Philosophical Exchange* (London: Verso, 2003).
[3] *Ibid.*
[4] Nancy Fraser, *Scales of Justice: Reimagining Political Space in a Globalizing World* (New York: Columbia University Press, 2010).

approach.[5] Robinson highlights the ways in which global restructuring has proceeded without attention to women's unpaid labor and their double work burdens.[6] Her analysis resonates with Arlie Hochschild's critique of "global care chains," through which women from the Global South are led to migrate to the United States and other distant and more affluent countries to take on paid but exploitative care work in households so that women there may work outside the home, while the care workers in turn have to leave their own children for years on end in the care of others.[7] A consideration of care work is seen as posing a challenge not only for many contemporary theories of distributive justice, but also in regard to the adequacy of current understandings of the list of human rights. In particular, I briefly consider the status of a right to care in the concluding section of this chapter.

Although not addressing care work as an economic factor, Honneth's theory implicitly ties justice in one of its aspects to care. In Honneth's account, recognition – and therefore justice, in his view – is understood in one of its senses as a matter of love and care. More specifically, he characterizes one of the three forms of recognition that he delineates as involving love, including in that category the caring activities involved in child raising.[8] In a parallel way, I suggest that there is a close relation between an important type of recognition and care, along with the related disposition of solidarity and the social empathy it involves.

Recognition and differentiation in the theory of global justice

I earlier suggested that the principle of *equal positive freedom*, when interpreted in a way that incorporates attention to differences, including cultural ones, can provide a regulative ideal for global justice. It enunciates a strongly egalitarian norm as a goal to be achieved through the construction of suitable economic, social, and political institutions. Given the existence of disparate political communities (whether national or transnational), the specification of institutional frameworks, along with the interpretation of the conditions included within human rights, can

---

[5] Fiona Robinson, "Care, Gender and Global Social Justice: Rethinking 'Ethical Globalization,'" *Journal of Global Ethics* 2, no. 1 (2006); and Robinson, *The Ethics of Care*.

[6] Robinson, *The Ethics of Care*.

[7] *Ibid.*, referring to Arlie Russell Hochschild, "Global Care Chains and Emotional Surplus Value," in *Global Capitalism*, ed. Will Hutton and Anthony Giddens (London: The New Press, 2001).

[8] See the discussion in Axel Honneth, "Recognition or Redistribution? Changing Perspectives on the Moral Order of Society," *Theory, Culture & Society* 18, nos. 2–3 (2001).

vary nationally and regionally. Such conditions for transformative human activity are themselves somewhat differentiated in social and cultural terms, and even vary among individuals, although it is most often not possible in politics to take direct account of strictly individual differences, because of the need to make policy for groups of people. The modes of realizing these conditions require substantial innovation in reforming existing institutions and developing new ones, which can variously extend to property law, to new modes of democratic procedure, and to a new emphasis on the provision of care and support for those who provide it.

In the view here, there is an interconnection between justice and care, a position for which other feminist theorists have also argued.[9] I have already indicated the ways the principle of equal positive freedom and the human rights themselves are founded in the fact of interdependence, which is stressed in care theories. Moreover, the conception of freedom foregrounds the idea of development, or even the growth of people over time, in a way analogous to feminist care interpretations. When justice is seen as drawing on care in its social and political import, I believe it becomes more sensitive to differences, of both individuals and groups, and links up with people's ongoing responsibilities towards others, beyond their claims to rights fulfillment. A care-influenced justice theory would focus on the social provision of the conditions for the meeting of needs, as an expression of people's mutual vulnerability. Keeping in mind that people's needs vary across their life stages, and that some people have greater needs than others, such a justice approach would support the range of these needs and also find ways to help caregivers in their essential work. It does not necessarily imply a notion of collective care, or a caring society in a holistic sense, although such a conception could usefully point to the importance of policies to support the various essential caring functions performed by individuals and groups within it.

In the same way that justice and care are interconnected, so too are human rights (the fulfillment of which is required by justice) and solidarity, as previously suggested. Caring for people at a distance and feeling solidarity with these individuals or groups not only provides needed motivation for taking their human rights seriously but also contributes to an understanding of their specific needs within given social contexts and thus is important to transnational efforts that aim to fulfill human rights. A caring and solidaristic attitude can also alert people to the impact of their decisions on the human rights of distant others, and help prevent

---

[9] My own argument on this point is in Carol C. Gould, "Philosophical Dichotomies and Feminist Thought: Towards a Critical Feminism," in *Feministische Philosophie, Wiener Reihe Band 4*, ed. Herta Nagl (Vienna: R. Oldenbourg Verlag, 1990).

decisions that would seriously curtail their rights. In terms of considering such wide effects of decisions, I suggested in Chapter 4 that human
rights importantly specify when people at a distance need to have input
into the decision in question. My proposal is that people can be regarded
as importantly affected by these decisions and policies and should have
input into them if their capacity to fulfill their basic human rights would
be seriously affected. This in turn gives rise to the need for devising forms
of transnational representation of these people in a way that goes beyond
caring attitudes or individual solidarity actions, although I would suggest
that it likely presupposes such solidarity. That is, social empathy with
the situation of distant others, along with sustained solidarity actions oriented to justice and the elimination of oppression and poverty, can help
in meeting the specific needs of others. Institutional reform and innovative design can then address concrete ways of taking their needs into
account within the emerging forms of global governance and eventually
of transnational democracy, in ways that are considered in Part III of this
book.

Recognition comes into the picture, first of all, in the basic idea of
human rights that is required in this perspective. Contemporary conceptions of human rights and their articulation in the existing international
covenants revolve around the two notions of freedom and dignity. I have
already proposed that the recognition of equal freedom is tied to the
requirement to be free from domination and oppression. The idea of
dignity implied in human rights, in a rather cross-cultural way, speaks
not only to the significance of the equality of agency and of people's
rights, including the centrality of meeting basic needs, but also points
to the crucial role of recognition. That is, for human dignity to be recognized it is necessary that equal respect be accorded to all persons (as
human) along with an affirmation of their equal worth. In addition, such
recognition presupposes the overcoming of domination, oppression, and
exploitation in practice. Needless to say, we cannot expect that all personal cases of oppression or domination can be eliminated but rather
that systemic or institutional forms will be overcome, as Iris Young and
others have emphasized.[10]

In recent decades, recognition has been taken more widely to highlight the importance of cultural group differences[11] and, as in Fraser's
reading, other aspects of individual and group identities. In Hegel's original analysis in the master–slave dialectic of the *Phenomenology of Spirit*,

---

[10] See especially Young, *Justice and the Politics of Difference*.
[11] See, for example, Charles Taylor, *Multiculturalism and "the Politics of Recognition"* (Princeton, NJ: Princeton University Press, 1992).

individuals as self-consciousnesses have a need for recognition, which initially gives rise to a struggle for power – indeed, a life-and-death struggle – when one confronts another self-conscious individual who has a similar need. We do not have to follow Hegel in the presumption of the inevitability of such conflicts, which in his view initially lead to one-sided modes of recognition before eventually (through the course of history) becoming reciprocal, at least in terms of the recognition of persons in law. I return to the analysis of recognition, its modes, and its ties to care in the next section. Here, we can observe the ways that the normative concept of recognition, which is involved also in human rights, makes room for differences, particularly for cultural ones, and also requires the critique of systemic domination and oppression. The need for recognition is in part a need for individuals and groups to be acknowledged as free and distinctive in their modes of expressing agency. It is thus not, in principle, a conception that requires strict sameness, but instead includes the recognition of people's specific needs and interests, at least to the degree that these can be taken into account at the level of politics and social life.[12]

Equal positive freedom and human rights take diversity and difference into account in both theory and practice in several ways, some of which have been well discussed while others are less obvious. We can indicate them in summary fashion here before moving to the analysis of care and solidarity in relation to recognition and redistribution.

Insofar as the modes of self-transformation involved in the expression of freedom are socially, culturally, and historically variable, the principle of equal positive freedom requires attention to these various forms of diversity, where the conditions required will vary somewhat, as will the institutional modes for realizing them. Although there is a certain commonality of basic needs across cultures, the interpretations of these needs differ and an account of global justice has to make room for that. An analogous point can be made about human rights, which are also subject to interpretations from different cultural perspectives. Especially prominent, too, are varying assessments of the weight and priority of human rights, and what to do when they conflict. This difficult problem of the interpretation of human rights and alternate ways of dealing with the conflicts that inevitably arise among these rights is an important theme in Chapters 8, 9, and 11.

Differential treatment and the management of diversity also come to the fore in the critique and overcoming of forms of oppression and

---

[12] For the importance of a political interpretation of care, see Tronto, "Human Rights, Democracy and Care;" and Tronto, *Caring Democracy*.

domination as required by equal positive freedom, inasmuch as various remedies will be appropriate for different contexts. This bears especially on establishing gender equality, which requires countering the disadvantages accruing to women because of both traditional forms of male domination and structural forms of injustice that often lead them to have a double burden of work within and outside their homes. Feminist social movements have cast light on these issues of structural injustice, which often seem to be exacerbated rather than lessened by economic globalization, at least in its neoliberal mode.

Movements for global justice have called for remedies that build difference into responses to neoliberal globalization. For example, in *A Better World is Possible!*, writers call for a new role for local communities to resist the forces of globalization, and they tend to embrace subsidiarity, or the notion that decisions should be taken at the most local level possible.[13] This might involve a focus on cities and towns, with issues of wider impact being considered within subnational regions, and then at the level of nation-states, or more broadly, supranational regions and where necessary at the global level.[14] In regard to the current institutions of global governance as well, there are calls for democratic accountability and responsiveness to multiple constituencies, where this goes beyond the transparency emphasized by critics like Joseph Stiglitz.[15]

Radical theorists have called for institutional innovation in developing forms of economic functioning and expanded opportunities for democratic decision-making.[16] I have also argued for democratic management at work and for democratic participation in decisions in a wide range of social and political institutional contexts.[17] Such participation requires active agency, along with responsiveness and receptivity, as

---

[13] International Forum on Globalization, "A Better World Is Possible!" (Report Summary, 2002, Excerpted) in *The Globalization Reader*, ed. Frank J. Lechner and John Boli (Oxford: Blackwell, 2008).

[14] The concept of subsidiarity has mostly been discussed in connection with the EU. See Andreas Føllesdal, "Subsidiarity, Democracy, and Human Rights in the Constitutional Treaty of Europe," *Journal of Social Philosophy* 37, no. 1 (2006); Andreas Føllesdal, "Survey Article: Subsidiarity," *The Journal of Political Philosophy* 6, no. 2 (1998).

[15] Stiglitz, *Globalization and Its Discontents*. It should be noted that Stiglitz has also called for new forms of representation of those affected within the institutions of global governance.

[16] "International Forum on Globalization, "A Better World Is Possible!" Report Summary, 2002, Excerpted;" Michael Menser, "Disarticulate the State! Bioregionalism, Transnational Combat, and the Maximization of Democracy," in *Democracy, States, and the Struggle for Global Justice*, ed. Heather Gautney et al. (New York: Routledge, 2009); and Carol C. Gould, "Envisioning Transnational Democracy: Cross-Border Communities and Regional Human Rights Frameworks," *ibid.*

[17] See especially Gould, *Rethinking Democracy*, chapters 1, 4, and 9, and the discussion in chapter 14 of this book.

features of what I call the democratic personality, and they contribute to the substance of democracy as well.[18] This sort of emphasis on responsiveness in turn shows the relevance of care, empathy, and solidarity not only to personal life but also to these more public domains.

Forms of recognition and social empathy

It is difficult to give a feminist reading of Hegel's struggle for recognition as a life and death struggle. Although women have not been absent from combat over the centuries, Hegel's model of violent struggle as humanizing is far from the sort of maternal thinking that Sara Ruddick describes as characteristic of women's (socially constructed) activities and identities.[19] Even Hegel's more benign elevation of the role of reciprocal recognition of equal rights through law can be subjected to critical scrutiny, in virtue of his emphasis on equality in law to the detriment of equality in politics, the economy, and the family. But it does not follow from this critique that the recognition of equal rights – whether legal, or more broadly political or social – should be entirely replaced by a care ethic. It is more plausible to propose that human rights (as a form of equal rights) need to be connected to care, empathy, and solidarity. We can now briefly point to some ways in which this connection can impact the analysis of recognition itself.

Let us consider again Axel Honneth's influential distinction among types of recognition, as based on love, or respect, or esteem. The first of these, in which people gain self-confidence through being loved, including as children within their families, entails a substantial role for care (although Honneth does not put it this way). The second form of recognition, respect, he sees as established in the recognition of equal rights in the law. The third type, namely, esteem, involves recognition through achievement and accomplishment, as part of a career, and is differentially allocated, especially in contemporary capitalist societies.[20]

I find Honneth's distinctions interesting and helpful. But I would instead propose another distinction, which resonates with the one he draws between his first and second categories. I would differentiate between what I have called *rigorous* recognition and *generous* recognition, or the recognition of abstract equality as against *empathic* or *solidaristic recognition*.[21] The first of these, the rigorous mode, involves a rational recognition of each person's equality and gives rise to notions like the

[18] *Ibid.*, chapter 10.   [19] Ruddick, *Maternal Thinking*.
[20] Honneth, "Recognition or Redistribution?"
[21] Gould, "Recognition, Care, and Solidarity," 243–56.

equality of citizens, with attendant norms of equal political rights and equal treatment before the law. Along these lines, many forms of cosmopolitanism seek to extend existing notions of citizenship to the global level, in the form of global citizenship.[22] We can say that the recognition remains formal and each acknowledges the other as having the very same rights and as equal in their dignity. The second, generous type of recognition, which I am here also calling empathic or solidaristic recognition, includes a more feelingful (as well as cognitive) understanding of the distinctiveness of the others in their concrete circumstances, including an acknowledgement of the difficulties they face, and an appreciation of their agency in that context.

I suggest that a fully adequate recognition of the human rights of others requires not only the first of these forms of recognition but also the second – more differentiated and generous – solidaristic type of recognition. Note that the recognition of difference here is not only an individual one, or even one that takes people's cultural affiliations seriously. It goes beyond these to an acknowledgement of people in their concrete social and economic circumstances. Solidaristic recognition thus presupposes equal rights but goes further in recognizing some specificity of people's needs and of their social context.

We can add that this sort of recognition embodies a caring attitude toward others, though when applied broadly it does not entail the strong senses of care relevant to interpersonal relationships close to home, among family or friends. At the institutional level of society and politics, recognition of human rights cannot require the recognition of others in the full richness of their individuality, nor a fully caring attitude toward every single individual worldwide. Nonetheless, it can require attention to the particular cultural differences and economic needs of others and of the groups with which they affiliate within their society. Moreover, it calls for an effort to interpret human rights norms in a way that is somewhat responsive to these particularities of societies and to cultural contexts of association, as will be discussed in some ensuing chapters.

Care work and global justice

A critical social theory of globalization should include an account of women's care burdens and the double load of unpaid and paid work they often perform. This needs to be explicitly theorized in an approach to global inequalities and within the political economy of

---

[22] See, for example, Nigel Dower, *An Introduction to Global Citizenship* (Edinburgh: Edinburgh University Press, 2003), and Luis Cabrera, *The Practice of Global Citizenship* (Cambridge: Cambridge University Press, 2010).

globalization.[23] Our norms of global justice accordingly have to take into account more than simply the issues of redistribution of wealth and income, resource transfers, or even the role of global corporations and property rights, all of which are crucial components of an adequate theory. There is a need to consider as well how to rectify the structural injustices that give rise to the inequalities implicit in the situation of women worldwide, to the degree that women are most often the responsible caregivers, both inside and outside of families. It is necessary to find new ways to explicitly support such care work, whether performed by women or by men, and whether inside households or in more public contexts.

The motivation for women to participate in "global care chains" is closely connected to unjust discrepancies between the Global North and South in resources, income, and wealth, along with differential positions within neoliberal globalization, and the theory and practice of global justice has to address this situation. The phenomenon of sex trafficking, with its economic motivations and pernicious personal effects, also needs to be analyzed within such a feminist global justice approach. Further, the effects of structural adjustment programs along with the actions of global corporations on women's care burden have to be examined and dealt with, as Fiona Robinson has effectively argued.[24]

Attention to these considerations regarding care work supports the idea proposed earlier that global justice requires more than redistribution, whether achieved through foreign aid, resource dividends, or new global taxation schemes,[25] although these are clearly significant. It requires recognition of women's equality and of the particular burdens they shoulder within contemporary political economies. The unequal allocation of care responsibilities points to the centrality of criticizing oppressive or coercive social, economic, and even political institutional arrangements as part of an approach to global justice. It also implies that new institutions that function in more egalitarian ways, including in equalizing the burdens of care, would be essential for the realization of human rights. Particularly important in this regard would be the fulfillment of economic rights to means of subsistence, but also to health and education, as Amartya Sen has argued.[26]

At a more general level, a focus on care should help to raise the status of economic and social human rights as on a par with civil and political rights, so they can have real purchase within the emerging, but still weak, human rights regimes, whether at national, regional, or global

---

[23] Robinson, "Care, Gender and Global Social Justice," and Robinson, *The Ethics of Care*.
[24] Robinson, *The Ethics of Care*.   [25] Brock, "Taxation and Global Justice."
[26] Amartya Sen, *Development as Freedom* (New York: Knopf, 1999).

levels. I have suggested that a care ethics approach lends support as well to taking the differences of individuals and groups seriously into account, to the extent that this is possible in politics. The attention to context and specificity implied in care ethics proposes at the political and legal level a role for *casuistry* in the interpretation and application of general norms, laws, and policies for particular cases. Such an emphasis on care also points to the importance of devising new ways to increase the *democratic responsiveness* and accountability of national and transnational organizations and institutions, and I consider this further in Part III. It can support as well a certain devolution of power to local communities, including cross-border ones, where possible.

In terms of the conception of network solidarity, we can evaluate the *solidaristic recognition* that may characterize such networks as an important aspect of movements for global justice. And given the interconnections that I have proposed with care, it is perhaps suitable to call these *care movements* as well. A further implication is that movements to bring about global justice would need to instantiate caring, responsive, and solidaristic modes not only in their goals but also in their own practices and methods.

A human right to care?

The view here does not see care ethics as a replacement for human rights but instead sees it as casting these rights in a different light. We can also ask whether human rights have a role to play in facilitating care globally, and how the rights currently formulated can best be applied to care. Beyond that, we can specifically ask whether a human right to care should be recognized normatively and perhaps added to the internationally recognized set of human rights acknowledged in law. Clearly, care is among the conditions for people's flourishing as self-developing and relational beings, whether this care is understood in terms of child-raising and the education and cultivation it requires, or in terms of providing opportunities to be cared for and to care for others at later stages of life. In this sense, it could plausibly constitute a human right, in the extended sense I have been discussing in this work.

However, recognizing a distinctive right to care would in some respects be redundant with existing rights recognized in both morality and law. If we look at the relevant set of rights in both the UDHR and in the International Covenant on Economic, Social and Cultural Rights,[27] we

---

[27] Universal Declaration of Human Rights, December 10, 1948; International Covenant on Economic, Social and Cultural Rights, adopted and opened for signature, ratification

can get a sense of the degree to which care is protected and facilitated, as well as some obvious defects in the way it is treated within those documents. A fuller analysis of the current status of care in international human rights would require reference to other covenants as well, including the Convention on the Rights of the Child and the Convention on the Elimination of all Forms of Discrimination against Women (CEDAW). The question of protecting and advancing care within a human rights framework is complex and barely addressed in the existing literature; so it can only be initiated here.

As currently understood, the human rights most relevant to the practice of care are enunciated in the UDHR primarily in Articles 22–6, which refer to several factors central to both caring and being cared for in contemporary societies. Interestingly, the "right to marry and to found a family" is treated earlier, in Article 16, among the civil and political rights, which also asserts that: "The family is the natural and fundamental group unit of society and is entitled to protection by society and the State."

Article 22 enunciates a right to social security, along with a general entitlement to the realization ("through national effort and international co-operation") of the economic, social, and cultural rights "indispensable for [a person's] dignity and the free development of his personality." Article 23 adds a requirement for "just and favourable conditions of work" and "just and favourable remuneration ensuring for himself and his family an existence worthy of human dignity, and supplemented, if necessary, by other means of social protection," and Article 24 adds a right to rest and leisure. Article 25 centrally specifies certain basic requirements that are aspects of care, even mentioning that concept directly:

(1) Everyone has the right to a standard of living adequate for the health and well-being of himself and of his family, including food, clothing, housing and medical care and necessary social services, and the right to security in the event of unemployment, sickness, disability, widowhood, old age or other lack of livelihood in circumstances beyond his control.

(2) Motherhood and childhood are entitled to special care and assistance. All children, whether born in or out of wedlock, shall enjoy the same social protection.

Article 26 states that there is a human right to education and indicates that "Education shall be directed to the full development of the human personality," while Article 27 adds to this a right "freely to participate in the cultural life of the community . . . "

and accession by General Assembly resolution 2200A (XXI) of 16 December 1966; entry into force 3 January 1976, in accordance with article 27.

Considering that only one of the original nine drafters of the UDHR was female (Eleanor Roosevelt), we can be pleased that care is treated as well as it is in that declaration. From the more feminist perspective of the present, however, the document falls short of the egalitarianism we legitimately expect. Most problematically, perhaps, it speaks of assistance for motherhood rather than parenting. Along somewhat similar lines, it refers to "a right to a standard of living adequate to the well-being of himself and his family," where it is likely that this literally was intended to refer to men and their families, although women did begin to enter the workforce in large numbers during the course of World War II, especially in the United States.

The document puts weight on those aspects of care tied to welfare and security, with little attention to the ways that public policy can support caregiving in families. Social services are mentioned, and so is disability. Yet, care work is not regarded as part of the work that the declaration refers to in its articles on work and labor. Nonetheless, it would be interesting to draw the implications of the rights enunciated there for such care work (including a limitation of hours and a right to rest and leisure). Education is mentioned but ways of supporting caregiving through childcare and early education are omitted, though here too, there is a base to build on in the recognition given to the distinctive needs of parenting (in the form of "motherhood") and childhood.

If we turn to the International Covenant on Economic, Social and Cultural Rights that specifies and incorporates these rights into international law, we can find a mention of care for children in Article 10 and an elaboration of the rights of children to protection and assistance, among other strengths, but we see some of the same problems that were observed in the Declaration. On the positive side, we find again the right to social security in Article 9, and then a fuller discussion of the family and children in Article 10. There the Covenant states that: "The widest possible protection and assistance should be accorded to the family . . . particularly for its establishment and while it is responsible for the care and education of dependent children." Helpfully, it also holds that: "Special measures of protection and assistance should be taken on behalf of all children and young persons without any discrimination for reasons of parentage or other conditions. Children and young persons should be protected from economic and social exploitation," and child labor should be prohibited. Beneficial for caregiving is the article's call for leave for working mothers before and after childbirth.

Noteworthy too is Article 7's call for "just and favourable conditions of work," including a "decent living for [workers] and their families."

We can appreciate Article 11's enunciation of "the right of everyone to an adequate standard of living for himself and his family, including adequate food, clothing and housing, and to the continuous improvement of living conditions," and a correlative right to be free from hunger. This article also helpfully discerns a connection between the reform of agrarian systems, along with the equitable distribution of food, and the goal of meeting adequate standards of living for all. Article 12 specifies a right to health in terms of a "right of everyone to the enjoyment of the highest attainable standard of physical and mental health," and sees it as requiring, among other factors, "the healthy development of the child." Finally, Article 13 formalizes "the right of everyone to education," again seeing it as "directed to the full development of the human personality and the sense of its dignity," and as working to strengthen "the respect for human rights and fundamental freedoms . . . education shall enable all persons to participate effectively in a free society." In this way, the article presumably points to some emphasis on civic education, including, potentially, in more cosmopolitan contexts.

As before, we can supplement the appreciation of the strong points of the Covenant with a critique of the document's one-sided protection of motherhood instead of the parenting that would represent a more egalitarian focus. Besides the important role played in caregiving by all parents, one can hope that the paid leave that it calls for upon childbirth could be extended to both parents, of whatever gender. Unsurprisingly, the Covenant, like the UDHR, opines on the role of the family in society seeing it as "the natural and fundamental group unit of society." Further, while the document argues for social security and elaborates the right to an adequate standard of living, it does not mention "the necessary social services, and the right to security in the event of unemployment, sickness, disability, widowhood, old age or other lack of livelihood in circumstances beyond his control," all of which were included in the UDHR in Article 15.

We have listed some of the strengths and also criticisms that can be made of the understanding of the economic and social rights as they pertain to the dimensions of care. The remaining question is whether it is necessary to go beyond these to recognize a right to care per se. At present, care is implicitly (and to a degree explicitly) protected and facilitated in a number of different ways in the UDHR and its elaboration in the International Covenant. These protections reflect the highly specific approach that these documents take, in making reference to present forms of social organization rather than characterizing the various rights as general features of any possible form of social life. This is not necessarily a drawback, since it has the advantage of making clearer how the various rights can be applied, while making implicit reference to the basic needs and interests that they protect.

Given this current approach to articulating economic and social human rights, would it be helpful to add an explicit right to care? Certainly, everyone needs to be cared for and indeed to actively care for others (at least at various times in their lives), and such caring could be said to express our relatedness to others. However, the concept of care has come to the fore only relatively recently, especially in the work of feminist theorists, and there are disparate views as to what should be included within it – as to whether it should be understood in terms of child-raising, parenting, and nurturance, or as a more general concept, in which case it has applicability not just to caring for but to caring about. These disagreements complicate the issue of proposing a human right of a relatively univocal or unitary sort and they also pose challenging questions of interpretation of such a right. Even care work itself has multiple aspects and applications, including not only care for children, but caring for the disabled, the elderly, the sick (and health care more generally). It could be extended to caring for friends and for members of our family generally, or to humanitarian forms of care.

Given this wide scope for care and the fact that there is not yet firm agreement on the relevant meaning of care (although we can discern evident family resemblances among the uses of the term), it may be best to hold in abeyance the possibility of a human right to care at this point, leaving that question for the future. Inasmuch as the current human rights documents do include elements of care, perhaps the focus could now be on strengthening the ways that care is treated within emerging human rights law. Welfare, education, and health care are already included (which is not to say these rights are fulfilled). More attention needs to be given to childcare and support for early childhood education. Clearly, the approach to care needs to become more egalitarian. Certainly more attention could be given to addressing the basic needs that people have for relationships more generally,[28] as well as for care within those relationships. Focusing on such needs extends the analysis beyond maternity leave and childcare. And it would have implications for how we understand some of the other rights, for example, health care, which are framed in terms of supporting the highest attainable standard of mental and physical well-being. Interpreting this with a focus on care, the right to health could be construed to involve finding ways to support

---

[28] On this need, see Gould, *Globalizing Democracy*, chapter 3.

productive and positive relationships, beyond the standard narrow focus on addressing illness, whether physical or mental.

Needless to say, advancing care within a society depends on more than getting it recognized as an aspect of people's human rights. To the degree that caring modes can facilitate not only friendships but also larger group forms of socially cooperative relations, care can play a role in the substance of democratic decision-making and public policy and in the ways these are carried out. A further elaboration of notions of public care and of policies that can support care work domestically and internationally would be important directions for research by feminist philosophers and others. So too would be the further elaboration of the connections of care, recognition, and global justice, some of which have been suggested in outline in this chapter.

8   Gender equality, culture, and the interpretation of human rights

Introduction

In a provocative article for the journal *Foreign Policy* some years ago, Ronald Inglehart and Pippa Norris argued that the true "clash of civilizations" between the Muslim world and the West does not concern the status of democracy, as Huntington and others supposed, but rather attitudes toward gender equality, divorce, abortion, gay rights, and so on. On the basis of surveys of values in these different cultural contexts, Inglehart and Norris concluded that there is wide agreement among Muslim and Western populations on the value of democracy. But such agreement is very much missing in regard to women's equality or what they call other "self-expressive" values such as tolerance for a variety of sexual lifestyles.[1]

In fact, the analysis that these authors offer poses troubling issues of research methodology, especially concerning how these culturally defined values are interpreted and more generally constructed, and how the various terms such as equality are used. But I am not concerned here with disputing their empirical results. Rather, granting that there remain significant differences in the valuation of women's equality and the perception of appropriate gender roles and identities in diverse cultural contexts, I want to consider the normative attitude that one can take to these differences, in light of a commitment to the value of women's equality.

Specifically, I will return to the much-discussed issue of how to approach differently constructed gender roles and identities in various cultures, and consider two conundrums that arise from a commitment to universal equality in that context. (Although not strictly paradoxes from a logical point of view, these certainly represent political paradoxes that

---

[1] Ronald Inglehart and Pippa Norris, "The True Clash of Civilizations," *Foreign Policy* 135 (2003). This article summarizes some of the findings in their co-authored book, Ronald Inglehart and Pippa Norris, *Rising Tide: Gender Equality and Cultural Change around the World* (Cambridge: Cambridge University Press, 2003).

this egalitarian commitment gives rise to.) I also examine the significance of women's human rights as a relevant set of norms for approaching these cultural issues. Divergent interpretations of these rights and of their relative weights can be seen to pose particular difficulties in adjudication. I examine a few such cases in the concluding section, including the use of religious courts for arbitrating family disputes and the much-discussed case of the headscarf.

Gender and two conundrums for feminist analysis

Gender has been treated by feminist theorists in the globalization literature in many ways, which can only be pointed to here. As discussed in Chapter 7, these analyses may understand globalization as "global restructuring," inasmuch as it involves the neoliberal control of economies by transnational actors, most especially, global corporations, with attendant demands for cheap labor, often combined with a diminution of social services. Women tend to be disproportionately employed in these forms of manufacturing (because of their supposedly "nimble fingers") or in the provision of services because they are less often organized and more subject to exploitation. Yet, these powerful globalization processes themselves are "masculinized," as revealed at a symbolic level, and often in practice as well, in the priority given to the masculine spaces "of finance capital over manufacturing, finance ministries over social welfare ministries, the market over the state, the global over the local, and consumers over citizens."[2]

Beyond this, it has been argued by Chandra Mohanty and others that these globalization processes are in fact racialized, in that black women may be least able to participate in this sort of modernization or may be most profoundly oppressed by it.[3] Other theorists have emphasized the rise in the migration of women, whether as domestic care workers in "global care chains,"[4] or in a quite different (and wholly uncaring) context, through sex trafficking.[5] Resistances to these various dimensions of globalization have themselves become more transnational, in the form

---

[2] Marianne H. Marchand and Anne Sisson Runyon, "Introduction," in *Gender and Global Restructuring*, ed. Marchand and Runyon (London: Routledge, 2000), 13.

[3] Chandra Talpade Mohanty, "'Under Western Eyes' Revisited: Feminist Solidarity through Anticapitalist Struggles," *Signs* 28, no. 2 (2002).

[4] Hochschild, "Global Care Chains."

[5] See, for example, Anne E. Lacsamana, "Sex Worker or Prostituted Woman?," in *Women and Globalization*, ed. Delia D. Aguilar and Anne E. Lacsamana (Amherst, NY: Humanity Books, 2004).

of women-led social movements or in more local manifestations.[6] Interestingly, the development of such locally organized programs has not diminished with globalization but has perhaps increased in this period.

At the same time, information and communication technologies, and global media more generally, have increased awareness of, and brought heightened attention to, practices that can only be anathema to believers in gender equality. These include the aforementioned sex trafficking in young girls, and also female genital cutting, which has received considerable critical attention in recent years. Needless to say, this does not exhaust the list: While sati and dowry killings have diminished, female infanticide and sex-selective abortions continue to contribute to millions of missing females, as Amartya Sen has observed.[7] Yet it is not only men who participate in these practices, but sometimes women support them as well and this poses a problem for the feminist critique, which I consider below.

It is perhaps important to stress, on the positive side, that the globalization of communications has not only made these oppressive practices more widely known but also has brought new appreciation of the diversity of cultures and has contributed to the emergence of so-called world cultures in several domains (for example, world music, including ethnic fusion, worldbeat, etc.). The interaction of cultures has also led to the scrutiny of gender practices both in post-industrialized societies and in more traditionally oriented ones (though not to an equal extent), and there has been some sharing of perspectives in both directions.

The persistence of practices like genital cutting that are inconsistent with women's equality poses persistent difficulties for feminist theorists. Respect for cultural differences and awareness of the negative consequences of imperialist impositions, or even judgments from the position of another culture, lead to a justifiable reluctance to criticize the practices of others, who are seen as equal in their differences. Yet, a commitment to equality for women would seem to require that such practices not be tolerated.

The seemingly incompatible requirements arising from universal human equality that constitute this first conundrum – to criticize or refrain from doing so – apply most sharply to traditional practices of the objectionable sort described above. In a different way they also apply to many instances of women's work in the context of economic globalization,

---

[6] Marianne H. Marchand, "Challenging Globalisation: Toward a Feminist Understanding of Resistance," *Review of International Studies* 29 (2003).

[7] Amartya Sen, "More Than 100 Million Women Are Missing," *The New York Review of Books* 37, no. 20 (December, 1990).

for example, where the work is routine and endlessly repetitive. In that set of cases too, feminists attuned to the different perspectives of others may well be unwilling to criticize the situation of women who appear satisfied by the new – though unequal – opportunities opened up by global corporations and free trade. Yet, these theorists rightly remain critical of the functioning of the capitalist economy that has contributed to providing only these sorts of work opportunities and that retains a strong preference for male workers in its reward structure.

In this case the conflict is perhaps not as stark, because one can appreciate that the situation may be relatively better than the previous ones the women endured. Nonetheless, the problem of a discrepancy in point of view and the idea that the subjects of criticism may not share the evaluation of their situation applies. These various tensions pose the difficulty for feminism of expressing criticism and working for change even when some of those who are in the putatively oppressed situation do not recognize it to be such.

Before addressing this conundrum, some clarifications concerning how oppression and domination are understood in this normative account may be helpful. There has been interesting work on the problem of explaining why people living in oppressive situations sometimes accommodate and accede to oppression. Theorists have used the concept of adaptive preferences,[8] or those of "false needs" or "deformed desires,"[9] if not the older troubled notion of false consciousness. My focus here is more narrowly on the relevant political and social norms for cross-cultural critique, rather than on a comprehensive ethical perspective, such as these views often presuppose. I have emphasized freedom as a social and political norm rather than autonomy, which I see as a more individual and ethical desideratum. I believe this allows us to sidestep the epistemological and moral questions engaged by the autonomy literature, as to whether people need to endorse their choices as their own. It also generally obviates the political criticism of others as lacking autonomy, which seems to deny them due respect.

In the view developed here, which analytically separates a capacity for choice from its development over time (seeing the capacity as a basis of equal recognition and thus of human rights), the capacity is *eo ipso* one's own, with the only exception being cases of literal force (or coercion in

---

[8] See, for example, Nussbaum, *Women and Human Development*, 116–18; Harriet E. Baber, "Adaptive Preference," *Social Theory and Practice* 33, no. 1 (2007).

[9] See, for example, Sandra Lee Bartky, *Femininity and Domination* (New York: Routledge, 1990), and Anita Superson, "Deformed Desires and Informed Desire Tests," *Hypatia* 20, no. 4 (2005).

the sense of violence).[10] However, the view also holds that full freedom goes beyond this capacity of choice or intentionality to involve access to a range of conditions. A crucial one is freedom from domination, oppression, or exploitation. (Although there are important differences among these three notions, for our purposes they can be considered together here.) Most often, oppression or exploitation proceeds not by efforts to directly bend the will of a person, or force them to do something, but indirectly, through controlling the conditions they need for their freedom. This is evident in the classic economic analysis of exploitation in Marx, where the power of capitalists over workers arises from their control over the means of production, leading to the need for the workers to cede control over their work for a given time to the capitalists (and produce surplus value for them) in exchange for a wage. Domination too can be framed in terms of control and often works via the conditions of action, including psychological ones. While the full meaning of oppression remains disputed,[11] it seems clear that it too operates on people (primarily identified by the groups to which they belong or are said to belong) via institutions or practices, and not directly in the way that force or violence would. We can thus keep our focus on the various conditions for overcoming domination, oppression, and exploitation, and on the constructive side those needed for realizing equal freedom, which stand opposed to these constraints.[12]

Turning to the second conundrum concerning a commitment to equality, we can discern an apparent tension between tolerating divergent modes of behavior or expression of individuals within a multicultural nation-state and tolerating cultural traditions in other nation-states or societies. Liberal-minded egalitarians often argue for extending tolerance towards people with highly unconventional lifestyles within a given country. Sometimes they also extend it to other peoples or nation-states.[13] But when faced with problematic cultural practices in other cultures or nation-states, liberal attitudes of tolerance are often replaced with

---

[10] For a discussion of some of the meanings of coercion, as well as the notion of power, see Carol C. Gould, "Transnational Power, Coercion, and Democracy," in *Coercion and the State*, ed. David A. Reidy and Walter J. Riker (Berlin: Springer, 2008).

[11] Two prominent approaches can be found in Young, *Justice and the Politics of Difference*, and Ann E. Cudd, *Analyzing Oppression* (New York: Oxford University Press, 2006).

[12] Interestingly, although Ann Cudd calls oppression "the fundamental injustice of social institutions," (*Ibid.*, 26) she does not follow my route in correlatively understanding justice as equal (positive) freedom (*Ibid.*, viii). Of course, this interpretation of justice has more implications than only the critique of oppression, but the latter is one of its fundamental implications on my view.

[13] Rawls seems to argue this way at various points in *The Law of Peoples*. Rawls, *The Law of Peoples*.

fundamental critique and efforts to eliminate the objectionable practices. How is it that people committed to universal human equality can apply the norm so differently in each context? Is this a true paradox of equality exposing an inconsistency at the heart of the concept and in the attitudes of those committed to its realization? Or is there another way to explain this divergence?

Feminist perspectives on gender equality across cultures and women's human rights

In her essay "Global Responsibility and Western Feminism," Alison Jaggar gives a helpful summary of the existing positions in the feminist literature and offers her own critique.[14] While sympathizing with the critique of violence and discrimination toward women offered by liberal feminists, Jaggar shares the concern of postcolonial feminist theorists to avoid imposing Western values on women in the Global South, along with any assumption of Western women's superiority. At the same time, she is attentive to the need, stressed by liberal feminists, to steer clear of the cultural relativism that has marked some postcolonial perspectives.

Jaggar's main recommendation, though, is for theorists to examine Western complicity in the oppression that is often experienced by women of the Global South, whether it has operated through military or economic coercion or other more indirect forms of imposition; she recommends that feminists engage in self-critique first and foremost. Although Jaggar notes that nonintervention or isolationism is no longer a possible posture, she advises that any interventions be cooperative and respectful, and undertaken with an awareness (and critique) of the power differential that is often involved.[15] I think that these points are well taken. And they are coupled in Jaggar's analysis with a useful emphasis on meeting the economic needs of women (and men) in the Global South.

Yet, I suggest that the examination of Western complicity in poverty and oppression needs to be supplemented with a positive account of human rights and their application to women in their diverse contexts. These rights can provide some guidance for actions and policies that can help to alleviate violence, poverty, and entrenched forms of discrimination, although their practical implementation will need to be taken as seriously as that of the standard list of civil and political rights.

---

[14] Alison Jaggar, "Global Responsibility and Western Feminism," in *Feminist Interventions in Ethics and Politics*, ed. Barbara S. Andrew, Jean Keller, and Lisa H. Schwartzman (Lanham, MD: Rowman & Littlefield, 2005).

[15] *Ibid.*, especially 193–5. See also Alison Jaggar, "'Saving Amina': Global Justice for Women and Intercultural Dialogue," *Ethics & International Affairs* 19 (2005).

The recognition that "Human Rights are Men's Rights," as Hilary Charlesworth has put it,[16] has led to extensive re-envisioning of human rights beyond their traditional role as constraints on the public domain of the state and its actors. Feminist theorists have shown how such rights can be reinterpreted to apply to the so-called private sphere in order to prohibit domestic violence against women and to prevent other violations of their bodily integrity, health, and well-being (such as genital cutting and other practices).[17] Rhonda Copelon has argued for reinterpreting the basic prohibition against torture to apply to rape and domestic violence,[18] while others have urged a focus on "bringing rights home" and on their applicability to nonstate actors more generally.[19]

The attention to women's human rights has led to an important emphasis on social and economic human rights (so-called "second stage" rights) as modalities for advancing women's equality. These rights have been taken both in general terms, as in the work of Sen and Nussbaum,[20] and also in specific ways that highlight women's labor outside and within the home.[21] These various approaches show how access to means of subsistence, meaningful work, and education can contribute to the diminution of oppressive practices, in that they are rendered less effective. Along somewhat related lines, some have advocated addressing genital cutting through the implementation of a right to health and to adequate health care.[22] And it is clear that such social and economic rights in fact

---

[16] Hilary Charlesworth, "Human Rights as Men's Rights," in *Women's Rights, Human Rights*, ed. Julie Peters and Andrea Wolper (New York: Routledge, 1995).

[17] See the essays in *Women's Rights, Human Rights* (New York: Routledge, 1995), and Rebecca Cook (ed.), *The Human Rights of Women* (Philadelphia, PA: The University of Pennsylvania Press, 1994), as well as Gould, *Globalizing Democracy*, chapter 6; and Carol C. Gould, "Women's Human Rights and the U.S. Constitution: Initiating a Dialogue," in *Women and the U.S. Constitution: History, Interpretation, Practice*, ed. Sibyl Schwarzenbach and Patricia Smith (New York: Columbia University Press, 2003).

[18] Rhonda Copelon, "Intimate Terror: Understanding Domestic Violence as Torture," in *The Human Rights of Women*, ed. Robin Cook (Philadelphia, PA: The University of Pennsylvania Press, 1994).

[19] See, for example, F. Beveridge and S. Mullally, "International Human Rights and Body Politics," in *Law and Body Politics: Regulating the Female Body*, ed. J. Bridgeman and S. Millns (Aldershot: Dartmouth, 1995).

[20] Amartya Sen, "Gender Inequality and Theories of Justice," in *Women, Culture and Development*, ed. Martha Nussbaum and Jonathan Glover (New York: Oxford University Press, 1995); Martha Nussbaum, "Human Capabilities, Female Human Beings," *Ibid.*; see also Martha Nussbaum, *Sex and Social Justice* (New York: Oxford University Press, 1999).

[21] Mary Margaret Fonow, "Human Rights, Feminism, and Transnational Labor Solidarity," in *Just Advocacy? Women's Human Rights, Transnational Feminisms, and the Politics of Representation*, ed. Wendy S. Hesford and Wendy Kozol (New Brunswick, NJ: Rutgers University Press, 2005).

[22] See, for example, Loretta Kopelman, "Female Genital Mutilation and Ethical Relativism," *Second Opinion* (October 1994).

have wide acceptance, at least in principle, across quite diverse societies (although not very much in the United States).

A focus on human rights can help address the conundrums I presented concerning the requirement of equality. Although not fully resolving these puzzles concerning the implications of our commitment to equality, this focus takes human rights to serve as legitimate constraints on the toleration of cultural practices: that is, such practices can be tolerated if they do not violate human rights,[23] and perhaps especially the basic ones. In light of this principle, we can see that the toleration or respect for unconventional sexual lifestyles or identities within a given society can be seen as fully compatible with the critique of practices by cultural groups (either within or without that society) that violate the bodily integrity of women and other of women's human rights.

With respect to the first conundrum – seeing equality as requiring the recognition and toleration of cultural differences (including oppressive ones) vs. requiring women's equal rights even when they conflict with cultural practices – the human rights focus advocated in this work would give priority to women's equality, if cultural practices seriously violate it. This follows from the deeply egalitarian and cosmopolitan reading given here of human rights themselves. This contrasts with such views as those referred to in Chapter 4, in which these rights are viewed as only minimal requirements holding on any given nation-state in a way that does not tie them to a strong principle of equality. (The latter view is evident in Joshua Cohen's account.) In my view, human rights specify the conditions – basic and nonbasic – required for justice as equal positive freedom. They follow from this equal freedom and are needed to protect and enable it. In this way, the equality of women has priority over these cultural practices. Nonetheless, individuals are understood here in relational ways, and thus are conceived as socially, culturally, and historically situated. These individuals and groups are differentiated, and therefore some variations can be expected in the conditions needed for self-developing activity, especially in regard to nonbasic rights. (Differences will enter the basic rights too in their application to individuals, for example, in accommodating physical differences or various handicaps as a condition for their treatment as an equal.) Later in this chapter, and in Chapter 9, I consider a few cases of diverging cultural or national

---

[23] I argued a similar point in Carol C. Gould, "Cultural Justice and the Limits of Difference: Feminist Contributions to Value Inquiry," *Utopia (Athens)* 21 (July–August 1996); and in revised form in Carol C. Gould, "Cultural Justice and the Limits of Difference," in *Norms and Values: Essays on the Work of Virginia Held*, ed. J. G. Haber and M. S. Halfon (Lanham, MD: Rowman and Littlefield, 1998). See also my discussion of this point in Gould, *Globalizing Democracy*, chapter 5.

interpretations of human rights or various weightings of the different rights in relation to each other, with a view to seeing how they can be accommodated.

In order for a reliance on human rights to avoid simply being an imposition of preferred Western mores, it has to meet certain other criteria: A crucial one is that the human rights standards have to be applied to criticize the situation in the United States and other post-industrial societies, and cannot be used one-sidedly to criticize only cultural practices within the Global South. As the anthropologist Sally Merry has argued, it is not as though the United States and other societies that strongly advocate for human rights are themselves culture free. Culture, if it is to be a viable concept, has to be seen as applying not only to so-called traditional cultures but to so-called modern ones as well, in that cultures consist of everyday practices, mores, and relatively stable expectations of actions and roles across the range of societies.[24]

I have suggested that any human rights critique of cultural practices needs to be coupled with a social, political, and economic analysis and critique of the conditions that have given rise to or contributed to the practices in question. Indeed, as Merry also points out, not all objectionable cultural practices are ancient, and current political and economic conditions can at the very least exacerbate them, as in the case of battering that is aggravated by contemporary wars and violence.[25] Further, the idea that these practices are entirely due to individuals in the "other" culture absolves Western societies and neo-liberal economics of any role in aggravating them.

An additional factor in understanding the normative acceptability of cultural practices is summed up in the question, "Who speaks for the culture?" as several feminist theorists have observed.[26] It is important that women be among the spokespeople, not only the rulers or male elites who are likely to be the ones benefiting from the status quo and thus interested in its perpetuation. Too often the representations of cultural and religious norms proffered by rulers and other elites are taken as definitive, where a more open and progressive reading of the variety of cultural

---

[24] Sally Engle Merry, "Human Rights Law and the Demonization of Culture (and Anthropology Along the Way)," *Polar: Political and Legal Anthropology Review* 26, no. 1 (2003).

[25] *Ibid.* See also Sally Engle Merry, *Human Rights and Gender Violence: Translating International Law into Local Justice* (Chicago, IL: University of Chicago Press, 2005).

[26] Arati Rao, "The Politics of Gender and Culture in International Human Rights Discourse," in *Women's Rights, Human Rights*, ed. Julie Peters and Andrea Wolper (New York: Routledge, 1995).

practices would be illuminating and perhaps also more accurate.[27] And as has been often noted, cultures are not homogeneous entities but rather incorporate different groups within them. In some cases, the objectionable practices may actually violate basic mores within the given cultural tradition and may be widely criticized (e.g., widow immolation or sati). It is a mistake to lump together such practices with others that are more fully supported by the cultural group in question. Finally, we need to keep in mind that, from the standpoint of both contemporary anthropology and social philosophy, cultures are appropriately conceived as relatively dynamic and changing, even though these transformations are sometimes slow and not very evident. And even relatively isolated cultures normally have some interaction with cultures and perspectives external to them.

Women's human rights as conceived here acknowledge that the equality of persons is not to be understood as sameness but rather as *equality through difference*, or perhaps *differentiated equality*. Equal positive freedom as a principle requires equal access to a range of different conditions that depend partly on people's social position, including correcting for the disadvantage arising from oppressive circumstances. Even people's needs for basic conditions of human life – including material needs, the need for recognition, and the need for relationships – are evidently differentiated socially and culturally despite the commonalities these abstract notions point to.

If we turn to the Convention on the Elimination of All Forms of Discrimination against Women (CEDAW), adopted in 1981, we can see that although it still lacks effect in international law (and in many ways does not go far enough in the changes it calls for), nonetheless, it recognizes that women's human rights presuppose the critique of oppression, as well as of lesser forms of discrimination.[28] The convention calls on state parties to prohibit discrimination against women, which it defines broadly in Article 1 as "any distinction, exclusion or restriction made on the basis of sex which has the effect or purpose of impairing or nullifying the recognition, enjoyment or exercise by women, irrespective of their marital status, on a basis of equality of men and women, of human rights and fundamental freedoms in the political, economic, social, cultural, civil or any other field." Note that this definition refers to the *effect* as well as the purpose of governmental measures and also does not limit

---

[27] Ann Elizabeth Mayer, "Cultural Particularism as a Bar to Women's Rights: Reflections on the Middle Eastern Experience," in Peters and Wolper, *Women's Rights, Human Rights.*

[28] The discussion of CEDAW in this section draws on Gould, "Women's Human Rights."

discrimination to that carried out through state action alone. Indeed, as is evident in the final phrase "in any other field," this discrimination can extend to that found in family affairs.

Article 2 calls on states to "pursue by all appropriate means and without delay a policy of eliminating discrimination against women," including that states should "embody the principle of the equality of men and women in their national constitutions or other appropriate legislation" (2a). Importantly, this article goes on to require them "to take all appropriate measures to eliminate discrimination against women *by any person, organization or enterprise*" (2e) and "to take all appropriate measures, including legislation, to modify or abolish existing laws, regulations, customs and practices which constitute discrimination against women." The phrase in 2e concerning eliminating "discrimination against women by any person, organization, or enterprise" can be taken to mean that the provision and indeed the Convention as a whole should apply to the private, nongovernmental sectors of society. It seems to require action against discrimination even among individuals. Other noteworthy features are its overall goal (in Article 3) "to ensure the full development and advancement of women," its endorsement (in limited terms) of affirmative action in Article 4, and its call on states in Article 5 "to modify the social and cultural patterns of conduct of men and women, with a view to achieving the elimination of prejudices and customary and all other practices which are based on the idea of the inferiority or the superiority of either of the sexes or on stereotyped roles for men and women."

CEDAW thus addresses the institutional framework for women's oppression and for their empowerment. Its requirement of equal rights for women goes beyond requiring a sex neutral opposition to sex discrimination per se and moves towards the elimination of discrimination against women specifically. It opposes laws that are detrimental in effect, even if they are neutral on their face, as well as those specifically harmful to women, such as the non-provision of obstetric services.[29] In contrast to the United States' intermediate scrutiny standard, CEDAW and other human rights instruments require that distinctions based on sex are deserving of the highest degree of judicial scrutiny, as Anne Bayefsky has argued.[30]

---

[29] Rebecca Cook, "State Accountability under the Convention on the Elimination of All Forms of Discrimination against Women," in *The Human Rights of Women*, ed. Robin Cook (Philadelphia, PA: The University of Pennsylvania Press, 1994), 236.

[30] Anne F. Bayefsky, "General Approaches to the Domestic Application of Women's International Human Rights Law," in *The Human Rights of Women*, ed. Rebecca Cook (Philadelphia, PA: University of Pennsylvania Press, 1994), 357.

In discussing CEDAW's strengths, Rebecca Cook has pointed out another of its advantages, namely, its import for state responsibility. She writes, "Although a state is not internationally responsible for a private act of sexual discrimination, it is bound to undertake means to eliminate or reduce and mitigate the incidence of private discrimination, and to achieve the result that such private discrimination should not recur."[31] Indeed, states are supposed to act to prevent anticipated violation of human rights, including those initiated by private persons. CEDAW's General Recommendation 19 further specifies this as applying to harms against women in the so-called private sphere of family and personal relations by calling on states to take "appropriate and effective measures to overcome all forms of gender based violence, whether by private or public act."

Needless to say, the CEDAW convention presently has the status more of a declaration than operative international law. But it represents some useful directions for the future. Beyond the legal changes it could enable would be institutional transformations in both politics and society that are needed to achieve fuller degrees of equality. In Part III I discuss some transformations of democracy that could be helpful, including new forms of democratic deliberation across borders. From the standpoint of this chapter, it is crucial to bear in mind that women will have to be permitted and enabled to play a large role in these discursive processes.

Interpreting and adjudicating women's human rights

We can now briefly consider a few cases in which rights pertaining to women and their families have been adjudicated, to see what is involved in holding human rights (and women's human rights, in particular) open to some differences in cultural interpretation. Some of these cases have arisen in an important new context for jurisprudence – namely, regional agreements on human rights. The most prominent of these agreements are in Europe, as instituted by both the Council of Europe and the EU. Agreements also exist, though they are not much used, in Africa (the African Charter of Human Rights), as well as in the inter-American context, with the American Convention on Human Rights of 1978 of the Organization of American States. Such regional agreements help to provide a framework for emerging forms of transnational cooperation and governance produced through economic, technological, ecological, and social forms of globalization. (Another element of this framework, forms of transnational democracy at regional levels, are discussed in the

---

[31] Cook, "State Accountability," 237.

concluding chapter of this book.) The various regional human rights agreements supplement existing international covenants by allowing a certain degree of subsidiarity and diversity of interpretation of the universal human rights for particular contexts.

One set of cases (already much analyzed) concerns laws – in France, Switzerland, Germany, and elsewhere – governing the permissibility of wearing religious headgear, with a focus especially on the Islamic headscarf for women – in the public sphere. The cases pointedly raise the question of whether the application of human rights can properly be understood to vary depending on the context. This variability was suggested by the European Court of Human Rights (ECHR) in *Sahin v. Turkey*, in its heavy reliance on the notion of a *margin of appreciation*, in the 2004 decision that affirmed the Turkish courts' ban on headscarves in universities. I think this notion of a margin of appreciation is suggestive, and is perhaps especially useful in the new regional jurisprudence concerning human rights. But an important question is who gets to participate in the interpretations of these rights and their implementation.

The issue of banning headscarves in public institutions, and especially in schools on the part of students or teachers, as well as the arguments one could mount against such legal prohibitions, is complex and cannot be resolved here. Some Western liberal feminists have tended to view the issue as raising autonomy concerns, not only in liberal democracies but also in Muslim majority societies like Turkey. Although they may see the oppressive aspects of the cultural practice where it is imposed, inasmuch as the requirement to wear the scarf may be required by prevailing male-dominant cultural practices, these theorists see the question as one of the freedom to wear what one pleases or as a matter of people's freedom to live a life of their own choosing. In the European context, they tend to place weight on Article 8 of the ECHR (respect for one's private life), although that article has not yet played a major role in the jurisprudence on this subject.[32] Or else, they may interpret the issue in more mainstream fashion as a matter of the freedom to manifest one's religion, as specified in Article 9 (of course, that freedom is not unlimited, as indicated in the second part of that article).[33] Others, like Seyla Benhabib, have emphasized the element of protest that may be involved in university women wearing the scarf, especially in France but also elsewhere in Europe.[34] Relatively few have promoted the arguments in favor of such

[32] Jill Marshall, "Women's Right to Autonomy and Identity in European Human Rights Law: Manifesting One's Religion," *Res Publica* 14 (2008): 177–92.
[33] Sharon Cowan, "The Headscarf Controversy: A Response to Jill Marshall," *Res Publica* 14 (2008): 193–201.
[34] Benhabib, *The Rights of Others*, 183–202.

bans that are based on secularism or laïcité, which has different weights in various European countries. It could be argued that such secularism not only has the status of a constitutional commitment, as in France, but also has itself become a cultural tradition there (and perhaps less so in Turkey). But interpretations of secularism along these lines would nonetheless have to interpret it in ways that also protect the minority rights of those living within that society.

In the 2004 case, the ECHR supported Turkey's ban on wearing the headscarf in universities, but we can wonder whether questions of dress, religious or otherwise, should be a matter of law. Still, autonomy or privacy arguments are distinctively liberal, whereas freedom of religious expression commands wider assent around the world. Some societies, including the United States, couple that latter freedom with a secular or neutral state, while others do not. Thus both the jurisprudence and the practices are unsettled and evolving. Even the established human rights instruments can point in different and possibly conflicting directions. What does seem clear is that human rights jurisprudence needs to be encouraged to move in directions that protect and enhance women's equality. For this, more women would need to be involved in interpreting these human rights themselves, including as judges. The participation of women in reinterpreting traditional Islamic requirements would be important as well. We can note in this connection the powerful work of theorists like Azizah Al-Hibri,[35] along with the more applied contexts of interpretation encouraged by Internet groups like Women Living under Muslim Laws (WLUML).

A political footnote here is that making laws against practices like the headscarf are likely counterproductive in any case (whether or not laws are justified on other grounds). Thus the prohibition itself may lead to strengthening people's interest in wearing it by way of protest.

Ayelet Shachar and Martha Minow have discussed another set of cases that implicate diverse rights of women and concern the varying boundary between the public and private spheres. In helpful nuance, they have addressed the status of religious courts (particularly Jewish and Islamic) as forums for arbitrating divorce and child custody disputes within family law, which has been considered by courts in the UK and in Canada.

---

[35] Azizah Al-Hibri, "Islamic Constitutionalism and the Concept of Democracy," in *Border Crossings: Toward a Comparative Political Theory*, ed. Fred Dallmayr (Lanham, MD: Lexington Books, 1999); Azizah Al-Hibri, "An Islamic Perspective on Domestic Violence," *Fordham International Law Journal* 7 (2003); Azizah Al-Hibri, "Developing Islamic Jurisprudence in the Diaspora: Balancing Authenticity, Diversity and Modernity," *Journal of Social Philosophy* 45, no. 1 (2014): 7–24.

Although not normally treated as a matter of human rights per se, the relevant policies and legal cases implicate issues of equal treatment under law, specific concerns of gender equality, and questions of religious expression. For example, a commitment to gender equality may well require that if such religious courts are to be used at all to arbitrate family disputes, their judgments should be subject to review by secular state courts. But if the review requires a post hoc appeal, it may put too much burden on ordinary citizens. Therefore, the conclusion would seem to be that regulation is required, or the procedures should not be permitted at all. But as Shachar and Minow discuss, perhaps new modalities for mediating the various normative desiderata will emerge.[36]

In contrast to the range of interpretations these cases support, we can note that there are others where the human rights violations are not susceptible to any flexible reading. For example, the case of honor killings in families contrasts with the headscarf issue in its clarity as a straightforward violation of human rights – to life and security of the person. It is evident that laws prohibiting some culturally mediated practices are mandatory in order to respect basic human rights. And in those sorts of cases, notions of a margin of appreciation or diverse regional applications would be out of place.

Provisionally, then, we can draw some conclusions from these various cases:

(1) Some cases of human rights violations, whether in the public or private sphere, do not permit of a margin of appreciation, and that is when they involve especially clear violations of what I have called basic human rights.

(2) The notion of a margin of appreciation can have a certain utility in regard to other human rights (nonbasic, though not inessential) where the cultural and historical context varies. Although human rights interpretation must adhere strongly to notions of fundamental human equality, including women's equality, some variation in interpretation can be expected and mutual learning among diverse cultural traditions would be appropriate.

(3) Women and other historically oppressed groups need to be given a place at the table, probably even a central place, in both the interpretation of human rights and in the ongoing interpretations of the religious traditions themselves.

---

[36] Ayelet Shachar, "Privatizing Diversity: A Cautionary Tale from Religious Arbitration in Family Law," *Theoretical Inquiries in Law* 9, no. 2 (2008); Martha Minow, "Is Pluralism an Ideal or a Compromise?: An Essay for Carol Weisbrod," *Connecticut Law Review* 40, no. 5 (2008).

(4) The fulfillment of human rights cannot be left to jurisprudential contexts or courts alone. They need to be taken as goals motivating the reform and creation of social, political, and economic institutions and policies that serve to realize them. As discussed in later chapters, these too can be subject to intercultural dialogue concerning their proper scope, interpretation, and forms of fulfillment over time.

9 The sociality of free speech: the case of humor across cultures

Introduction

Free expression has most often been considered as a right or capacity of individuals. Although free expression has been theorized for its political import, the social dimensions of such speech or expression have received less scrutiny. An exception perhaps has been the philosophical reflection on dialogue, though even that has often been viewed through the lens of democratic deliberation. Of course, all speech as communication is social by nature. This chapter attempts to delineate some of the less obvious social dimensions of freedom of expression, both as a phenomenon and, to a degree, as a right. The analysis focuses especially on the exemplary use of speech in the telling of jokes. The connection of jokes to a particular audience that understands them and to which they are directed will be seen to raise interesting questions both of inclusion and exclusion that are especially relevant to the possibilities for cross-cultural speech. Although jokes, and humor more generally, are in some ways idiosyncratic, I think that they may nonetheless help to reveal some of the limitations and possibilities of understanding speech and communication in increasingly dominant transnational contexts.

Taking off from Ted Cohen's helpful work *Jokes: Philosophical Thoughts on Joking Matters*,[1] this chapter first considers what jokes presuppose about the individuals or community that hears them, and some of the problems that can arise when they are taken as derogatory towards another culture. It then looks at some of the ways that jokes can facilitate social and political protest. The chapter goes on to briefly consider other

---

[1] Ted Cohen, *Jokes: Philosophical Thoughts on Joking Matters* (Chicago, IL: University of Chicago Press, 1999). Much of the analysis and many of the jokes in the first section of this chapter are drawn from Cohen's insightful book. Although there are other published versions of several of these, for example, in William Novak and Moshe Waldoks (eds.), *The Big Book of Jewish Humor: 25th Anniversary* (New York: Collins, 2006); and Thomas Cathcart and Daniel Klein (eds.), *Plato and a Platypus Walk into a Bar. . .* (New York: Harry N. Abrams, 2007), I found Cohen's versions to be generally the funniest and most accessible, so I include them here.

forms of social speech, and especially deliberation, along with its role in the functioning of voluntary associations and social movements. These various analyses provide a basis for some tentative conclusions about the sociality of free speech, about the conditions for avoiding exclusionary or oppressive speech, and concerning whether a global audience for humor and other forms of social expression is possible, or perhaps even desirable. Although the main focus is not on the basic philosophical justification of the right to free expression, these social aspects of speech suggest some additional factors for this justification.

Jokes, communities, and exclusion

Consider this philosopher's joke, as presented in Ted Cohen's book.

The president of a small college desires to improve his school's academic reputation. He is told that the best way to do this is to create at least a few first-rank departments. It would be good to work on the mathematics department, he is told, because that would not be too expensive. Mathematicians do not require laboratories or even much equipment. All they need are pencils, paper, and wastebaskets. It might be even better to work on the philosophy department. The philosophers don't need wastebaskets.[2]

In his interesting and influential analysis of humor, Ted Cohen points out that many jokes are conditional, as this one is. They require some background knowledge supplied by a particular audience, and are often best appreciated by that audience.[3] Here is another, rather different, example that Cohen presents:

Early one morning a man awoke in a state of terrible anxiety because of a dream he had been having. He immediately called his psychiatrist, and after making a special plea because of his distress he was granted an appointment that morning even though it was not the day for seeing his psychiatrist. When he arrived at the doctor's office, he said, "I had the most awful dream you can imagine. In it I raped my mother, killed my wife, and seduced my daughter, and more things worse than those. I woke up shaking and sweating, and I called you immediately. Then I had a quick piece of toast and some coffee, and ran down here to see you."

"What?" said the psychiatrist. "You call that a breakfast?"[4]

Although one certainly does not have to be Jewish to appreciate this joke, Cohen thinks that it depends on knowing that many psychiatrists are Jewish and that Jewish mothers are excessively concerned about food. (I would say it is enhanced with that knowledge, but still comprehensible

[2] Cohen, *Jokes*, 14. [3] *Ibid.*, 12–14. [4] *Ibid.*, 15.

without it.) Cohen calls these sorts of jokes *hermetic*, though their degree of accessibility can vary considerably.

Some jokes can be read at different levels, depending on the audience and its background knowledge. An example is the following joke, approachable in several ways:

> A musician was performing a solo recital in Israel. When he ended the last selection, a thunderous response came from the audience, including many cries of "Play it again." He stepped forward, bowed, and said, "What a wonderfully moving response. Of course I shall be delighted to play it again." And he did. At the end, again there was a roar from the audience, and again many cries of "Play it again." This time the soloist came forward smiling and said, "Thank you. I have never been so touched in all my concert career. I should love to play it again, but there is no time, for I must perform tonight in Tel Aviv. So, thank you from the bottom of my heart – and farewell." Immediately a voice was heard from the back of the hall saying, "You will stay here and play it again until you get it right."[5]

Cohen points out that this joke does not presuppose much more knowledge by way of background than about what music recitals are like. But he observes that its reception is improved by knowing something about the confident music audience to be found in Israel. And it is enhanced even further perhaps by knowing about the Jewish religious requirement that when the Bible is read in the synagogue, those hearing it should announce any errors they discern in the reading, which the reader then is then expected to repeat until the passage is read entirely correctly.[6]

Beyond drawing on shared background knowledge in this way, jokes, in Cohen's account, involve what he calls an *affective* conditional, that is, "their success (their capacity to amuse) depends on the affective disposition of the audience."[7] Accordingly, they will be funnier if the listener shares not only perceptions but also some degree of feeling with the person telling the joke and with other members of the audience.

According to Cohen, these examples suggest that when jokes are successful and evoke a shared response of laughter, it is because they establish a certain intimacy with the audience, an intimacy borne of a shared sense of community. This involves two aspects in his view, first, "a shared set of beliefs, dispositions, and preferences, et cetera – a shared outlook on the world," and second, "a shared feeling – a shared response to something."[8] In this way, we can observe that jokes presuppose and also evoke a degree of empathy among the members of the community. Cohen goes on to suggest that laughing together realizes, if briefly, the hope "that

[5] *Ibid.*, 23.   [6] *Ibid.*   [7] *Ibid.*, 21.   [8] *Ibid.*, 28.

we are enough like one another to sense one another, to be able to live together."⁹

But generally speaking, it helps not to be a member of a group against whom a joke is directed. Thus many jokes are likely to affect people differentially depending on their group affiliation. Indeed, as Cohen points out and as is widely understood, many of these jokes take as their topics enduring stereotypes, whether or not the stereotypes are still actively subscribed to. Among such jokes some are relatively benign and can even be self-directed against one's own group in a sort of joshing way or else to pre-empt or subvert criticism by outsiders. A number of Jewish jokes fall into this category. Here's one tale that Cohen presents, which he suggests is accessible to both Jews and non-Jews, but which may have a deeper resonance for Jews:

Abe and his friend Sol are out for a walk together in a part of town they haven't been in. Passing a Christian church, they notice a curious sign in front saying "$1,000 to anyone who will convert." "I wonder what that's about," says Abe. "I think I'll go in and have a look. I'll be back in a minute; just wait for me."

Sol sits on a sidewalk bench and waits patiently for nearly half an hour, and then Abe reappears.

"Well," asks Sol, "what are they up to? Who are they trying to convert? Why do they care? Did you get the $1,000?"

Indignantly, Abe replies, "Money. That's all you people care about."¹⁰

And here's a lighthearted one:

A group of Jews decided to take up competitive rowing, and so they formed a crew and began practicing. Months later they had competed several times, and always they not only lost, but came in so far behind that they thought something must be wrong with their approach. They sent one of their number off to England to observe the Oxford/Cambridge race, and then to the Ivy League to see the rowers there. When he returned, he was asked if indeed these other crews had a different technique.

"Well, he reported, "they have *one* guy *yelling*, and *eight* guys *rowing*."¹¹

But there can also be jokes that turn on stereotypes that are more offensive. In contrast to the set of jokes with which I began this chapter that specifically turn on *including* members within a community, or sharing features of group affiliation good-naturedly with an audience, there are many ethnic jokes of a mocking variety that tend to *exclude* communities

⁹ *Ibid.*, 29.   ¹⁰ *Ibid.*, 27.   ¹¹ *Ibid.*, 42.

from joining in the laughter, since the joke is about them. So for example, we have the following jokes, all of them not only exclusionary but offensive in various ways:

What does it say on the bottom of a Polish Coke bottle?
Open other end.[12]

Or this one:

The thing about German food is that no matter how much you eat, an hour later you're hungry for power.[13]

Or another Polish joke that plays on stereotypes:

A Polish man walks up to a counter and says, "I want to buy some sausage."
"You want Polish sausage?" asks the clerk. "Kielbasa?"
"Why do you think I want Polish sausage?" replies the man indignantly. "Why wouldn't I want Italian sausage, or Jewish sausage? Do I look Polish? What makes you think I'm Polish?"
The clerk responds, "This is a hardware store."[14]

In a lighter and more generous vein, the following joke turns on ethnic stereotypes but is partly self-critical:

On a flight to Israel in late December: "This is your captain speaking. This is the culmination of El Al Flight 761, and we welcome you to Ben Gurion Airport in Tel Aviv. Please remain seated with your seat belts fastened until the plane has come to a complete halt and the seat belt signs have been turned off. [Pause] And to those of you who are still seated, we wish you a Merry Christmas and a Happy New Year."

If we keep in view the pervasiveness of group stereotypes in jokes and elsewhere in life, as well as the importance for successful jokes of some affiliation by members of the audience and the teller, we can wonder whether it is possible to share jokes across communities or cultures, and even more so in global contexts. Indeed, we can ask whether the "community of amusement" presupposed in many jokes (in Cohen's felicitous phrase) would even be a good thing if it came to be extended globally.

---

[12] *Ibid.*, 21.   [13] *Ibid.*
[14] *Ibid.*, 73. In the final chapter of his book, Cohen insists that many jokes remain funny despite their portrayal of ethnic stereotypes, even particularly detestable stereotypes (much worse than those included here). He does not give any arguments to support his opinion on this matter, and I believe his otherwise trenchant analysis is not convincing at that point. I expect I am not the only one for whom the salience of a joke's moral obnoxiousness overwhelms the possibility of finding it funny.

Would such universal communication presuppose that all important cultural differences among people were eliminated (which would evidently be an unfortunate development)? Clearly, some jokes are more fully universal or at least intercultural than others – those concerned with the standard challenges presented by growing up, by marriage and the family, and by death. But what about the vast array of other jokes, which may be conditional and dependent on context, and what of their potential to hurt?

The conception of what we could call a *global community of amusement* would seem to parallel the notion in the global justice literature of a thoroughgoing cosmopolitanism, standing over against particularist conceptions that emphasize retaining the central role of nation-states or of local communities. But even if we advance a more modest notion to the effect that *overlapping communities of amusement* are desirable, the need for shared communities of understanding raises the question of the possibility or effectiveness of intercultural dialogue and communication not only in the realm of jokes but in speech more generally.

Remaining for now on the terrain of humor, we can observe that some not very funny "jokes" have in fact provoked considerable consternation, and indeed even violence, internationally in recent years. Although not the main focus of analysis here, these efforts at humor (or better, sarcasm, in some cases) raise difficult issues in regard to free speech. A noteworthy example is provided by the set of Danish cartoons published in the daily newspaper *Jyllands-Posten* in 2005, which depicted the Prophet Muhammad in troublesome ways. Most problematic, perhaps, was one cartoon that portrayed him with a turban in the shape of an ignited bomb with verses from the Koran inscribed on it. Although there have by now been extensive scholarly analyses of the issues raised by the publication of these cartoons,[15] vexing practical problems arose from the anger that their publication occasioned, including a threat of terrorist actions by members of Al Qaeda against Danish targets around the world.[16]

It is apparent that the images of a religious prophet published in the mass media of Western countries in which certain sectors of the population have experienced repeated verbal attacks and thoroughgoing criticism are quite a different sort of humor than the jokes with which I began this chapter, which are typically told among friends or colleagues. Indeed, in the intercultural context, a controversy may arise comparable

---

[15] See, for example, Robert Post, "Religion and Freedom of Speech: Portraits of Muhammad," *Constellations* 14, no. 1 (2007); Sune Laegaard, "The Cartoon Controversy: Offence, Identity, Oppression?," *Political Studies* 55 (2007); and Tariq Modood, "The Liberal Dilemma: Integration or Vilification?," *Open Democracy* (2006).

[16] *New York Times*, September 5, 2008.

to that concerning domestic hate speech, and difficult problems confront us concerning the limits of freedom of expression in public discourse, in the press, and in the arts. A relevant case here concerned the Repertory Theatre in Birmingham, UK, which produced a play "Behzti" (meaning "Dishonor" in Punjabi) authored by a British-born female Sikh play-wright. Members of the local Sikh community requested changes in the play, and after a dialogue between theater management and the local Sikhs ended in stalemate, a demonstration erupted outside the theater, which led to violence and the closing of the production. The issues in that case were not only about religious and secular values, but implicated questions of race, gender, and culture.[17] This case brings into relief for us not only the meaning and possible limits of freedom of speech, but also the dangers that can arise from attempts to constrain it.

These cases concern the treatment of religious or ethnic minori-ties within given nation-states, themselves liberal, and the philosophi-cal ground has been relatively well-trodden in that context (although the question of defining and dealing with hate speech remains vexing). When questions of free speech and toleration arise transnationally, I believe they can become even more difficult to negotiate. Granted, freedom of expres-sion has standing as a human right in the UDHR and in the International Covenant on Civil and Political Rights,[18] but determining its significance cross-culturally is difficult. With the further development of transnational communication, especially through social media, along with the intensifi-cation of regional cooperation, whether economic or political, it may well become necessary to come up with new ways of protecting and enabling freedom of expression in regional and global contexts.

It can be expected that in transnational contexts, crucial issues arise (as they also have within nation-states) concerning the ways in which

---

[17] Ralph D. Grillo, "License to Offend? The Behzti Affair," *Ethnicities* 7, no. 1 (2007).

[18] Article 19 of the Universal Declaration of Human Rights (UDHR) affirms that "everyone has the right to freedom of opinion and expression; this right includes freedom to hold opinions without interference and to seek, receive and impart information and ideas through any media and regardless of frontiers."

Article 19 of The International Covenant on Civil and Political Rights (entered into force in 1976) stipulates: "(1) Everyone shall have the right to hold opinions without interference. (2) Everyone shall have the right to freedom of expression; this right shall include freedom to seek, receive and impart information and ideas of all kinds, regardless of frontiers, either orally, in writing or in print, in the form of art, or through any other media of his choice. (3) The exercise of the rights provided for in paragraph 2 of this article carries with it special duties and responsibilities. It may therefore be subject to certain restrictions, but these shall only be such as are provided by law and are necessary: (a) For respect of the rights or reputations of others; (b) For the protection of national security or of public order (ordre public), or of public health or morals."

speech may contribute to oppression (and not just give offense), whether religious groups should be regarded as comparable to ethnic groups in this respect (and thus whether there is something akin to racism in the derogatory treatment of Muslims), and how much weight to give these considerations of oppression and discrimination as qualifications on freedom of speech. I will return to some brief consideration of these matters later in the chapter. But it is evident from the review already presented that factors concerning the recognition of people and their cultural differences introduce features of sociality that need to be reckoned with in an adequate account of freedom of expression.

Jokes, protest, and resisting oppression

We can consider a different type of joke and its significance for freedom of speech and its sociality. These are protest jokes, which exist in many traditions. Consider the following two sets of jokes from the former Soviet Union:

First, we have two typical Soviet jokes from the time of terror, 1928–56:

What is the difference between India and Russia?
   In India one man starves for the people, and in Russia the people starve for one man.

Two Russians discussed who was the greater man, Stalin or President Hoover.
   "Hoover taught the Americans not to drink," says one.

"Yes," replies the other, "but Stalin taught the Russians not to eat."

From the time of routine oppression (1957–85), we find the following examples:

What is seven kilometers long and eats potatoes?
   A Polish meat queue.

Why is the Soviet system superior to all others?
   Because it successfully overcomes problems that no other system has.[19]

And here's another Soviet joke of indeterminate date and provenance:

What is the difference between a party in New York and a party in Moscow?
   In America, you go out and find party.
   In Soviet Russia, party find you!

---

[19] These two sets of jokes, in their varying historical contexts, are drawn from the account in Christie Davies, "Humour and Protest: Jokes under Communism," *International Review of Social History* 52 (2007): especially 295, 99.

These examples suggest the important role played by jokes in protest-ing harsh and oppressive regimes. They are sometimes one of the few available avenues of freedom of expression in times of oppression, and they can serve to mock leaders or make fun of difficult economic short-ages. Jokes can even provide some help in coping with extremely chal-lenging circumstances or even trauma, allowing emotional release, as well as constituting covert forms of communicating people's opposition to authoritarian regimes. Yet, it is interesting to observe, following Christie Davies in his article "Humor and Protest: Jokes under Communism," that jokes as protest may become more prevalent when conditions ease a bit, that is, when these become routinely oppressive rather than utterly terrifying.[20] This is likely to be due to the extreme danger of telling jokes in a time of terror.

Davies resists the conclusion, however, that jokes in themselves are a strong form of protest or resistance. As he points out, in times of actual resistance or revolution, jokes tend to disappear and utter seriousness takes over. But jokes in some ways serve to keep resistance alive when alternative forms of action are unavailable and also serve to bring people together in their protest and struggles.[21] In this way, Davies's findings lend some support to Cohen's thesis concerning the way that jokes bind a community or communities together, in this case, the rather far-flung array of oppressed people protesting Soviet rule.

A more recent example of this binding power was the popularity and influence of Bassem Youssef's jokes and satire, presented on his very pop-ular TV program in Cairo, Egypt, "Al Bernameg." The effectiveness of his jokes and the way they helped to constitute a community of protest was evidenced by the efforts the regime made to jail Youssef on various defamation and libel charges and thereby to curtail his effective criticism. To this threat Youssef replied at one point, "If we back down, that would be the end of our brand. Our brand that we use sarcasm and humor to combat stereotypes and to combat the status quo."[22] And as the preem-inent humorist Jon Stewart added, during a supportive appearance he made on Youssef's TV show, "If your regime is not strong enough to handle a joke, then you don't have a regime."[23]

The use of speech to resist oppression, whether in serious or joking ways, points to another social and political use of speech that I want to highlight here. That concerns the right to protest or to demonstrate, a

---

[20] *Ibid.*, 299–301.   [21] *Ibid.*

[22] www.npr.org/2013/04/24/178675692/egypts-jon-stewart-says-he-won-t-back-down-amid-charges

[23] www.youtube.com/watch?v=kEO2Rd3sJbA

dimension of free speech that has sometimes been curtailed in the past period in the United States. (Of course, it is even more fully repressed in many other countries around the world.) Noteworthy and disturbing were the preemptive searches, seizures, and arrests of activists that marked the start of the Republican National Convention in Minneapolis in September 2008. There, some of the young people organizing housing and food for protestors were arrested at gunpoint even before the convention or any demonstrations began and were charged with felony crimes under the Patriot Act. Moreover, through that convention period, twenty-four credentialed journalists who were covering the demonstrations were arrested, as were a total of over 800 protestors as well, nearly all of them engaged in lawful and peaceful protest. (Some bystanders were included in the arrests as well.) More recent cases were the mass arrests of peaceful protestors, including the use of pepper spray and sometimes harsh forms of police violence, during the Occupy Wall Street movement.[24]

The right to protest and to demonstrate is in fact one of the key aspects of freedom of expression and is of considerable importance for a democratic politics. It is, however, sometimes neglected in philosophical or political accounts of free speech, and is increasingly honored in the breach in practice. In fact, as Holloway Sparks has suggested, dissident speech and activism, often carried out by women in recent decades, is crucially important if people are to be self-governing.[25] (She cites Rosa Parks as a central example of a courageous activist individual, but there have been many contemporary examples as well.) The argument is that it is insufficient simply to protect speech for those who disagree and who are able to express this effectively within conventional modes of deliberation and participation, that is, within representative systems of government. There needs to be room for dissent by those who seek to challenge the prevailing structures of power, or who are marginalized or oppressed within a given society and who thus do not participate with others as deliberative equals.[26] Sometimes their dissent can be effectively organized through NGOs, but sometimes it is best expressed through demonstrations or even nonviolent civil disobedience. Such forms of dissent importantly supplement and bring into the public sphere views

---

[24] For an analysis of Occupy Wall Street, see Michael Gould-Wartofsky, *The Occupiers: The Making of the 99 Percent Movement* (Oxford: Oxford University Press, 2015).

[25] Holloway Sparks, "Dissident Citizenship: Democratic Theory, Political Courage, and Activist Women," *Hypatia* 12, no. 4 (1997).

[26] *Ibid.*, 83–4. Sparks writes that "dissident democratic citizenship can usefully be conceptualized as the public contestation of prevailing arrangements of power by marginalized citizens through oppositional, democratic, noninstitutionalized practices that augment or replace institutionalized channels of democratic opposition when those channels are inadequate or unavailable."

that are not represented by the existing party system, or by lobbyists, or by elected officials and the (increasingly) corporate media.

Other distinctively social forms of free expression

I have so far discussed two of the social dimensions of free speech. One concerns the power of speech, and in particular jokes, to include or exclude and possibly to contribute to oppression, particularly in regard to minority ethnic or religious groups in a national or global context; the second dimension is the role of speech in protest and resistance. In order to articulate some of speech's other social facets, we need to step outside the domain of humor, and briefly turn to Habermassian discourse theory (as well as some theories of deliberative democracy). In that theoretical approach, people are understood as free to enter into the discourse or deliberative process and to communicate freely with others whom they regard as equals, at least ideally.

Freedom within discourse or deliberation theory has the aspect of being uncoerced (again, ideally). It also presupposes some background conditions of social and economic equality. These requirements point to the way that issues of justice influence the possibilities of free speech, as Alistair Macleod has argued.[27] The freedom of the participants in these discourses or deliberations is supposed to be not only equal but reciprocally recognized by each as they relate to each other through discourse. Some feminist theorists in particular have raised questions about those who are silenced because they are marginalized in various ways. Moreover, the emphasis that such accounts place on the rationality of discourses (people are to be moved by "the force of the better argument") makes the theories quite idealized in relation to real politics. Even ideally, there is undoubtedly a role to be played by empathy (as feminist theorists have proposed), or by the "enlarged" mentality or understanding that Hannah Arendt emphasized. One can object as well to the separation – at least in Habermas's version – of the communicative from the expressive, where the former is understood as interactive and the latter as more a matter of individual activity. My own theory sees these two aspects as intrinsically interconnected, as is evident in the very notion of freedom of expression.

The ways that discursive approaches are expected to work transnationally has not yet been fully articulated by theorists. To the degree that there are inequalities of power or of social condition as the background for discourse, the latter cannot be expected to instantiate the

---

[27] Alistair Macleod, "Free Speech, Equal Opportunity, and Justice," in *Freedom of Expression in a Diverse World*, ed. Deirdre Golash (New York: Springer, 2010).

freedom, equality, and reciprocity of all potential participants. In addition to addressing oppression and domination, as well as the economic inequalities that can interfere with the time and interest needed for deliberative discourse, there would need to be ways to build in a social critique and a self-critique of bias, ideology, and other distorting factors, as a way of moving towards the requisite uncoerced, open, and genuinely equal discourse. (This is part of the notion of concrete universality, discussed previously.) We have seen the disarming role that genuine self-criticism can play in the case of jokes. The case is similar for discourse, to the degree that such self-criticism can open a space for freer (less defensive) and more equal expression on the part of others.

A final social aspect of freedom of expression is even less often articulated than the previous ones, although it was adumbrated in the role of NGOs in sometimes organizing dissent. This concerns the ways in which freedom of expression can be protected and, perhaps more importantly, *enabled* by social organizations and social movements, and not only by governments. Free speech has been traditionally theorized as a right to be protected against interference by governments (e.g., from censorship) or as a right of individuals in a minority to speak out or to dissent from the rulings of majorities within a democratic system. The right to protest goes beyond this, as we have seen, and deliberative democrats have additionally pointed to the role of freedom of expression within discourses in the public sphere. We need to add the function that voluntary associations and other groups in the nongovernmental sphere – and especially social movements and NGOs – can play in protecting and enabling freedom of expression for those active within them and for wider circles of people. On the world stage, human rights INGOs, social movements, and independent media organizations have called attention to the stifling of free expression in various countries and attempt to facilitate openness to alternative forms of social, political, and legal organization that would give voice to silenced minorities. Organizations like Amnesty International and International Pen have attempted to confront repressive governments that block political criticism by making appeals to "national security" needs and fear of terrorism. Such international organizations, along with social movements of a less institutionalized sort, may work on behalf of people imprisoned for their beliefs or their ethnic membership.

Sociality and the human right to free expression

Highlighting the social features of free expression does not imply that individuals are subordinated in this account. Rather, the significance and value of individuality remains intact when it is understood in terms of a social ontology of individuals-in-relations. To recognize that individuals are partly constituted through their social relations and that their agency has material and social conditions does not diminish the significance of their own self-transformative power and their capacity to change these relations over time (though most often only by cooperating with others). In this account, then, agency itself can be collective. And we have seen in the discussion of protest how freedom of expression – especially as dissent – most often takes collective forms. Further, numerous jokes routinely make reference to, and take aim at, the cultural groups to which people belong.

Freedom of expression as a legal human right can be seen to be a matter of basic liberty, which serves as a crucial protection of people's choices and their self-transformative activity. As noted, these proceed through people's expression and communication with others, whether in speech or action, through art, science, work, culture, and so on. Freedom of expression is standardly held to fall under the so-called negative liberties, requiring especially "freedom from" interference by the state or government. The account given here is less classically liberal in adding to this the need to be free from oppression, domination, and exploitation (although those requirements have not yet been included among standard lists of human rights).

Besides its connection to agency and autonomy, the right of freedom of expression has been justified as a condition for inquiry and for discovering truth in the "marketplace of ideas" (following Mill in *On Liberty*). It is essential as well for democratic participation and deliberation, and thus for effective politics and for shared governance. On these grounds, and especially the first – in which expression is close to our very agency itself, whether personal or joint and also enables the cultivation of relationships – it seems to me that free expression is a high value and should be given expansive protection. Assuredly, a constraint can be posed by the fact that the agency in question is to be taken as *equal* agency. That normative constraint, and the correlative need to be free from oppression and to be recognized and respected by others, can set some limits to the legitimate exercise of freedom of speech. In the first instance, this is an ethical point of critique and it does not necessarily imply that derogatory uses of speech should be made illegal, though that may sometimes be justified.

In terms of the philosophical justification of the human right to freedom of expression, we can see that the recognition of the sociality of free speech suggests new avenues for justification, and argues in favor of a large scope for its practice. Although freedom of expression is correctly viewed as a right of individuals, because these individuals are social beings who need and value their associations – personal, group, and cultural – we can see that speech is important not just for a democratic politics, or for truth in a marketplace of ideas, or for individual autonomy, but for creating, perpetuating, and changing these multiple affiliations, as well as for people's communication across these groups and cultures, and for the organization of movements for social change. This observation reveals a connection between freedom of expression and freedom of association, besides the usual connections that the right is regarded as having with the values of privacy and autonomy.

The recognition of these social factors supports an enlargement of the rights to protest and to organize (and not only in politics, but at work as well). Moreover, taking free expression as an equal and effective right of everyone lends weight to positive efforts to support and cultivate people's expression, for example, through education. It requires attention to enabling vulnerable or marginalized people to exercise their expressive rights, preferably directly but if necessary through representatives. Further, to the degree that free expression is centrally required for members of a democratic community as human rights, it would count against present tendencies to attribute free speech rights to corporations.

An interesting feature of free speech rights internationally is the difference that attends their legal interpretation in various countries, as well as how they are weighed in relation to other basic rights and interests. These differences constitute a good test case for the claim I have made previously that there can be some margin of appreciation in regard to human rights, in which their interpretation can be seen to vary somewhat in different social, political, and cultural contexts without their losing force as human rights. I cannot go into a full discussion of the various aspects of this complex issue, particularly as a matter of law. It is worth noting, however, that societies and governments that strongly protect freedom of expression may take rather discrepant approaches to legal prohibitions on hate speech and on the rights of dissenters. This is evident in the comparison between the United States and Canada, both of which see freedom of expression as a core feature of liberal democracy, but which differ in various ways in their constitutional language (between the US Constitution and the Canadian Charter of Rights and Freedoms) and the role of the courts in relation to the legislature and to the states or provinces.[28] We can also understand that particularities of history count heavily in Germany's strict prohibitions on hate speech. Other values, like justice and the related notions of freedom from oppression and

---

[28] See the helpful discussion in Kent Greenawalt, "Free Speech in the United States and Canada," *Law and Contemporary Problems* 55, no. 1 (1992).

nondiscrimination, can be implicated in these somewhat divergent treatments of the legal right. Some deference to local history and other features of social context is probably required, provided that this human right retains a central place, given its importance for democracy, autonomy, and sociality.

A global community of amusement?

Finally, we can return to the question of whether our goal should be the creation of a world in which jokes can be universally understood. Certainly, those jokes that concern shared challenges of human experience are most accessible cross-culturally. Yet, even in those cases, the concern about linguistic differences would remain. But more significant, few of us would want to see the particular communities that share laughs among themselves disappear. Perhaps, then, there could be overlapping networks of communities of amusement. And it would undoubtedly be good for people to be able to join and participate in the laughter of groups other than their own – even distant ones – if they are willing to make the effort to learn about and understand whatever mores, practices, and nuances of language are required to understand the relevant jokes. Normatively, it is clear too that outsiders should not be barred from understanding or appreciating this humor because of racism, hatred, or oppression. But to accomplish something like this transnational understanding in the real world, we probably need more than jokes (though they are undoubtedly helpful in the main). We would need the cultivation of empathy, the development of solidarity movements, and even more, forms of structural and institutional social change. I discuss some of those institutional changes in Part III, on interactive democracy.

10 Violence, power-with, and the human right to democracy

Introduction

We have described some positive normative directions that are enabled by globalization's facilitation of communication across borders. But equally striking is its facilitation of transnational forms of violence. Over the past period, we have witnessed salient examples of transnational violent terrorist attacks, as on 9/11, as well as transnational responses to them via the introduction of a coordinated security apparatus and the extension of forms of militarization across borders. Numerous other globalized forms of violence also permeate contemporary politics, including the proliferation of private military firms, transnational criminal and sex trade networks, and new forms of war-making tied to global economic and political processes.[1]

In this chapter, I want to consider how our conceptions of power and democracy can be expanded in order to better counter these forms of transnational violence. The empirical democratic peace hypothesis – that democratic states tend not to go to war against each other – is often introduced as evidence to support democratization as a way to mitigate violence between nation-states. But it is not clear whether or how such a hypothesis could apply to more transnational forms of violence, carried out especially by nonstate actors. Moreover, the conceptual interrelations that underlie this peace hypothesis and especially the connections between power, democracy, and violence are not well understood.

Standard approaches to violence presented in older philosophical doctrines of just war also do not fit easily with the new realities, and those doctrines themselves have been subject to effective criticisms by feminist scholars who see them as male-biased in various ways.[2] In the legal domain, newer notions of genocide and of crimes against humanity, along

---

[1] For a helpful discussion, see Richard Devetak and Christopher W. Hughes, *The Globalization of Political Violence: Globalization's Shadow* (London: Routledge, 2008).
[2] See, for example, Laura Sjoberg, *Gender, Justice, and the Wars in Iraq* (Lanham, MD: Lexington Books, 2006).

with the more recent conception of the responsibility to protect (R2P), have been elaborated; and the International Criminal Court and various war crimes tribunals importantly allow for cross-border prosecution of a subset of cases of heinous violence. But I would suggest that the normative and legal directions provided by both just war theory and these newer conceptions, despite their considerable relevance, do not sufficiently link up with human rights theory and practice, or indeed with democratic theory and its implementation. Even more significantly, they do not speak to the varieties of power and the corresponding political and social changes in its exercise that would be needed in order to make the resort to violence less commonplace.

The sections that follow address some of the interrelationships between democracy and human rights, on the one hand, and those political and social transformations in the use of power that might mitigate transnational forms of violence, on the other. I approach these complex relations in the first instance by building on the work of Hannah Arendt, Iris Young, Amy Allen, and Laura Sjoberg, in order to develop the contrast introduced by Arendt between violence and power, and then to elaborate this opposition more specifically as one between violence and what has been called *power-with*. I go on to suggest that power-with can be understood as a more cooperative and empathic mode of social and political power, in a way that ties it to the enriched interactive conception of democracy for which I argue in this work. Yet, besides its reference to the sort of collaborative power involved when people act in concert with shared ends, I propose a new networking interpretation of power-with, suitable to emerging transnational interconnections, online and off. Forms of both democracy and power-with (in its various senses) can also be seen to presuppose access to basic economic and social conditions of life and well-being, as specified in human rights. In the concluding section, I draw some implications for bringing human rights to bear on the critique of violence, with a view to understanding the conditions for lessening violence's gravity and scope. My analysis supports the conclusion that beyond appealing to human rights norms of life and security of the person, the diminution of violence in the contemporary world requires the fulfillment of a broader range of human rights, including those to means of subsistence and to political participation in new, and increasingly transnational, democratic forms.

Violence and power

In her book *On Violence* (1969), Hannah Arendt famously distinguishes violence from power. In that work – written during the Cold War and at the height of the student movement of the 1960s – Arendt frames violence as an instrumentality or means to an end, distinguishing it from power, which by contrast "corresponds to the human ability not just to act but to act in concert."[3] Although in some ways unfairly critical of both the student and the black power movements of the time, as well as of theorists like Sartre and Fanon who were active then, Arendt elaborates some helpful contrasts between these two modalities of violence and power. She gives power what could be called a social interpretation, writing that: "Power is never the property of an individual; it belongs to a group and remains in existence only so long as the group keeps together."[4] And she is concerned also to distinguish power from command, rule, or domination, inasmuch as these latter concepts would tie power to violence on her view. Arendt sees violence, especially in war and in nuclear armaments, as becoming more elaborated in its potential, and deadlier in its impacts, with the rapid technological development and the dominance of means–ends rationality during the twentieth century. According to Arendt, violence can readily destroy power, yet cannot create it. "Out of the barrel of a gun grows the most effective command, resulting in the most instant and perfect obedience. What never can grow out of it is power."[5]

Arendt originally developed the notion of power in her work *The Human Condition* (1958), where it is understood to arise when people live together in a "condition of plurality." In what she calls the public space of appearances, people reveal themselves to each other in speech and action, and when they act together power exists, but only as a continuing potentiality. Even in this earlier work, the distinction Arendt wanted to draw between power and violence is evident:

What first undermines and then kills political communities is loss of power and final impotence; and power cannot be stored up and kept in reserve for emergencies, like the instruments of violence, but exists only in its actualization. Where power is not actualized, it passes away, and history is full of examples that the greatest material riches cannot compensate for this loss. Power is actualized only where word and deed have not parted company, where words are not empty and deeds not brutal, where words are not used to veil intentions but to disclose realities, and deeds are not used to violate and destroy but to establish relations and create new realities.

Power is what keeps the public realm, the potential space of appearance between acting and speaking men, in existence.[6]

[3] Hannah Arendt, *On Violence* (New York: Harcourt, 1969), 44.
[4] *Ibid.*   [5] *Ibid.*, 53.
[6] Hannah Arendt, *The Human Condition* (Chicago, IL: University of Chicago Press, 1958), 200.

Interestingly, Arendt also endorses nonviolent forms of popular revolt as displaying "an almost irresistible power even if it foregoes the use of violence in the face of materially vastly superior forces."[7] She continues, "To call this 'passive resistance' is certainly an ironic idea; it is one of the most active and efficient ways of action ever devised . . . The only indispensable material factor in the generation of power is the living together of people."[8]

Arendt's last remark – that the only crucial material factor in generating power is people living together – has an unfortunate implication, however, for it seems to deprecate the wider range of material factors that support the exercise of power, and in this way I believe it shows the limitations of her otherwise trenchant analysis. In her apparent efforts to distance herself from Marxist modes of analysis, or perhaps simply because of the attraction the Greek polis held for her as a model of political community, Arendt unfortunately sharply separates the sphere of action (where power comes in) from those of labor and work. While Marx, following Hegel, operated with a conception of objectification that at one and the same time had social and natural dimensions, and put forward an enlarged conception of labor and action that involved at the same time an account of interaction (e.g., in the importance of the social relations of production), Arendt tends to relegate economic relations to the status of merely necessary background conditions of freedom. Concurrently, she is forced to regard family life and the differential roles of women within it, and any domination or oppression in that context, as merely private concerns, and the family itself as only a preparation for the preeminent sphere of public action and speech.[9] We will see that this diminution of the life of production and reproduction has consequences for an understanding of the conditions for both promoting power and mitigating violence. So does the privileging of politics or the public domain as the exclusive arena for the exercise of the sort of social power Arendt extols in her work.

In a helpful essay "Violence against Power," Iris Marion Young uses Arendt's distinction between violence and power as the basis for a critique of most forms of humanitarian intervention in the contemporary world. Already in Arendt's own work, the distinction between power and violence correlates with the further idea that power can be legitimate, but violence – both thinkers hold – can only be justified, and cannot be legitimate per se.[10] Power comes into being through founding acts that serve to legitimate it, on Arendt's view, and as Young points out in

---

[7] *Ibid.*, 200–1.   [8] *Ibid.*, 201.

[9] For my own more extended critique of Arendt and Lefort along those lines, see Carol C. Gould, "Claude Lefort on Modern Democracy," *Praxis International* 10, nos. 3–4 (1991).

[10] For Arendt's view on this, see Arendt, *On Violence*, 52.

explicating Arendt's remarks in *On Revolution*, requires institutional forms for its preservation and embodiment in law.[11] Young, in turn, uses Arendt's distinction between the legitimate and the justifiable to suggest that the use of violent means for intervention, even with humanitarian ends, can sometimes be justified, but can never be legitimate.

While suggestive, it is not clear where this hard and fast distinction between the legitimation of power and the mere justifiability of violence would leave contemporary efforts to establish a responsibility to protect as more than a hortatory call to action. Though R2P emphasizes the use of nonviolent means of protection, and views the use of violence as a last resort, it does not rule out the latter, if required to prevent mass atrocities. Young's claim would also seem to negate any utility in determining legitimate authorities – and especially the UN – that could engage in peacekeeping functions, or eventually also possibly in peacemaking ones. That is, it is not clear why the use of violence cannot sometimes also be legitimate or lawful. And conversely, legitimate authorities can be called to account for, in the sense of being required to justify, their application of laws.

Perhaps more significant, Young does not provide an analysis of the notion of coercion. Something like coercion would seem to have a role to play even in the best-governed societies, since forms of coercion would presumably be needed for law enforcement in the interest of establishing or preserving justice. Nonetheless, we can say that both theorists are clearly right to avoid characterizing the political function of states simply in terms of legitimate control over the means of coercion or like notions (as they are traditionally described). The emphasis both of these theorists place on power understood apart from violence or even coercion thus helps us to avoid conceiving of state power simply as dominion over a territory or as a monopolization of the means of violence. Moreover, it potentially sets the stage for a democratic reading of power and its role in curbing violence for which I argue in later sections of this chapter. Although Arendt understood power as primarily established in legitimating moments, it is possible, I will argue, to tie the understanding of power to ongoing democratic forms of both governmental and social organization.

Power-with

Read a certain way, we can see Arendt's notion of power as pointing to the contemporary notion of *power-with*, a concept that has been

[11] Iris Marion Young, "Violence against Power," in *Ethics and Foreign Intervention*, ed. Deen Chatterjee and Don Scheid (Cambridge: Cambridge University Press, 2003), 259.

emphasized in recent feminist theory and elsewhere. Thus, as Young points out, in an interpretation of Arendt: "Power consists in collective action. Power is the ability of persons jointly to constitute their manner of living together, the way they organize their rules and institutions through reciprocal self-understanding of what the rules are and how they foster cooperation." Young adds, "Those who engage in collective action must communicate and cooperate, discuss their problems and jointly make plans."[12]

Laura Sjoberg likewise sees such a concept as ingredient in Arendt's interpretation of social power as the "human ability to act in concert and begin anew."[13] Sjoberg goes on to propose that "Power-with is about cooperation, regardless of and around any power-over domination. It is collaborative, not competitive; relational, not reactive. Distancing power from domination makes space for creative political actions by marginalized actors to destabilize power-over. Empathetic cooperation inspires power-with, which is the opposite of coercive force."[14] She also writes, "Empathetic cooperation is solidaristic in nature. Solidarity is acting together."[15]

Sjoberg's account at this point largely follows Amy Allen's interpretation of the tripartite character of power, as *power-over*, *power-to*, and *power-with*. (Note that this division does not line up exactly with Lukes's three dimensions of power,[16] although most power theorists regard power-over as one of its aspects.) In brief, Allen understands power-over "as the ability of an actor or set of actors to constrain the choices available to another actor or set of actors in a nontrivial way," with domination being an especially important application of this type of power, in which the constraint over the others' choices "works to the others' disadvantage."[17]

Power-to is interpreted by Allen in terms of individual empowerment, as when women resist male domination and empower themselves (or are empowered through participating in caring relations with others), despite the existence of domination. Allen writes, "I define 'power-to' as the ability of an individual actor to attain an end or series of ends."[18] In this reading, power-to is seen as individualistic, which in my view is not required by the concept (as is indeed evidenced by the very case cited of caring relations with others). Moreover, others, such as C. B. Macpherson, have interpreted power-to in terms of the notion of self-development

---

[12] *Ibid.*, 254.

[13] Sjoberg, *Gender, Justice, and the Wars in Iraq*, 69, citing Arendt, *On Violence*.

[14] Sjoberg, *Gender, Justice, and the Wars in Iraq*, 69.

[15] *Ibid.*

[16] Steven Lukes, Power: A Radical View, 2nd ed. (Palgrave Macmillan, 2004).

[17] Amy Allen, "Rethinking Power," *Hypatia* 13, no. 1 (1998): 33–4.   [18] *Ibid.*, 34.

rather than empowerment as such. Although Macpherson took such self-development to apply to individuals, in some ways it seems applicable to forms of cultural development or collective self-transformation, but this reading would bring power-to close to the third sense of power.

This final aspect of power, or power-with, is defined by Allen as "the ability of a collectivity to act together for the attainment of a common or shared end or series of ends." Solidarity, understood as a sort of collective empowerment, with particular reference to the feminist movement and its self-understanding is an application of power-with on Allen's view. She defines such solidarity as "the ability of a collectivity to act together for the shared or common purpose of overturning a system of domination."[19] Although Allen relates her own conception of power-with to Arendt's notion of acting in concert, I would suggest that the thrust of Arendt's concept of power is somewhat different, in that she does not seem to be thinking of social movements generally as exemplary of this notion (although the nonviolent resistance under Gandhi that Arendt cites approvingly would fit with Allen's own emphasis).

Sjoberg uses the analysis of power and especially of power-with to advance a feminist interpretation of just war principles. This represents one possible direction for rethinking the norms for war and violence in the context of globalization. In her book *Gender, Justice, and the Wars in Iraq*, Sjoberg makes some interesting, though highly idealized, suggestions regarding what she calls "Feminist Just Cause." She proposes that justice here requires dialogue among citizens, guided by empathy, and should involve inclusive and participatory forms of deliberation about the proposed war. These dialogues, she writes, "would pay attention to the physical and political needs of those at the margins who would be most affected by war-making and war-fighting." Because many will suffer from the fighting, Sjoberg holds that

[T]he state going to war must have just cause against the people that the war will affect rather than only the state that the war is against. Feminisms justify this attention to the individual 'enemy' because normally those people least culpable for the 'just cause' that one state claims against another are most affected by the horrors of traditional just wars.[20]

Sjoberg calls for public participation in determining the justice of the war and a consideration of the war's potential impact on the people of the warring country as well as on those outside its borders who will be affected, along with its implications for eventually restoring peace among

[19] *Ibid.*, 35–6.   [20] Sjoberg, *Gender, Justice, and the Wars in Iraq*, 78.

the belligerents. Likewise, in her account of *jus in bello* (justice in the war), Sjoberg holds that it is necessary to consider not only the standard effects on civilians but also on long-term infrastructure and health and all factors that enable the people of a country to recover *post bello*. Needless to say, these suggestions are normative and some would say entirely impractical, but they are interesting and important nonetheless in challenging our usual understanding of just war principles and in suggesting new directions for their interpretation.

Sjoberg's analysis touches on the potential transnational application of the notion of power-with, pointing to the possibilities for cross-border deliberation and empathy; and we have seen Allen's reference to social movements as an important domain for the exercise of power-with in the struggle against domination. However, most analyses of power-with have focused more narrowly on cooperative activities at the national level. It seems clear that beyond those, it could apply to the emerging forms of transnational solidarities and cross-border democratic participation characteristic of some contemporary social movements that were discussed in previous chapters, as well as to modalities of social networking and online collaborative interaction, and even to incipient regional and global forms of cooperation at the institutional level, which are considered in Part III. Is it possible to interpret power-with, then, not only in terms of common activity or acting in concert within a given nation-state, but also in terms of a newer network notion in which various groups may act in solidaristic or quasi-democratic ways with others at a distance?

In the transnational solidarities that may hold among individuals, groups, civil society associations, or members of social movements, we discern overlapping network relationships aimed at providing aid in order to alleviate suffering or to achieve justice. These forms of solidarity tend to differ from the more traditional forms that hold within a single community, inasmuch as the networks involved are often loosely and "horizontally" organized and tend to be based on voluntary association. They may involve a readiness to offer mutual aid, and include some elements of "fellow feeling" and social empathy. In recent years, such networks have made extensive use of the Internet for organizing and have also disseminated their work and established outreach through social media. These sorts of networks – whether of institutions or individuals – do not understand themselves to form a unified community, although they share some overlapping aims and can agree, often consensually, to work together on a certain project. Instances of such projects range from post-disaster recovery in New Orleans, Indonesia, Haiti, and most recently in New York City (with Hurricane Sandy), as well as responses to the democratic uprisings of 2011 in North Africa, the Middle East, and the southern periphery of the Eurozone.

Such networking involves overlapping associations most often oriented to particular causes, and it can exist among institutions, individuals and groups, as well as among political communities. It is in fact a form of association that the Internet – as a network of networks – encourages and facilitates, especially by enabling the storage and delayed retrieval of information and communications (discussed further in Chapter 12). The overlapping groups within a network can affiliate differently for varying purposes and may operate consensually and collaboratively on specific projects, rather than making use of formal democratic procedures (e.g., majority voting). Such groups are increasingly using video and teleconferencing to facilitate the participation of people situated at a distance.

The question is: what form of power-with is involved in this kind of networking? It is most often a weaker one than acting in concert, but it can be effective to the degree that people collaborate on specific projects with a view to achieving general common aims such as overcoming suffering or specific instances of exploitation or oppression. The networks can mobilize groups with very different compositions and identities, each of which draws on its own set of resources while sometimes sharing them in mutually supportive ways. I would call this conception one of *networking power*, and the sort of power-with it evidences *synergistic power*. Here, people or groups lend their power to a common cause, and combine their agency variously to accomplish overlapping shared aims and projects. In light of this analysis, we can now go on to briefly consider the import of such synergistic power for democracy, along with the more prominent form of power-with as acting in concert.

Power-with and democracy

Our analysis of the notion of power-with – as acting in concert and as networking power – suggests some interesting implications for understanding democracy. Its first sense evidently ties into a conception of democracy as a mode of decision-making concerning collective or common action oriented to shared goals, referred to in earlier chapters in terms of the idea of "common activities." We have seen that beyond elections and majority rule, this notion requires more opportunities for participation and deliberation than on traditional accounts of democracy (though it is not justified solely or even primarily by appeal to the values of deliberative proceduralism). And democracy in this sense applies not only to political communities but to economic and social institutions as well.

Thus understood, democratic decision-making in contexts of common or collective activity involves something analogous to the cooperative activity that in Arendt's and Young's view characterizes social power. In this usage, democracy largely takes place in public, as a locus for people to exercise their freedom in action and speech (to use Arendt's terminology), and to be recognized by others. Although Arendt did not especially emphasize the equality of agents that would be needed for this fuller conception of democracy, we can see a manifestation of social power or power-with in the forms of deep democracy previously alluded to.

Arendt herself seems to find social power less in democracy than in acts of founding characteristic of some revolutionary moments, such as the American Revolution. Nonetheless, she also made room (in her *On Revolution*)[21] for councils as participatory democratic forms of organization, however temporary, which presumably also display social power, or power-with.

If we turn to the feminist interpretations of power-with, we see the central role they give to dialogue based on empathy with the situation of others, and their emphasis on cooperative modes of problem solving founded on the equality and agency of participants. Although not developed as a theory of democracy, the account suggested by Sjoberg appeals to the need for an inclusive approach to deliberations (in her case about justice of the war), in which it is necessary for participants to take account of the impacts of decisions on all those affected. The feminist emphasis on empathy stands in contrast with Arendt's approach, since she eschewed the notion,[22] though she appealed to a sort of enlarged thinking that involves some elements we think of as empathic, such as taking into consideration the perspective of others. Interestingly, Arendt sees this sort of imaginative bringing of the other close in thought to have been adumbrated in Kant's Third Critique (rather than in the explicitly moral or practical Second Critique).

While highly idealized and normative, the various elements of dialogue and empathy among free and equal participants in common activity thus seem not only characteristic of power-with but also of the enriched conception of democracy sketched above. Granted, such normative notions are barely realized at all in existing forms of democracy, which may not even be able to maintain free and fair elections, let alone the demanding modes of responsiveness and recognition of equal agency discussed here. Nonetheless, at the normative level, the close connection

[21] Hannah Arendt, *On Revolution* (New York: Viking, 1963), 263–73.
[22] Hannah Arendt, *The Life of the Mind* (New York: Harcourt, 1989), 257–8.

of notions of strong or deep democracy with conceptions of power-with is striking.

A further question concerns the potential democratic import of networking power-with. Certainly, this can apply to transnational participatory forms short of fully organized or institutional democracy, as in some cross-border social movements. The features of empathy, collaboration, and openness to participation that are held to mark power-with may characterize such movements, if they are inclusive and nonhierarchical in organization. While these movements, or also networked NGOs, most often do not function in formally integrated ways or necessarily employ full-scale majority voting procedures, the relations within them can be quasi-democratic to the degree that they operate consensually or through tacit agreements to harmonize their actions with each other. Thus networked activist groups or NGOs may retain the power of vetoing a joint activity or opting out, but they may also compromise or go along, perhaps on the basis of expectations of reciprocity or mutual aid when needed. Where institutions are involved, the relevant networks have thus far been mainly those of civil society and have less often involved international organizations or nation-states. A clear exception has been the use of networking consultative methods in the EU. But that example also clearly presents the drawbacks that may ensue where consensus is required, inasmuch as that can actually block action, particularly perhaps in those formal and bureaucratic contexts.

Democracy and the mitigation of violence

Turning now to this chapter's motivating question of the mitigation of transnational violence, we can consider the import of the earlier distinction between power and violence for both power-with and democracy. I suggested that one of the main directions for understanding power, at least in the accounts of Arendt, Young, and Sjoberg, is in terms of power-with, in contrast to power-over as domination, structural or otherwise, and power-to, if conceived in opposition to power-over, where it constitutes an individual's overcoming of oppression. This suggests that the contrast of power and violence may be manifested in a contrast between power-with – for example, in the form of passive resistance – and violence. But if we bring strong versions of democracy into the picture, as themselves exemplifying power-with, then it would seem that democracy itself (in this highly normative reading) contrasts with violence as well. That is, conceptually, the opposition discussed earlier between power understood in terms of social power that can be legitimated, and violence as an instrumentality that can only be justified, is paralleled here in a distinction between strongly participatory notions of democracy and violence. This contrast suggests that conceptually, strong democracy and violence are opposites.

While there is much to be said for this reading, it moves a bit quickly. For one thing, it is possible that some forms of power-with may need to resort to violence in extreme cases, in particular, where it may be needed to counter violence. Thus, where people are oppressed and rise up, it may not always be possible to avoid violence, even though it would be preferable to do so. When such revolutionary activity meets profound repression, it is difficult to avoid all use of violence, although passive resistance is the normatively desirable course (and sometimes can be more effective, as Arendt points out). For the most part, these cases of resort to violence are usually instrumental, rather than legitimated by law, and thus do not challenge the distinction that Young, following Arendt, sees between power and violence. Yet, as noted, the Arendt-Young approach gives no account of coercion, including legitimate uses of it in law, where it may be required for the sake of assuring or restoring justice when people have wronged others. It is implausible to regard the use of coercive force in such cases as illegitimate (as they would seem to be on Young's account), although in these cases too there would be a normative preference for non-coercive alternatives.

It is plausible, I think, to suggest that democracy in its strong or deep sense contrasts with violence conceptually and, where fully implemented, democracy in this richer sense could be expected to work to keep violence at bay. Note how this constitutes an interesting revisioning of the well-known democratic peace hypothesis at the normative level. Here it is not simply that democratic states are observed to avoid warring with each other (for the most part). The suggestion here is that the very conception of democracy in its connection to power-with stands opposed to violence. Likewise, transnational solidarity networks and movements oriented to global justice are themselves often explicitly non-violent and can serve to bind people together across borders in what could be called proto-democratic ways. They thereby could be expected to serve the same interests of peace as do more organized forms of democratic communities.

Yet, it must be granted that the prospect of diminishing violence through deeper forms of democracy – whether in common activity or networking forms – would seem to extend only as far as democracy does. For one thing, while conceptually democracy and power-with contrast with violence, this does not yet speak to the possibilities of violence between democratic organized states and constituencies external to them. Indeed, the above analysis suggests that new forms of transnational democracy would be required if violence between states is to truly diminish.[23] Likewise, transnational networks may be forced to confront violent repression or may themselves fail to be inclusive of outsiders. Put in terms of power-with, we can say that insofar as diverse peoples lack contexts of collaboration and solidarity with each other, it is likely that their relations will continue to be marked by forms of conflict and even violence.

The human right to democracy, the interdependence of human rights, and the minimization of violence

To approach transnational violence, we have investigated the connection of power to violence, and specifically in the form of power-with, which brought us back to the conception of democracy and its potential for mitigating violence. We can finally observe that human rights have a bearing on this issue as well. Recalling the arguments developed in Chapter 4 to the effect that democracy should be understood as one of the human rights, we can see how the recognition of this right, along with the traditional rights of life and security, could be useful for more adequately dealing with contemporary violence. Likewise, it can be observed that economic rights (e.g., to means of subsistence), while seemingly unrelated to these civil and political rights, in fact play a significant role in this process.

Recall that human rights are understood in this work not primarily as legal rights holding against states (though they are also that) but as *moral* or more broadly *normative* rights. Although they may begin as the social claims of individuals, they need to be fulfilled by means of specific political, economic and social institutions (and also hold against the variety of these institutions). It is plausible, as Robert Goodin has argued, to see these more delimited institutions as appropriate practical frameworks for their realization, and in this way as essential instrumentalities for human rights fulfillment.[24] Moreover, institutions themselves, including but not limited to governments, not only enable such fulfillment, but can themselves threaten individuals' liberties in various ways, and thus some of the human rights are reasonably oriented to constraining the actions of such institutions, and notably the state and its government. In both of these

---

[23] See Daniele Archibugi, "From Peace between Democracies to Global Democracy," in *Global Democracy: Normative and Empirical Perspectives*, ed. Daniele Archibugi, Mathias Koenig-Archibugi, and Raffaele Marchetti (Cambridge: Cambridge University Press, 2011).

[24] Robert Goodin, "What Is So Special About Our Fellow Countrymen?," *Ethics* 98, no. 4 (1988).

functions – that is, as enabling and as constraining – human rights can be seen to be institutional, in ways that go beyond interpersonal obligations of each to all others.

The human right to democracy, in particular, has been conceived here as having a more general form than the recognized requirement for free and fair elections, with universal suffrage, along with the right to participate in the governance of one's country (as recognized in the UDHR and the Civil and Political Covenant). I have interpreted this right of democracy as one of the codetermination of common activities, stemming from the requirement that people enjoy equal effective freedom or agency, not only with respect to their individual goals and pursuits, but also in all contexts of collective activities oriented to shared goals where these serve as conditions of their self-transformative activity. Such common activities are also arenas for the exercise of power-with. In Part III, we see how forms of democratic participation can apply not only to political communities at various levels but to a wide range of institutions, including economic firms. I also develop the second criterion for the applicability of democracy in transnational contexts – namely, the all-affected principle – and explore some new directions for implementing it.

The relevant set of human rights for addressing violence consists, then, not only of the standard rights to life and security, but also the human right to democracy. It is customary to see violence as a threat to the life of the person when it takes the form of killing, or a threat to the security of the person more generally when it poses the danger of bodily harm. These rights to life and security call for the protection of people by the state and also require that individuals refrain from violating these rights of others. But if it is the case, as we have seen, that violence contrasts not only with power-with but with robust forms of democracy, and if democracy in this more than minimal sense is a human right, then an adequate approach to minimizing violence would need to support the establishment of broader and deeper forms of democracy, including forms of participation and deliberation, in local and national communities and in transnational instantiations (whether organized or movement-based). Although life and security may have a claim to being among the most basic types of human rights, democracy is important as well, in order to establish law-governed, rational, and empathic conditions for solving problems and resolving conflicts. This connection of democracy to peace and the minimization of violence have begun to be recognized instrumentally and in practice, though primarily in the weak form of the democratic peace hypothesis. In this chapter, I have suggested that there are deeper conceptual and normative interconnections between democracy and the avoidance and mitigation of violence, whether national or transnational.

It is worth noting, too, that the fulfillment of various economic and social rights can contribute to minimizing violence and establishing more peaceful modes of conflict resolution. This has sometimes been recognized in practice (for example, in claims that development is helpful in eliminating the conditions for terrorism),[25] but it has not been much worked out in theory. For the present, it will suffice to emphasize that the extension of democracy and its concomitant growing recognition as a human right will likely play an important role in supporting the effective protection of rights of life and security. Likewise, the protection of the latter rights, along with basic economic and social rights, clearly gives people a better chance to participate in democratic processes and take some part in the governance of their country. These rights also support people's abilities to have some say about the important social and economic institutions of which they are members, and which affect them.

An important proviso should be indicated in conclusion, however: recognizing the normative desirability of democracy does not provide grounds for powerful states to impose it around the world. (Besides this, as I suggest elsewhere in this work, democracy needs to be understood in more cross-cultural and open ways than it has been.) Nonetheless, recognizing the connection of democracy to power-with and its contrast with violence, as argued here, gives us an additional avenue for approaching the profound contemporary problems posed by conflict, force, and coercion. It serves to reminds us how the growth of democracy as a deep form of social power needs to be primarily the work of people themselves, in their efforts to replace forms of oppressive power or power-over with more collaborative modes of power-with.

If we are interested in practical suggestions for countering or minimizing transnational violence, the above conceptual connections are certainly insufficient. However, I suggest that they go part of the way to reframing the issues that are posed by the new forms of violence pointed to at the outset, whether as terrorism, or cross-border militarization or securitization, or transnational criminal trafficking, or new forms of war-making. Inasmuch as these modalities are increasingly transnational, so the ways to counter them have to go beyond concerns of national security, and indeed beyond concerns of security per se. Even an emphasis on the newer notion of human security is insufficient. Attention needs to be given to the constructive forms of power pointed to by the notion of power-with and to the development of new, increasingly transnational, forms of democracy that can embody such power-with. These new forms

---

[25] See Lloyd J. Dumas, "Is Development an Effective Way to Fight Terrorism?" in *War after September* 11, ed. Verna V. Gehring (Lanham: Rowman & Littlefield, 2003).

include modes of regional democratic cooperation, as shown in Part III, but also the types of transnational solidarities involved in social movements that cross borders. It may also involve the introduction of new sorts of transnational representation, such as is called for in proposals for a global people's assembly or regional parliamentary bodies.[26] And it certainly requires the innovation of modalities for input by distant others into the institutions of global governance, including opening new forums for online deliberation and decision. Less radically, and possible in the present, is the introduction of human rights impact assessments for the transnational decisions of powerful decisions, mentioned in Chapter 1.

Beyond these structural changes, however, the opposition elaborated in this chapter between violence and forms of power-with – whether as collaborative power or deep democracy – suggests the need for a set of social changes at the level of transnational relationships, and not only within given nation-states. The account implies that attention should be given to the cultivation of empathy and reciprocity in the relations among people in social life, whether within institutions or interpersonally. And it centrally lends support to the importance of opening up new forms of constructive democratic dialogue and collaboration across borders. Such dialogues across borders are the focus of Chapter 11.

[26] See Richard Falk and Andrew Strauss, "On the Creation of a Global Peoples Assembly: Legitimacy and the Power of Popular Sovereignty," *Stanford Journal of International Law* 36 (2000); Raffaele Marchetti, *Global Democracy: For and Against* (London: Routledge, 2008), and Daniele Archibugi, Mathias Koenig-Archibugi, and Raffaele Marchetti (eds.), *Global Democracy: Normative and Empirical Perspectives* (Cambridge: Cambridge University Press, 2011).

Part III

Interactive democracy – transnational, regional, global

11 Diversity, democracy, and dialogue in a human rights framework

Introduction

With the growing awareness of the power and scope of global interconnectedness in its various dimensions, and the new importance of the institutions of global governance, hopes have increasingly been placed on the development of a global public sphere of discourse and deliberation. The idea is that within this sphere – or better, spheres – dialogue can take place among diverse people from a range of cultural perspectives and that by mobilizing this dialogue it may be possible for people around the world to provide input into the decisions and policies of global governance institutions and other global actors that increasingly impact their lives. If people cannot participate directly, given their numbers, then this global public sphere may perhaps function to facilitate the representation of their views by NGOs or others. The recent literature emphasizes the role of inclusive deliberative processes at the transnational level that would strive to take into account the viewpoints of those at a distance who are affected by these policies but who have not thus far been powerful enough to influence their formation or direction.[1] And, recognizing the limitations of earlier overly rationalist models of deliberative democratic process, a broader array of features have entered the picture as desirable components of such dialogic procedures, including empathy and responsiveness, as called for by feminist philosophers and some political theorists.[2]

In this chapter, I examine the possibilities for intercultural dialogue and for more effective deliberative processes in a global public sphere, largely in online contexts, but also involving opportunities for face-to-face

[1] See, for example, James Bohman, *Democracy across Borders: From Dêmos to Dêmoi* (Cambridge, MA: MIT Press, 2007). For my own account, see Gould, *Globalizing Democracy*, esp. chapters 2 and 9.
[2] See, for example, William Rehg, *Insight and Solidarity* (Berkeley: University of California Press, 1994); Iris Marion Young, "Communication and the Other: Beyond Deliberative Democracy," in *Democracy and Difference*, ed. Seyla Benhabib (Princeton, NJ: Princeton University Press, 1994).

interactions. I consider some ideas for bringing transnational forms of dialogue and deliberation into the "epistemic communities" of the institutions of global governance and influencing other powerful global actors such as corporations. Interestingly, the global public sphere has to a degree been transformed online into a mélange of public and private, particularly on social networking sites like Facebook, which blend relatively private and personal disclosures to friends with groups and causes that represent more traditional associative or political contexts for activity and communication. New, more interactive and participatory forms of activism make use of YouTube, Twitter, and cellphone technologies. Chapter 12 focuses more directly on contemporary online networking in informal as well as formal spheres, and especially on its role in helping to bring about democratic change. I consider there the import of networking for participatory rather than mainly deliberative forms of democracy (though the two are not in opposition).

As I proposed previously, transnational dialogue and deliberation, whether in newly formed regional communities or within international organizations (governmental or nongovernmental) can helpfully be framed by human rights agreements that are adopted at regional, as well as at global, levels.[3] We can see the importance of these frameworks for institutional transformations in democracy (considered in Chapters 13, 14, and 15). The motivation for this recommendation stems from the recognition that globalization has generated an increasing number of cross-border communities, whether they are centered around ecological, economic, or political concerns, or take the form of voluntary associations (e.g., on the Internet). Such communities may be locally cross-border, or regional, or fully global. In order to protect the rights of individuals and communities interacting within these broader contexts, new regional agreements on human rights are needed, to supplement those already in existence (in Europe and the EU, in Africa and in the inter-American context), along with the global agreements that have already been introduced. But we will see that these new agreements themselves raise issues of the diversity of cultures, and would seem to require some degree of dialogue and deliberation in both their drafting and interpretation.

In a brief final section, this chapter attempts to connect democratic deliberative processes in this sort of human rights framework with the idea of the rule of law in the context of globalization. "Democracy" and "the rule of law" are often uttered in the same breath. It will be of interest then to ask whether the rule of law should be understood purely as a matter of formal legality, as it is frequently understood, or whether

---

[3] See Gould, *Globalizing Democracy*, especially chapters 8 and 9.

human rights underwrite deliberation,
deliberation produces human rights.

chicken-and-egg paradox?

its value should be understood as integrally tied up with those of human rights and democratic participation and deliberation.

Problems in extending dialogue and deliberation across borders

Unlike some other democratic theorists, I do not take dialogue as foundational for the justification of global norms nor do I regard the notion of deliberation as the primary meaning of democracy in transnational contexts. Rather, as I have argued, norms need to be grounded in a social ontology of human beings in relationships, and democracy requires more than deliberation. It requires actually making decisions (with majority rule as the leading possibility here, though not the only one), as well as forms of mutual recognition among persons, along with broad opportunities for participation in social, economic, and political life. Moreover, democracy presupposes the fulfillment of a set of human rights, including economic and social ones, and in political societies requires a constitutional framework – implicit or explicit – that sets out appropriate procedures and that protects the rights of all, including those of minorities residing within them. Yet, deliberation is certainly a crucial feature of democratic processes that seek to foster some measure of agreement about common interests and that aim at decisions based on inclusive, rational, and empathic procedures, involving reciprocal recognition of the equality of participants and an equal consideration of their importantly affected interests. Dialogue, too, is a central feature in the interpretation and application of transnational norms and serves as a condition for their emergence as more than projections of one-sided ways of life.

Significant problems – both theoretical and practical – emerge from the fact that dialogue and deliberation increasingly extend across borders. Aside from the, by now, standard question of how to construe dialogue among people with different cultural backgrounds, we can ask what factors contribute to making cross-border deliberative processes effective. How is it possible to enable deliberative input into the policies of global governance institutions by those affected by their decisions? How can stakeholders have a say in the decisions of multinational corporations or even perhaps of nation-states, given that distant others are often importantly affected by their policies and activities? My interest in this connection is especially on enabling participation by people of the Global South in the "epistemic communities"[4] of global governance

---

[4] Peter Hass (ed.), "Special Issue on Knowledge, Power, and International Policy Coordination," *International Organization* 46, no. 1 (1992).

what about intra-cultural deliberation & the potential for misunderstanding?

institutions, and I also touch on some of the fundamental questions involved in structuring transnational dialogues.

Online dialogue and deliberation provide an especially promising locus for new forms of deliberation by wider publics concerning the policies and decisions of these global institutions. Several theorists have looked to online information to help achieve greater openness and transparency, if not also accountability, in the institutions of global governance.[5] In the domestic context, much has been written about the role of facilitation, about the use of deliberative forums in e-government or e-democracy, and the problem of the digital divide.[6] Although it is possible to open the deliberations of national and global governance bodies to contributions by remotely situated publics, it is necessary to avoid the over-romanticism that has characterized some discussions of these possibilities, and to ask an array of hard questions.[7] There are concerns about who will be included – will they be credentialed participants or else people at large, or both of these at different stages of policy making? Will people be permitted to participate anonymously, or will authentication and the identification of participants be required? Who will take seriously all the potential input, and how will it be sifted down? Or will something like public ombudspersons suffice? Already there is digital overload – multiple arenas with large numbers of often-anonymous participants, or where they are not anonymous, their participation may be limited to email or to bounded and partly closed social networking sites.

The Internet has enabled growing opportunities for blogging, petitioning, commenting, and communicating about social and political issues, and has been highly important for political organizing and for networking social movements. However, so far, relatively few public, deliberative forums have risen to the level of substantial influence over policy, even in domestic contexts, not to speak of global levels. Instead of the open discussion among people with different perspectives that has been thought to be required in deliberative politics, many online discussions groups have been limited (most often self-limited) to like-minded participants. Where there may be an admixture of different viewpoints represented, as on some blogs and journalistic comment sites, we find that instead of reasoned argument, there is quite often shouting, assertions with little argument, and so on.

 Sunstein

---

[5] See Stiglitz, *Globalization and Its Discontents*.

[6] On the latter, see, for example, Pippa Norris, *Digital Divide* (Cambridge: Cambridge University Press, 2001).

[7] See also Andrew Chadwick, "Web 2.0: New Challenges for the Study of E-Democracy in an Era of Informational Exuberance," *I/S: A Journal of Law and Policy for the Information Society* 5, no. 1 (2009).

'digital overload'. / exclusive / – irrelevant / self-limity.

None of this gives reason to doubt the power and potential of Internet communication for politics. We have recently observed its formidable possibilities in organizing and mobilizing people, for example, in the pro-democracy movements in the Middle East, both in processes of revolutionary overthrowing of autocratic regimes or in narrower protests, for example, concerning the fairness of a given electoral process or around economic insufficiencies. Online organizing has also characterized social movements elsewhere, whether in connection with the World Social Forum or solidarity struggles in Latin America, or Occupy Wall Street and its offshoot, the 99 Percent movement. The relatively recent dominance of mobile communication and computing, including cellphones and text messages, has thus far proved of considerable utility for such social and political movements, as has the proliferation of social networking sites (e.g., Facebook and Twitter), which supplement the older web-based forms of computing and communication.

Yet, all these forceful possibilities do not immediately transfer to inclusive processes of orderly deliberation, though they can – at least in principle – enhance the responsiveness of governments and of existing democratic decision procedures. It is evident that many people are interested in having a say about politicians and their decisions, and would take advantage of meaningful opportunities for input into these decisions, if it were clear that their participation would affect legislative processes and public policies. Such participation would have to go beyond the currently dominant and rather random forms of polling and surveys. The question remains how such public contributions and online deliberation processes can be structured in order to be maximally effective, and also how to address the cross-cultural and transnational dimensions they have.

This analysis of cross-border dialogue and deliberation focuses primarily on two key issues that have descriptive and normative dimensions. The first of these has been relatively under-theorized in the deliberative democracy literature. That concerns the presence of systematic misunderstanding, especially in cross-cultural contexts, which I take up later in the chapter with a proposal concerning highlighting contested categories in these online deliberations. The second is the continuing barrier posed to equal participation by global inequalities and the digital divide (though that divide is beginning to contract in regard to basic Internet access). These two themes are interrelated in highlighting how power disparities and oppressive historical and current conditions can enter in the very way transnational discourses are framed.

Two additional relevant issues can be noted here and will come up in Chapter 12. One concerns the intensification of governmental surveillance, restrictions, and interventions into these online discussions.

Each of these internet-facilitated movements have failed / been incoherent? (In their own terms).

C what are we asking of these movements?

Another is the difficult question of the language used in cross-border deliberations, and in particular the current domination of English for these purposes, at least in contexts of trade and diplomacy.

Norms of democratic discourse and human rights in intercultural global contexts

If we go back to the characteristics of discourse demarcated in the iconic discussions of it (especially in Jürgen Habermas and later in Seyla Benhabib and others) as well as in the democratic deliberation literature (Joshua Cohen, John Dryzek, James Bohman, Amy Guttman and Dennis Thompson, Iris Marion Young, and others), we can note the essential claim that people are supposed to be free and equal to enter into the dialogue or discourse. Moreover, they are (normatively at least) regarded as reciprocally related in terms of opportunities for listening and being heard, and are supposed to use reasoning to achieve agreements that take into account the perspectives of others.[8] Going somewhat beyond the original emphasis on rational argument in coming to agreements on "generalizable" or shared interests, feminist theorists have focused attention on the importance of a felt understanding and responsiveness toward the positions and needs of others, and on giving a voice to marginalized people within the dialogues.

While I have reservations about taking deliberation or discourse as *constitutive* of democracy,[9] it clearly is a central feature of *effective* democracy, if democratic decision-making is to be more than an aggregation of interests or a pure compromise between antagonistically defined positions. This is not to say that consensus has to be achieved in all these deliberations or that it is even reasonably understood as the aim. But some measure of agreement that goes beyond pure power struggles or

---

[8] Jürgen Habermas, *The Theory of Communicative Rationality*, trans. Thomas McCarthy, vol. 1 (Boston, MA: Beacon Press, 1985); Jürgen Habermas, *Moral Consciousness and Communicative Action*, trans. Lenhardt Christian and Nicholsen Shierry Weber (Cambridge, MA: MIT Press, 1990); Jürgen Habermas, *The Inclusion of the Other* (Cambridge, MA: MIT Press, 1998); Seyla Benhabib, *Situating the Self* (New York: Routledge, 1992); Joshua Cohen, "Deliberation and Democratic Legitimacy," in *The Good Polity*, ed. Alan Hamlin and Phillip Pettit (New York: Blackwell, 1989); Joshua Cohen, "Procedure and Substance in Deliberative Democracy," in *Democracy and Difference*, ed. Seyla Benhabib (Princeton, NJ: Princeton University Press, 1996); John Dryzek, *Discursive Democracy* (Cambridge: Cambridge University Press, 1990); James Bohman, *Public Deliberation: Pluralism, Complexity, and Democracy* (Cambridge, MA: MIT Press, 1996); Amy Gutmann and Dennis Thompson, *Democracy and Disagreement* (Cambridge, MA: Belknap Press of Harvard University Press, 1996); Iris Marion Young, *Inclusion and Democracy* (Oxford: Oxford University Press, 2002).

[9] See Gould, *Globalizing Democracy*, chapter 1.

simple compromise is normally regarded as a goal of these discourses, and held to be achievable through rules that ensure reciprocity, freedom and equality of participants, and so on. However, when such dialogue or deliberation occurs across borders, whatever inequalities may have marked national or domestic discourses are compounded by the deep inequalities that pervade many North–South relations, as well as by divergences in cultural practices, and by language differences.

Questions of scope are posed as well, inasmuch as the extent of the *demos* or public, or of membership in the community of discourse, is radically in question in transntional deliberative contexts. I have discussed this question of scope and proposed two criteria that are relevant: the first involves the extension of traditional notions of political and other communities to cross-border or transnational contexts and centers around a notion of common activities. Here the criterion is the constitution of an ongoing community understood as oriented to shared goals, where these may be embedded in relevant practices and institutions. Normally there is an intensional aspect, that is, the community understands itself to be a community or collectivity and to be oriented to the goals in question. The second criterion involves the use of the all-affected principle to demarcate those at a distance who should be able to provide input into discourses and decisions when they are importantly affected by a given decision or policy.

This still leaves open the question of how to determine who is "importantly" affected. I earlier proposed a particular interpretation of "importantly affected" for the global context, to delineate who should have some input into the decisions and policies in question. I argued that when people are affected in their possibilities of fulfilling their basic human rights they can be considered "importantly affected" and should have rights to provide input into those decisions or policies. Where decisions significantly bear on whether people can meet their economic means of subsistence, that is, basic economic human rights, these affected people need to be able to influence or affect the decisions that are made.

Given this normative requirement of hearing from dispersed publics, the question arises of how it can proceed if it involves communication with people in societies that may not allow open discourses or are not democratically organized. In such societies, some people are thought to be unable or unqualified to participate, even if the technological means for them to do so are available. This constitutes a conundrum or paradox, which can be added to the earlier puzzles concerning equality. Here, too, a key case concerns women who may be discriminated against or oppressed or held to be inappropriate participants. A seemingly easy solution to extending deliberation across cultural borders would be to give a place at

what about misogynistic cultures?

the table to excluded women and other marginalized or unequal groups. However, doing so often presupposes the very equality and openness of societies and their democratic organization that we are hoping to produce by the extension of democratic deliberation transnationally and that have in fact been lacking in the society in question. This is *a conundrum of deliberative democracy* in cross-border contexts.

In the epistemic communities of global governance institutions as well, such as the World Trade Organization (WTO), the World Bank, and the IMF, power and participation have tended to be limited to elites, so that giving a say to broader publics and a fortiori to marginalized groups is difficult to accomplish or even to envision. Dealing with this problem involves two aspects – one is cultural and political, where the required free and equal participation confronts existing dominant cultural norms or practices, and the second is social and economic, namely, the challenge of enabling participation by people who are dealing with poverty or various forms of oppression.

The requirement that we hear from women or oppressed groups arises in answer to the apt question: "Who speaks for a culture?" We can quite rightly object to simply accepting definitions of cultures promulgated by dominant groups or governments or others who benefit from the proposed cultural definition. (And, as previously noted, we can object to the unified notions of culture that these dominant interpretations often imply.) Oppressive, and even coercive, practices are specifically insidious in suppressing alternative interpretations of cultural traditions and norms that would likely be offered by marginalized groups if they had equal access to the educational and leisure opportunities, as well as to the powerful positions needed to advance their own cultural or religious interpretations.[10]

We have seen that universal norms like human rights are open to a certain range of local interpretations, as Martha Nussbaum has also suggested,[11] and we have taken note of some degree of cultural or political variability in the priority given to various human rights (regardless of the UN understanding of them as equally essential). But the possibility of tolerating deeply inegalitarian or oppressive cultural *practices* is more difficult than tolerating statements in *discourses*, and I have proposed that the limit to the practices is set in principle by a range of human rights, which have certain inelastic dimensions of interpretation, in virtue of

---

[10] See also the discussion in Kok-Chor Tan, *Toleration, Diversity, and Global Justice* (University Park, PA: Penn State University Press, 2000), chapter 6.

[11] Nussbaum, *Sex and Social Justice*; Martha Nussbaum, *Creating Capabilities: The Human Development Approach* (Cambridge, MA: Harvard University Press, 2011).

their connection to people's equal (positive) freedom. In any case, the recognition and tolerance extended to a wide diversity of customs cannot eliminate the possibility of criticism of unjust or oppressive practices, and several authors have pointed to the important distinction between offering criticism and attempting to *enforce* agreement.[12]

If discourse is to take into account and acknowledge inequalities in the starting positions and background life-world of participants, it needs to proceed with self-awareness of these factors in the interlocutor's own case, including awareness of relative (and unearned) privilege. Such discourse is enhanced by a degree of social theoretic understanding of oppressive social conditions and the ways that diverse participants may have benefited from them. These critical and self-critical aspects of the discursive process involve attention to relevant differences, in order to compensate for them with a view to establishing real equality among the participants.

An idea of this sort may have been behind Iris Young's concerns with special representation for oppressed groups and with the possibility of a veto to be exercised by them in deliberations about policies that importantly affect their interests.[13] Whether or not those specific proposals are desirable or realistic, they point to the significance of taking into account the diversity in concrete circumstances that people bring to deliberations. They require, in turn, a contemporary version of the critique of ideology, that is, of one-sided and distorting perspectives that can arise from the differently constituted life-worlds and different relational standpoints that people bring to the deliberations. Needed here is some awareness of the degree to which advocating a position serves one's interests and presupposes a particular standpoint and a set of background cultural and historical practices, which may themselves entail elements of oppression or residues of colonialism. Another challenge concerns the need, as one author puts it, to "attend to what remains unspoken, who is absent, and those who the words are unlikely to reach."[14]

Deliberative discourses are more likely to succeed if they are based on the achievement of reasonable levels of economic well-being among participants. Henry Shue recognized this sort of interdependence early in the philosophical discussions of human rights in his argument that

[12] See especially Martha Nussbaum, "Women and Theories of Global Justice: Our Need for New Paradigms," in *The Ethics of Assistance*, ed. Deen Chatterjee (Cambridge: Cambridge University Press, 2004).

[13] Young, *Justice and the Politics of Difference*.

[14] Loren B. Landau, "Can We Talk and Is Anybody Listening? Reflections on Iasfm 10: Talking across Borders: New Dialogues in Forced Migration," *Journal of Refugee Studies* 20, no. 3 (2007).

Deliberating discourses rather than systems per se.

the realization of basic rights to democratic participation and subsistence mutually implicate each other.[15] Subsistence is required for democratic participation and opportunities for genuine participation help to insure the realization of people's rights to subsistence. We can see how this observation supports a strong connection between global justice and democratic deliberation across borders, themes that have often been treated separately in the literature.

Democratic deliberation online

There have been exciting developments in online communications, including new opportunities for discussion across borders, particularly enabled by social networking and media. At the level of national politics, online activity has exerted considerable influence in recent U.S. elections and has become a regular part of e-government. Blogs and online organizing and e-petitions have been prominent, and there are increasing technological opportunities for deliberative forums and collaborative planning, as well as new opportunities for the public to provide feedback into ongoing policy discussions. Nonetheless, it is easy to overstate the significance of such online activities, including in regard to the emergent deliberative forums that specifically aim to enhance democratic participation through sophisticated online software. Most of these democratic forums in practice have been local, but even when open to distant others, they have so far been subject to a certain randomness in regard to who hears about them and who gets to participate in them. Especially evident is the small number of participants in these forums to date.[16] It is an open question whether they can be said to be representative of citizen views generally, or even of the views of those who participate in them. Further, like most online communities, they seem to have a tendency to discourage dialogue among people with conflicting perspectives, while encouraging discussions among those who agree. While this is probably felicitous from the standpoint of political organizing, it is not conducive to meeting norms of deliberation among people with fundamentally divergent political views.

Further, the entire online sphere can be subject to the charge of being exclusionary in view of the digital divide. Aside from the costs of access, many effective cross-border dialogues take place only among elites drawn from various national governments, or else operate within the upper

---

[15] Shue, *Basic Rights*.

[16] Chadwick, "Web 2.0"; Euripides Loukis and Maria A. Wimmer, "Analysing Different Models of Structured Electronic Consultation on Legislation under Formation" (paper presented at the From e-Participation to Online Deliberation, Fourth International Conference on Online Deliberation, Leeds, UK, 2010).

echelons of the institutions of global governance themselves. Civil society organizations themselves may have trouble being representative of their members or of the people they are trying to help; and sometimes their leadership is self-selected from among the most active participants in the organization.

Within the range of online dialogues, then, it would indeed be a step forward to find ways of representing the interests of distant people who are increasingly affected by globalization, but that remains a challenge for the future. There are promising technological developments, for example, the Issue-Based Information Systems (IBIS) platform, which facilitates the mapping of issues, arguments, and dialogues themselves. Besides the deliberations within global governance institutions, it would be desirable to enable dialogues that elicit stakeholder input in the management of global corporations. But we need to acknowledge that, at present, broad consultations with stakeholders or enabling their participation in key decisions remains an elusive goal. We can see that in all of these developments, there is a need to avoid giving the mere appearance of participation if the real power still resides with governmental elites or large corporations, whether at national or transnational levels. In these cases, it sometimes seems that proposals of deliberative democracy may only serve to obscure the facts on the ground.

Despite these admitted difficulties, I would like to propose a feature that should be included in future deliberative designs for the global public sphere, and which has not yet received sufficient attention. This is the importance of highlighting the contested normative or descriptive concepts that arise in the course of these discourses and providing a way for participants to become aware of their different meanings. We do not have to subscribe to Gallie's notion that many normative concepts are *essentially* contestable – with deep and irremediable divisions concerning their meaning – to observe that the contrasting uses of them when unacknowledged can generate misunderstandings and block agreements.[17] This is not, of course, to imply that ethnic, cultural, and political disagreements are reducible to disputes about words, nor that they are correctable without attention to other factors as well, especially disparities in economic and political power. Nonetheless, if dialogue proceeds at cross-purposes, it exacerbates misunderstandings and makes the requisite deliberation in the public sphere and the institutions of global governance less likely to occur.

If we grant that in dialogue and discussion among widely distributed participants, the cultural locations and backgrounds of these dialogue

---

[17] W. B. Gallie, "Essentially Contested Concepts," *Proceedings of the Aristotelian Society* 56 (1956): 167.

participants will influence their uses of language, then it may well be that the terms used in the discussion will sometimes have different meanings for each of the interlocutors. This is likely to lead to misinterpretation, and accentuate disagreements. For example, value terms like *just* or *unjust* and even supposedly descriptive terms like *terrorist* can have different meanings in different contexts. It would be helpful, then, to develop a software environment that could provide input to the various speakers when the terms they use have multiple meanings within the context of the discussion. This software would highlight the contested terms, present a range of different uses and meanings to the users, and enable these authors to choose which of these they intend, thereby also helping them also to become aware of the alternate interpretations.[18] Initially, this process would probably have to be limited to text-based discussions whether through email, chat, texting, or more formal forum sessions, but eventually there might be an analog developed for video communications as well. If participants become more aware of the one-sidedness of their interpretations, as well perhaps of their own background assumptions, it is possible that agreements will be facilitated.

Of course, we see that even where disputed meanings are acknowledged, as when conflicts erupt among contributors to Wikipedia concerning alternate interpretations of the terms or topics, there is no easy harmony to be achieved. Nonetheless, awareness of perspective can be helpful. We can hope, too, that dialogue can be coupled with dialectic, as discussed in the Introduction to this book. That is, disagreements do not necessarily lead to either a relativism of perspective or mere compromise (though the latter can surely sometimes be helpful), but can involve the search for a new and broader perspective that incorporates the conflicting views.

In regard to the second issue with deliberative opportunities in global contexts, namely, the persistence of the digital divide, we can observe the importance of developing not only new technologies, but also new opportunities for face-to-face discussion and new modes of representation for people affected by the policies of the powerful governance institutions. Despite the utility of mobile technologies for global interactions, in addition to the older forms of Information and Communication Technologies (ICTs), there seems to be no substitute for some component of actual rather than virtual dialogue among people affected by policies or plans. In regard to new forms of transnational representation, this could involve literal representatives, hopefully chosen democratically, or it

---

[18] This idea was developed in research and discussion with Arun Sood and Peter Mandaville of George Mason University.

linguistic difficulties.

could involve new forms of deliberative polling or deliberative democracy among representative individuals,[19] in this case representing those affected by the policies or transnational plans in question. Such deliberative polling has been mainly advocated for local and national politics, but it is relevant to global politics as well. It would appear most easily achievable there if it were to proceed online, though this raises again the question of how to manage the digital divide for such cases. It is clear, then, that creating new opportunities for dialogue does not in itself solve the problems of what I called informational poverty[20] or of actual poverty that necessarily limits the time people can spend in cross-border political discourse or deliberation. These problems again crucially highlight the importance of having our discussions of democracy and of global justice – and specifically of economic human rights – proceed in tandem.

Framing democratic deliberation

I have suggested that democracy in all its aspects – deliberative, participatory, and electoral – needs to be framed by human rights protections, as embodied in constitutions and in regional agreements,[21] as well as through more informal rules for democratic procedures in social or economic organizations. These institutional contexts need to be bound by understandings of the various procedures to be employed, whether involving rules or laws, though on my account democracy extends beyond procedure to involve substantially equal recognition among persons, and even beyond that, a notion of democracy as a way of life.

Human rights have been embodied in law, and democratic procedures too may be formalized in law and they also eventuate in laws in the case of legislation. The question therefore arises of how the "rule of law" can be understood in this connection. What is its relation to democracy and human rights, to which it is often linked? Without attempting to treat the complex notion of the rule of law adequately here, we can observe that the priority suggested in this work for a normative conception of human rights (and the conception of justice as equal positive freedom from which they follow), along with a strong conception of democracy,

---

[19] See, for example, Mark Warren, "Citizen Representatives," in *Designing Deliberative Democracy: The British Columbia Citizens' Assembly*, ed. Mark Warren and Hilary Pearse (Cambridge: Cambridge University Press, 2008).

[20] Carol C. Gould, "Network Ethics: Access, Consent, and the Informed Community," in *The Information Web: Ethical and Social Implications of Computer Networking*, ed. Carol C. Gould (Boulder, CO: Westview Press, 1989).

[21] See the discussion of the relation of a constitution to human rights, and the issue of the constitutional circle, in Gould, *Globalizing Democracy*, chapter 1.

has implications for understanding the important notions of law and the rule of law. In this view, respect for human rights would be a qualification not only on proper actions of government but on the laws themselves. And some degree of democracy may already be implied in one aspect of the rule of law, namely, when it is seen as contrasting with authoritarian uses of power or coercion.

A normative approach that privileges a broad conception of deliberative and participatory democracy, where it applies to a range of social and economic institutions as to political societies, would stress the ways in which laws are one subset of the broader set of rules through which people can codetermine the institutional spheres of their activity in society, and thereby bring openness, fairness, and predictability to their interactions. If one takes seriously the notions of openness and revisability so often associated with the rule of law, one can recognize the need for democratic ways of transforming laws, at least insofar as laws are thought to originate in legislatures (though interpreted by courts).

Claiming that human rights and democracy should inform the rule of law brings us squarely up against those approaches that instead see the rule of law as purely a matter of formal legality, centering on features of generality, publicness, predictability, and so on, rather than of any type of substantive equality. Some theorists accordingly argue that the value of the rule of law needs to be strictly separated from the values of human rights and democracy.[22] In such conceptions, the rule of law can be used for good or ill, in the same way that a technology can be put to good or bad uses. It is also objected that it is confusing to simply lump together numerous values under one heading, and that therefore a "thin" theory of the rule of law is to be preferred.[23] However, one can wonder what good can be found in laws formally promulgated by an otherwise authoritarian or fascist regime. Clearly, there might be some reduction in anxiety in having such laws and the punishment for their infraction predictable, but that would be surpassed by the much greater anxiety involved in having a deeply unaccountable government or one that suppresses dissent, or more generally in having no role for people to shape the common life of the body politic.

Another problem with such formalist views is that laws most often entail some degree of coercion in their implementation. Although such coercion may sometimes be just – when it is required to prevent significant harms to others or to insure fundamental equality – it nonetheless involves

---

[22] See the discussion in Charles Sampford, "Reconceiving the Rule of Law for a Globalizing World," in *Globalization and the Rule of Law*, ed. Spencer Zifcak (New York: Routledge, 2005).

[23] *Ibid.*

some loss of freedom. This sort of loss is only justifiable, it would seem, when it is required by justice, which further suggests that justice needs to qualify a rule of law if law is to merit our respect. It seems clear then that the rule of law needs to be qualified not only by the notions of human rights, and democracy, but also by that of justice.

Nonetheless, there is evidently value in the features often cited as part of a rule of law, simply on their own account. In Brian Tamanaha's summary account, for example, we have the (interrelated) three cluster concepts of a "government limited by law" emphasizing "restraint of government tyranny," in which "officials must abide by currently valid positive law," along with the existence of restraints on the government's power to make the laws;[24] "formal legality," including such features as "public, prospective laws, with the qualities of generality, equality of application, and certainty," which also emphasizes "a rule-bound order established and maintained by government;"[25] and the "rule of law, not of men," according to which people are "not to be subject to the unpredictable vagaries of other individuals,"[26] and which is tied centrally to rule by judges and most often a separation of powers. Joseph Raz has emphasized such features as: that laws should be prospective, open, clear, and relatively stable; that law-making should be guided by general rules, and so on; and that the judiciary should be independent, among other important factors.[27]

Yet, the aspect of formal legality, despite its importance, needs to be qualified by democracy and human rights, since if it is put in the service of pernicious ends, it can actually lose whatever value it may otherwise have had. That is evidently the case for particular unjust laws. But it may also characterize an entire system of law if that were introduced to systematically deprive a group of people of their basic rights. Further, without having an origin in people's own decisions or that of their representatives, the law can be said to dominate over people rather than serving as an instrumentality of their own self-control or collective self-determination. If freedom from domination is a significant aspect of our notions of freedom and equality, then this too argues for an intrinsic coupling of the rule of law with democracy and human rights. Of course, it is also the case that law and the rule of law are needed for protecting people's human rights and in structuring democratic legislation within political societies. So, these concepts are interdependent in that way as well.

---

[24] Brian Tamanaha, *On the Rule of Law: History, Politics, Theory* (Cambridge: Cambridge University Press, 2004), 115.
[25] *Ibid.*, 119.   [26] *Ibid.*, 123.
[27] Joseph Raz, *The Authority of Law: Essays on Law and Morality* (Oxford: Clarendon Press, 1979), 214–19.

The quasi-foundational approach here, which gives priority to the equality of humans taken as social beings with human rights that must be fulfilled, in no way implies that dialogue and cultural diversity have no role to play in understanding the values of the rule of law, or of human rights, or democracy. For example, as argued previously, dialogue from various cultural perspectives was crucial in the process of the articulation of human rights in the UDHR and in their subsequent elaboration in the Covenants and other international agreements. Accordingly, these rights came to include not only civil and political ones favored by the United States but also a fundamental set of social and economic entitlements advanced by states in Eastern Europe and the developing world, and more recently have incorporated third stage group and development rights promulgated in part by countries in the Global South.[28]

As argued in earlier chapters, expanding networks of social relations are also important conditions for the emergence of these normative conceptions and for their subsequent interpretation and application. I have referred to this as concrete universality, in which a process of critical dialogic interactions enables normative notions to become less one-sided and more multi-faceted, without however losing their range of core significances, which I suggest depend in various ways on people's equal freedom and dignity. It is clear that recognizing these processes of development does not thereby entail a relativist approach to the norms and values. But the theory here is harmonious with pluralist approaches that aim to acknowledge the diversity of individuals and cultures and the variety of forms that democracy and law may take, which are nonetheless compatible with this fundamental equality. An important future step is to make room for expanded conceptions of deliberation and participation within a human rights framework that can speak to the present situation of globalization. My suggestion here is that dialogue across borders and cultures will play an important role in insuring that this expansion proceeds in a non-dominating way, with a view to global justice.

---

[28] Carol C. Gould, "Two Concepts of Universality and the Problem of Cultural Relativism," in *Cultural Identity and the Nation-State*, ed. Carol Gould and Pasquale Pasquino (Lanham, MD: Rowman & Littlefield, 2001), and in revised form as chapter 2 of Gould, *Globalizing Democracy*. For a somewhat related argument, see Allen Buchanan, "Human Rights and the Legitimacy of the International Order," *Legal Theory* 14 (2008).

12   What is emancipatory networking?

Introduction

In recent years, we have witnessed significant democratic transformations initiated by people who have been able to mobilize and organize in part through the use of social media and, more generally, ICTs. The two most prominent cases were the revolutionary overthrow of various autocratic governments in the course of the Arab Spring of 2010–11 and its aftermath, and the Occupy Wall Street/99 Percent movement of 2011–12, following on the rebellions and participatory methods initiated by the *Indignatos* in Spain. Predictably, perhaps, these progressive democratic movements have been followed, in the first case, by instability, renewed repression, and violence in several of the Arab countries, and, in the second, by a decline of interest and participation in Occupy and the 99 Percent movement, marked also by increased dissension about tactics and strategies in both of these contexts.

What can we learn about the democratic potential of the Internet from these two cases? Going beyond online deliberation as discussed in Chapter 11, how can online networking be used to foster participatory democracy at this historical juncture? Given that the Internet in its social and political functions and its underlying technology continues to evolve rapidly, we need to try to avoid the rapid obsolescence that can mark discussions of this type. It would be helpful to keep the analysis at a somewhat general level, and focus on key features of contemporary democracy, online and off, that we want to enhance, and some rough directions for encouraging those enhancements in the future development of ICTs.

Aggregative vs. networking logics

In an interesting article reflecting on Occupy Wall Street's use of social media, Jeffrey Juris contrasts what he calls the "logic of aggregation" of that movement with the earlier networking logics that he chronicled

both failed, as Gould acknowledges

in the Global Justice movement of the late 1990s, especially centering around the "Battle of Seattle."[1] According to Juris, what is sometimes referred to as hashtag Occupy (#Occupy) – in view of the prominence of Twitter and other social media in its functioning – displayed a "logic of aggregation" that brought together individuals who were not primarily associated with institutions such as NGOs and collected them at particular places. Juris claims that because of its emphasis on inclusiveness and on participatory democratic procedure (especially in its General Assemblies), #Occupy focused on agglomerating people and their disparate views without coming up with concrete plans of action. And, in fact, the movement was characterized by a rather sharp divide between those who wanted to take action in support of standard political processes and those who maintained a purer and more comprehensive opposition to the status quo. Twitter and other social media are well suited to bringing large groups of people together at particular times and places, but apparently less suited to uses that could help those people achieve agreements on longer-term courses of action, or establish lasting institutional forms that could extend the participatory forms of democracy they seek.

By contrast, according to Juris, the Global Justice movement represented a networking logic that emerged, for the most part, among existing NGOs and other established institutions (if countercultural ones). Partly modeling themselves on developments in Latin America, the existing associations and institutions were able to use the Internet to network and to come up with joint policy proposals. This in turn gave them more enduring power, Juris thinks. Overlapping networks of individuals, groups, and relatively stable institutions helped to create such relatively long-lived associations as the World Social Forum and Indymedia. Though the Global Justice movement, like Occupy Wall Street, made important use of consensus and other collaborative forms of decision-making, Juris argues that existing organizations and institutions have a major role to play in a progressive movement's success. We can add that the use of these democratic modes undoubtedly contribute to its legitimacy as well.

I would disagree with the sharp separation that Juris draws between Occupy and the Global Justice movement, especially given the large number of people involved in Occupy's 99 Percent movement who were representatives of diverse institutions such as labor unions, NGOs, and churches and synagogues. Moreover, OWS evidently used a networking logic to advance its activities in various ways, particularly online, and it especially encouraged networking among the various Occupy sites and

---

[1] Jeffrey S. Juris, "Reflections on #Occupy Everywhere: Social Media, Public Space, and Emerging Logics of Aggregation," *American Ethnologist* 39, no. 2 (2012).

social movements as aggregationist
↳ fulfilly role of parties?

working groups. These "logics" should also not be taken to be determined by available technologies, but rather by the forms of organization and mobilization they involve.

Nonetheless, there are two important points that we can discern in Juris's account that provide cautions for democratic uses of the Internet. The first concerns the difficulties that emerge from the prevalence of rather atomistic lifestyles and their online correlate of fragmentation, where people seem increasingly disembedded from given communities. Thus it was already a considerable accomplishment to mobilize individuals en masse to participate in the Occupy protests and to have a subset of those people take part in the General Assemblies. With the influence within that movement of anarchist theory, along with a strong commitment to consensus decision-making, it took Occupy Wall Street some time before viable methods of coming to agreement could be implemented, and agreements were never achieved on a set of demands.[2] Still, the large number of working groups on diverse topics, such as labor and ecology, played an important role in establishing continuities among various participants, as did the creation of a living community at many of the Occupy sites, including the provision of meals, a library, a medical tent, and so on. The second point we can take from this analysis, which is discussed further below, concerns the importance of institutions, whether existing or new ones, if democracy is to flourish in new ways appropriate to emergent transnational contexts.

What both the Arab Spring and the Occupy movement suggest is not just the role of counterpublics in newer uses of the Internet.[3] Beyond this, they reveal the effectiveness – if of a transitory sort – of more participatory modes of democratic protest and organization. This contrasts with a traditional account of democracy, along with its correlate of e-government. It also suggests the viability of going beyond the emphasis on online deliberative democracy that has been the main focus of discussions of the Internet and democracy in recent years, at least among political theorists.[4] While the examples we have witnessed of more participatory modes have thus far relied mainly on what could be called the power of crowds, for example via crowd-sourcing, a deeper look will discern some possibilities for moving to more steady and organized forms of democratic participation. I discuss some of these possibilities in what follows, beginning with the still important deliberative framework and

---

[2] For a comprehensive study of the development of the Occupy movement, see Gould-Wartofsky, *The Occupiers*.

[3] Lincoln Dahlberg, "The Internet, Deliberative Democracy, and Power: Radicalizing the Public Sphere," *International Journal of Media and Cultural Politics* 3, no. 1 (2007).

[4] Adam See, "Participatory Politics and New Media: Towards a New Communitarianism" (Unpublished manuscript, 2012).

proceeding to a more participatory one, in the context of new forms of democracy beyond borders.

From e-government to e-deliberation to e-participation

In order to address the potentials of online participation, it will be helpful to keep in mind not only the new technological developments that can facilitate this participation but also the modes of mainly offline democracy that characterize the present increasingly transnational context and that pose the need for expanding opportunities for this participation. Discussions of democracy on the Net often take democracy in its traditional sense as pertaining exclusively to forms of government within nation-states. They also tend to focus on the forms that such democracy tends to take, whether electoral processes and voting, or the relation of representatives to citizens, or the relevance of rational choice perspectives for decisions. I believe that the Internet has implications not only for the forms of democracy – whether on or offline (e.g., deliberative, participatory, electoral) – but also for the scope of democracy. If the dominant rather sclerotic and bureaucratic forms of politics are to somehow become more participatory, we need to attend to both increases in scope and improvements in the form of contemporary democracy.

The new type of democracy that is normatively desirable and facilitated by contemporary social developments is what I am calling "interactive democracy." In the usage here, interactive democracy is not limited to online manifestations, that is, to democracy on the Net, although the Web, and the Internet more generally, does facilitate such interactivity. More broadly, the term points to the ever more intense interrelations among people within a democracy and between existing democratic political communities; it also suggests processes of growing regionalization, the emergence of transnational communities (whether online or off), and the multiplicity of overlapping networks among groups in economic, social, and political life, which can organize themselves democratically if they choose.[5] The conception is founded on an interactive (and active) conception of individuals, as *individuals-in-relations.*

Much has recently been made of the interactivity of "Web 2.0." As popularized by Tim O'Reilly in his influential account of Web 2.0 principles, including collective intelligence, the importance of data, "rich user experiences," and so on,[6] this second-generation web development has included an emphasis on user-generated content, online collaboration

---

[5] See also Gould, "Envisioning Transnational Democracy."
[6] Tim O'Reilly, "What Is Web 2.0? Design Patterns and Business Models for the Next Generation of Software," (2005), www.oreilly.com/lpt/a/6228.

the definition of interactive democracy.

and sharing of information among users (as in Wikipedia and collaborative editing software), video repositories, and an extensive use of social networking sites. More recently, mobile smartphones and their apps (some free and some paid for) have come to prominence. Information and data follow people on multiple devices and increasingly exist in the "cloud." These developments correlate with an emphasis offline on horizontal networks among people and groups, and are said to bring with them a democratization of information and of the Internet itself, in the form of blogs, tagging, posting, and commenting (whether on journalistic or social media sites).

Clearly, while these developments open collaborative and interactive opportunities, they also bring perils, so it is important to avoid romanticizing their potential for democratic enhancement, as we also saw with online deliberation. In online networking, we can find fragmentation of attention, thin relationships, and sometimes a preference for the virtual over the actual. User-generated content can enable the manipulation of information, with a consequent erosion of trust. Where it involves news gathering, the information generated is often unreliable and disorganized. Crowd-sourcing can help find missing persons, fund worthy projects, or monitor public officials, but it is prominently used for marketing purposes, and can be used for harassing people, or in discriminatory ways. The profiles people post on social networking sites like Facebook are increasingly subject to data mining for commercial purposes, and have enabled extensive government surveillance. The private information posted on those sites is increasingly in the public domain, and in many cases is archived indefinitely. Moreover, it is not clear that the forms of interactivity and participatory politics that these technological developments facilitate can even begin to balance out the effects of Super PACs and other large donors that currently profoundly influence politics offline (at least in the United States).

The scope of democracy, online and off

As discussed in earlier chapters, we can discern three contexts for democracy, where the first two of these involve an appeal to the "common activities" notion. One is the case of democracy within political societies and localities, as well as in smaller-scale institutions (including economic ones, discussed in Chapter 14) operating within nation-state borders. Related to these, though taking a distinctively transnational form, are the various cross-border communities that have emerged with globalization, such as ecological groupings that see themselves as communities, social movement networks that connect through video and other means, and also Internet forums of various sorts. In these "communal" cases, we can speak of equal membership and equal rights of participation for the members, whether they are citizens or residents or members of an economic firm or other institution. The third case is the rather different one in which global actors (e.g., global governance institutions, or nation-states, or global corporations) are increasingly connected to distant others via the external impacts or effects of their decisions or policies. In such cases, I have argued for the need to solicit democratic input from these affected people, though not necessarily for equal rights of participation.

It can be surmised from this tripartite division that somewhat different forms of democratic participation are appropriate to the various cases, rather than a one-size-fits-all approach. In particular, the third type of case admits of differential impacts and hence differential rights of input, whereas the common activities criterion supports equal rights of democratic participation. In the case of being affected at a distance, I think we need to actually hear from people, including in regard to any tradeoffs that may be necessary. There is also no necessary presumption that the distant others are less affected by the decision or policy in question than are the powerful decision makers – they may be more affected and so have commensurately greater rights of input.

It seems clear that this last arena for democracy, that is to say, hearing from those affected, is particularly amenable to the use of the Internet, in terms of the possibilities it offers to solicit and receive input from broader publics. But the problem arises of how to manage differential inputs. Moreover, new processes along these lines run up against the standard difficulty that afflicts all efforts to hear from these publics, namely: who will listen to them? Simply enabling people to raise concerns will not suffice unless these concerns, or even more strongly, people's participation and deliberation in regard to the policies or decisions themselves, are taken seriously, indeed so seriously as to affect the policies themselves. New institutional forms are thus required if we are to use the Net for such democratic input.

Chapter 11 called attention to the problem of cross-cultural understanding or, often, misunderstanding. It is not possible to simply assume that participation or deliberation across borders will proceed in English, though translation software is rapidly improving. The problem of the lack of univocal meanings for the terms of the discussion remains, as does the issue of contested concepts across varying cultural and national borders. Clearly, if clarifying deliberations could be engendered, they would help to sort out these various meanings and the respective worldviews that frame them. Nonetheless, the possibility of such deliberations is precisely what is in question, and they often cannot even get off the ground because of these cultural misunderstandings and mistakings. This can be called *the paradox of cross-cultural deliberation*.

Respect for diverse cultural interpretations of terms comes up against an especially hard question in regard to a core value of the Internet, namely, open access to information, particularly because of its close connection to freedom of expression. Some cultural or national perspectives regard other values as having priority over freedom of expression (even in Western countries), for example, equality and nondiscrimination norms requiring strong prohibitions against hate speech. Alternative priorities may lead states or cultures to support Internet censorship, which apparently contravenes the requirement of openness. Various cultural or political perspectives may not perceive any connection between freedom of expression and open access to information (or else may breach it in practice).

An interesting example of such divergent approaches to the value of openness was the Yahoo case of 2000 in which a French court ordered Yahoo to prevent access in France to Nazi auctions or any sites displaying Nazi sympathy or Holocaust denials. As Joel Reidenberg points out, this decision was consistent with French norms, and does not apparently violate international human rights, as they are presently construed at least.[7] I have previously argued that human rights (taken as moral and not only legal rights) set an appropriate limit on the toleration of cultural practices, such that if such practices violate these rights, we can at least be critical of them (though the issue of legitimate international intervention to enforce these rights is a separate question and would rarely be justified). In order to avoid the consequence that Internet censorship is acceptable, then, one would have to argue that current legal interpretations of human rights as permitting it are misguided, which is certainly a possibility. Still, it is difficult to argue that the U.S. interpretation, which gives supreme scope to civil and political rights like freedom of expression to the detriment of social and economic rights, is the only or best one. In any case, given the centrality of the apparently contested norm of free and open access to information, it seems that the recognition of a margin of appreciation for some local differences in human rights interpretations poses special difficulties for the openness that would be needed for using the Internet for democratic purposes.

Informational privacy

In an early article on democratic participation on the Net in 1989, "Network Ethics: Access, Consent, and The Informed Community,"

---

[7] Joel R. Reidenberg, "The Yahoo! Case and the International Democratization of the Internet," *Fordham Law & Economics Research Paper*, http://papers.ssrn.com/sol3/papers.cfm?abstract_id=267148.

which appeared in my collection that year entitled *The Information Web*, I proposed as a principle maximally free and open access to information consistent with the rights of privacy (and in some cases, property).[8] In that article, I also argued for the relevance of the *principle of informed consent*, which had previously been used in medical ethics, for this new domain of network ethics. While I think these principles are still sound as general normative guidelines for this domain, it is clear that the situation is much more complicated than it then appeared. As emerging from DARPANET and NSFNet, the Internet was originally designed for collaborative scientific research, with its inherent commitment to free and open access to information (despite the sometimes questionable foci of the research itself). This scientific origin apparently led to design decisions to make the Net itself decentralized and open. Subsequently, the development of commercialization on the Web and its ever-increasing use for surveillance purposes (both governmental and corporate) threaten these values of free and open communication and access to information, although happily the Net itself has so far largely retained its initial decentralized architecture.

In the United States, it currently seems nearly impossible to implement the strong privacy protections that the principle would require in regard to control over information about individuals (the EU seems exceptional in having more protections in place). On social networking sites such as Facebook, people post all types of personal information. While this can contribute to enhanced forms of interpersonal communication and sociability, along with sometimes creative merging of actual and virtual social identities, the information can be used (and is used) for surveillance purposes, even when people attempt to keep the information restricted to close networks of friends. Moreover, online networking most often leaves permanent traces, at least as currently designed. Data mining for commercial purposes and the use of that information to tailor advertising to particular individuals is extensive.

Most troubling from the standpoint of informational privacy are the vast government security databases, from which it seems nothing online can be hidden. The only secrecy seems that of the databases themselves and the uses to which they are put, along with the design and policy decisions of closed environments like Facebook. Increasingly, some of this secrecy is being breached by hacktivists. But reliable and reasonable procedures that could protect some measure of users' privacy and informational control are lacking. The proposal of informed consent regarding uses of information about oneself remains almost wholly ideal, if it is to

---

[8] Gould, "Network Ethics."

be applied to particular uses of specific pieces of information, particularly where "big data" is involved.

However, the principle of informed consent remains relevant if it is taken as a desideratum that applies to classes of information about groups of people. It would then be understood to require a high degree of transparency in regard to the procedures and laws to be applied to these larger uses of information, and the requirement for democratic control by polities over these procedures. Where it is a question of the operation of courts, which may be asked to approve covert surveillance and interpret the relevant laws, the interests of the people affected need to be represented in the deliberations of these bodies, and the policies and laws governing these various processes need to be open to deliberation within a polity and receive their consent to the rules. It is evident that these rules should permit gathering only of relevant information for particular security purposes, rather than enabling blanket policies of comprehensive data gathering in advance of particular threats. In these various ways, the notion of informational privacy can still be recognized as a legitimate constraint on uses of information, and the Web's important role in facilitating the sharing of free and open communication preserved.

Forms of democracy on the Net

Turning now to the question of the forms of democracy on the Net, we note that most attention has thus far been paid to supporting electoral and representative democracy, as well as replicating deliberation online. There remains wide opposition to e-voting per se, because of the opening it is thought to present for manipulation or outright fraud. The focus has been on preparations for elections, by informing and mobilizing voters. Efforts to democratize the representative and executive functions have resulted in "e-government" (and the newer e-governance at more global levels), with two-way communications between representatives and their constituencies, along with placing many government services online, whether at municipal or national levels. Some progress has been made regarding the norm of transparency, though much more would need to be done to make it widespread and effective (and the powers mobilized against this remain substantial).

We have seen that the focus in political theory has been on deliberation online, including software development for such dialogues, most often proceeding with moderators or facilitators. Practically, the deliberative model has been applied in some local and national forums that attempt to generate citizen interest, and through their discussions arrive at proposals that could influence public policy, but as noted these have garnered few participants.[9] The idea of deliberative polling online has been attempted in select environments. Along these lines, in 2012, Ireland organized a constitutional convention made up of a total of 100 representative citizens and parliamentarians to draft some amendments to its constitution. Forms of deliberative polling could be especially effective in the new contexts of transnational governance, where it is difficult to organize large numbers of participants in dialogues, but where representative samples of stakeholders would be easier.

What has been omitted from the discussions of online deliberation until recently, whether positive or critical, is the potential of the Net for introducing participation in democratic decision-making. Crowd-sourcing was used to draft a set of basic laws for a new Icelandic constitution, subject to a referendum and subsequent action by parliament. Twenty-five members of the public initially drafted proposals and received comments on Facebook and Twitter. More radically, we have seen that Occupy Wall Street operated with general assemblies, which attempted to implement open and consensual decision-making. Generally, however, the possibility of introducing participation in direct and egalitarian forms has been dismissed as utopian. Theorists instead call for hearing from the broader public online, as when opportunities may be opened for commenting on prospective policies or imminent laws. The problem is that such participation is necessarily sporadic, subject to the digital divide, and often no one is required to read what the members of the public say should be done, let alone take it seriously in policy making or legislation. Although politicians have increasingly been paying attention to polls, there is little way for people to contribute to the questions asked there or to propose new questions. In the United States, politicians also frequently employ focus groups to hone their "message," and increasingly keep up with comments made about them at social networking sites, but the influence on policy is largely absent.

Clearly, much more can be done to intensify and regularize democratic participation in decision-making, without undermining representative government where it exists. One possibility is to implement more participatory modes in the local and smaller-scale contexts in which it could directly affect policy and procedure, and potentially be taken seriously. These contexts include economic firms, as well as local municipalities and towns. Chapter 14 will develop the argument for the extension of democratic rights of participation to firms, taking Mondragon (the sixth largest corporation in Spain and a worker-managed success story) as a model case in point. Some of the resulting participative functions can

---

[9] Chadwick, "Web 2.0," 16–17.

be transferred online, although the degree to which self-managing firms have done that is unclear.

Likewise, within cities or other local political units, or newer cross-border associations, actual participation in decisions or policy making is plausible, even in the short term. We can cite the important example of participatory budgeting, which began in Porto Alegre, Brazil, but now extends even to some city council districts in New York City.[10] Other groups oriented to social justice goals have successfully networked, shared information online, and have begun to make decisions collectively there. An example is provided by the sharing of effective tactics and strategies by way of videoconferences in the Movement for Justice in El Barrio, which has held *encuentro* meetings online with likeminded groups from South Africa, El Salvador, Mexico, and elsewhere around the world.[11] It is noteworthy that such activist groups often define themselves in highly inclusive ways, such that they are open to further networking with new groups, in the interest of overcoming oppression or achieving the forms of justice they seek.

Regarding larger units, I think that political theorists of democracy on the Net will need to come up with innovative models for enhancing participation. There is already considerable political concern manifest on social media and in blogging and commenting online. The question is how to mobilize this to bring it closer to actual political processes and make it effective there. There is also a need to construct new forms of representation for popular input into transnational policies (as discussed in Chapter 13). Even more radically, I have suggested considering some form of delegate assemblies to supplement existing forms of representative democracy. These assemblies could be addressed to pressing problems, or they could be standing units, structured in terms of the principle of subsidiarity, where the constituencies may not even have to be geographically defined, but could be organized functionally or by economic sector.

Besides facilitating new forms of deliberation and participation, "emancipatory networking" should use online interactivity to contribute to what I have called "the democratic personality,"[12] or more generally, in Dewey's terms, "democracy as a way of life." With other feminist theorists, I have argued for the need for forms of equal recognition in more "private" domains of life, for example, in the family, required both in itself

[10] www.participatorybudgeting.org/
[11] Michael Gould-Wartofsky, "Here Comes the Neighborhood: The Housing Movement Goes Global in East Harlem," *The Huffington Post* (March 25, 2010).
[12] Gould, *Rethinking Democracy*.

and as a necessary support for the flourishing of democratic citizenship.[13] Increasingly, equal recognition needs to have a cosmopolitan aspect such that it extends not only to those resident in a territory (whether they be citizens or not) but extends to those within one's region and in fact globally. (As we have seen, this is not to say that there is no place for political community, nor does it imply the abolition of nation-states). Furthermore, the democratic personality requires cultivating both agency and receptivity (including listening skills), as well as a disposition to empathy and solidarity, with compatriots and with distant others. We have seen that empathy involves a cognitive aspect of understanding the practical situation and perspective of others, as well as an affective component of "feeling with" others.

How can the Net contribute to the recognition of others as equal, along with helping to generate the required agency, receptivity, and disposition to empathy, including with those situated at a distance? Clearly these are large questions that I can only pose but not answer here. To a degree, the Internet's aspects of openness and extension of access to information and to the life experiences of concrete others around the world has aided in expanding the scope of recognition. However, it can also enable people to more easily link up with groups that seek to exclude others (e.g., various hate groups), who are likewise able to mobilize effectively online.

The paradox of anonymity

In conclusion, we can focus on a puzzle that the above desiderata pose for a crucial feature of life on the Net, concerning the contested issue of anonymity. We can sketch what can be called *the conundrum of anonymity*.

Viewed in terms of the desirability of mutual recognition of persons, as equal participants in dialogue and decision-making online, anonymity can evidently have the powerful effect of rendering people equal, in that it abstracts from any of the standard features that might be used to discriminate among them, and instead gives the major role to what they say and how they present themselves online. In these respects, it can also free people to speak as they please. But at the same time, it frees them to discriminate or to speak uncivilly or even hatefully toward others. It can concomitantly lead to an absence of taking responsibility for the various interventions that people make online. Thus we can say that anonymity

---

[13] Gould, "Feminism and Democratic Community Revisited." See also Jane Mansbridge, "Feminism and Democratic Community," in Democratic Community: NOMOS XXXV, edited by J. Chapman and I. Shapiro (New York: New York University Press, 1993).

at one and the same time can foster equality and inequality, recognition and misrecognition.

What can be done about this conundrum? Presumably resolving it would require differentiating democratic contexts in which the anonymity is productive from those in which it is on balance harmful. For example, where discussion and dialogue is mainly expressive, preserving anonymity could be appropriate, while for organizing purposes or for making actual decisions or policies, speaking in one's own name, with the requisite authentication and the resultant accountability, would need to be given priority. Although people are now comfortable in speaking in their own names on such private/public spaces as Facebook and Twitter, their willingness to do so in broader arenas would probably require the extension of trust and civility beyond those relatively protected spheres, along with the diminution of the fear of reprisal and negative judgments that currently pervades the online domain. Perhaps the democratization of the transnational realm would be of some help in that respect. At present, however, the pervasiveness of forms of negativity, even within national contexts, makes the achievement of the requisite online civility seem like a distant possibility. Chapter 13 explores some directions for conceiving of more transnational, or even fully global, forms of democracy.

13 Structuring transnational democracy: participation, self-determination, and new forms of representation

Introduction

What sort of democratic political transformations will be needed to empower the emerging transnational communities that are growing in importance as the sovereignty of traditional nation-states is becoming partially eroded? With the intensification of economic globalization, the increase in shared ecological and economic interests across borders, extensive migrations, and transnational social movements, we can ask what political and social forms would enable a measure of democratic control over these transnational phenomena on the part of people involved in them or else deeply affected by them. Currently, much global economic activity involves forms of transnational power exercised by large corporations, accompanied by wide inequalities and severe ecological problems. At the same time, politicians within nation-states seem unable to deal with these consequences and are generally unresponsive to constituent needs. In this situation, it is not surprising that many people feel that they lack any democratic say over the conditions of their own life activity. With the growth of global governance institutions, nation-states are no longer the only significant actors in international politics, as Buchanan and Keohane have argued.[1] We can ask, looking ahead, what would effective democratic reforms look like at the transnational democracy level? Would full global democracy be a solution here and would it be desirable?

Where it is not rejected altogether, global democracy is often thought of in either/or terms: either it entails the implementation of full-scale world government, or else it is limited to innovations within the existing system of nation-states and international organizations, in particular, the introduction of loose federations of nation-states at regional or

---

[1] Allen Buchanan and Robert O. Keohane, "The Legitimacy of Global Governance Institutions," *Ethics & International Affairs* 20, no. 4 (2006).

international levels, or else the strengthening of existing international institutions, for example, through the addition of a Global People's Assembly at the UN.[2] This characterization of the options omits a distinctive feature of contemporary globalization, namely, the emergence of cross-border communities and transnational associations, which require new ways of thinking about the norm of democracy in a deeply interconnected world.

Many critics dismiss the entire project of establishing global or even transnational democracy on the grounds that it is either impossible, given the current state system, or else undesirable, since it would entail a unified government for everyone or some form of supranational state. It is observed that no global *demos* exists, and there is only a weak global public sphere, where both the *demos* and the public sphere are seen as prerequisites for democracy (based on the experience with nation-states). I think that these criticisms are well taken, but I would reject the conclusion that we can make no sense of viable transnational democracy, and perhaps of more fully global forms. If we remain with the current interpretation of political communities as sovereign nation-states and with democracy limited to its present formations, then globalizing democracy is probably impossible. And if we take it to mean a world government, then it is undesirable, for the reasons discussed below.

These critics are also correct that there is no global demos, in which everyone can participate equally as a citizen in a single world polity, and no effective global public sphere. But I think that it is probably a mistake to seek such a global *demos* and a single globalized public sphere; and it would be an impoverished view of transnational democracy that would see it as entailing a singular government replacing smaller forms of associations. In contrast, the emerging multiplicity of interacting transnational public spheres might make possible a richer, and potentially more democratic, form of transnational association.

A single world government is undesirable mainly because of the possibilities it would introduce for world tyranny.[3] Just as authoritarian regimes can come to power via elections in sovereign nation-states, so a similar possibility cannot be ruled out for a democratic world government, despite the safeguards that would be introduced. But it is more difficult to fault other contemporary proposals for loose federations of nation-states at regional and international levels, or for strengthening of international institutions with, for example, a global peoples' assembly.

---

[2] Falk and Strauss, "Global Peoples Assembly."
[3] See also the discussion in Walzer, *Arguing About War*, chapter 12.

nor a single, unified global public sphere.

with a single world government.

In regard to the first of these, the further development of regionalism is of considerable interest, following on the lead of the EU (despite its recent problems), and I discuss regional forms of democracy in Chapter 15.

However, to the degree that regional federations are built up as aggregations of nation-states, where the latter remain the decisive units, federations or confederations cannot adequately address the new cross-border communities within them (or that intersect with them). Crucial global justice concerns that separate world regions into relatively well-off and impoverished ones are also not dealt with by this regionalism proposal. Global corporations too, which are often problematic actors under current globalization, tend to escape the reach of both regional bodies and nation-states. Yet another limitation of such regional federations concerns the difficulty they face in dealing with ecological impacts of a more fully global nature, most especially the urgent crisis posed by climate change. Moreover, there remains an important role for the idea of the self-determination of nations or peoples, associated at present with nation-states, especially in protecting against intervention. Is there an effective way to keep self-determination in place in view of increasing transnationalism?

A second contemporary approach to more global forms of democracy emphasizes adding to current international institutions new forms of representation of people as global citizens. A key proposal along these lines is for a People's Assembly in the UN, which would be popularly elected rather than serving to represent governments.[4] This would be a worthwhile innovation, but it is hard to see how this one body could deal with the myriad new issues that confront a more globalized world, particularly given the powerful nation-states that would continue to dominate international relations.

To address this range of issues, this chapter begins with a brief review of the two criteria for democratic participation, including replies to some objections. I then touch on the question whether the interactive forms of democracy that these criteria support are compatible with the older norm of self-determination and the related prohibition against forcible intervention into other nation-states. An argument is then presented for democratic accountability on the part of global governance institutions. Finally, some practical implications of the democracy criteria for institutional transformation and design are considered, with special reference to new directions for *transnational representation*.

---

[4] Falk and Strauss, "Global Peoples Assembly."

Refining the criteria for the scope of democracy

As discussed in Chapter 4, the consideration of the appropriate scope for democratization makes appeal to two concepts, "common activities" and impact on human rights. The first is an interpretation of democracy as rule by the people or popular control and requires equal rights of participation in decisions concerning institutions with shared goals and practices. This approach rather easily applies to new cross-border associations and communities, since it does not prioritize the nation-state in its fundamental conception. To the degree that forms of common activities with shared ends are becoming increasingly cross-border, it follows that democratic participation and representation are relevant to these new contexts as well. Indeed, there have been interesting developments along these lines, not only in the large-scale and established context of the EU, but in emerging smaller-scale communities, both of a locally cross-border sort – whether ecologically or economically based – or in new forums enabled by Internet communications, for example, among political activists or in some discussion-based groups. However, it is not the case that this model of common activities or preexisting communities of interest extends globally in a way that would require a single *demos* with traditional democratic participation and representation.

Several potential problems have been raised against this common activities view, which can be considered briefly. One set of concerns has been aptly posed by Pablo Gilabert: Given the variety of common activities, what is to be done when they overlap and conflict with each other? Which communities should be given priority? In addition, it might seem that the concept is so broad that it proliferates communities; its application could then become indeterminate in much the same way that the unrestricted "all affected" principle is.[5] I think that the second part of this objection – concerning the proliferation of communities – is not decisive, since the proposal is explicitly one for extending the scope of democracy; it thus endorses a requirement for democratic participation within a wide range of associations and communities beyond those currently recognized (where this is admittedly a rather ideal possibility in the present). The desirability of networks of overlapping communities further mitigates the problem here, since they could be mutually enriching and stand in solidarity with each other, as discussed in Chapter 5.

The first problem cited is more difficult, however – namely, what to do when communities or spheres of common activity conflict with each other. It is partly because of the pervasiveness of such conflicts that states

---

[5] Gilabert, "Global Justice, Democracy, and Solidarity."

have evolved over time. Their broader frameworks can provide important adjudicative functions when disputes arise. But that fact does not establish that nation-states are different in kind from other institutions and communities as potential arenas for democratic decision-making, although the range of the activities and of the shared goals and projects that states embody are more extensive. Even smaller-scale institutions than the state (e.g., transnational corporations), and certainly also localities like cities, have to deal with and adjudicate internal conflicts, where some of these are not only between individuals but also among the smaller organizations that make them up.

Another set of objections comes from those who think an emphasis on political agency is too demanding, particularly with globalization. Thus Daniel Weinstock objects to this emphasis as unrealistic and as ineffective in meeting people's interests. On his view, only a more delimited set of institutions of global governance can be justified, if they were instrumental to meeting people's fundamental interests.[6] But I think the criticism Weinstock gives misconstrues the argument for rights of democratic participation. It is not that participation is simply good in itself (although it does bring benefits to those who make use of it); and the argument is only for rights of participation not for obligations to participate. In the account I give, democratic participation serves freedom, and some of what Weinstock counts as fundamental interests come in as either aspects of, or conditions for, freedom. Thus democracy is in this sense instrumental to people's goals and projects in my own view as well. However, I think that an emphasis on equal agency and its conditions is to be preferred to the "bundle of interests" perspective. In fact, the importance of agency is brought in by Weinstock as well, though in what might seem a somewhat backhanded way. Specifically, he identifies nondomination as among people's fundamental interests.[7] I suggest that this implicitly recognizes the importance of the freedom and equality of agency to democracy, which is at the core of my account.

The "common activities" criterion does have a serious limitation, and that is its incompleteness as an account of the scope of democracy. Thus the model sees democratic modes of decision as applicable wherever people are organized (either voluntarily or traditionally) into institutions or communities. Such a model has increasing practical applicability to new communities that are literally cross-border, for example, where ecological

---

[6] Daniel Weinstock, "The Real World of (Global) Democracy," Special Issue on Democracy and Globalization, ed. Carol C. Gould and Alistair Macleod, *Journal of Social Philosophy*, 37, no. 1 (2006).

[7] *Ibid.*, 12.

interests are shared among neighboring communities across nation-state or more local borders, and to noncontiguous transnational communities of limited purpose such as those that may develop on the Internet. But interpreting the principle of democracy in this communal way does not suffice to address the need to open the institutions of global governance, or indeed even the decisions of traditional political communities, to input from people increasingly affected by their decisions, who often reside in locations remote from the institutions and from the major participants within them. So I have argued that there is a need for an additional principle beyond "common activities" and have proposed a variant of the "all affected" principle as relevant there. In particular, when people at a distance are impacted in regard to their possibilities for fulfilling their basic human rights by way of the decisions and policies of transnational or fully global institutions, they have rights of input into those decisions.

Because of the centrality of democratic participation in people's having the ability to realize and protect their human rights, including economic and social ones – according to the argument initially presented by Henry Shue[8] – it follows that they should have substantial input into the decisions that affect their rights fulfillment. The role of democratic input can also be gleaned by considering that people are themselves usually best able to identify and characterize their own needs. This suggests the superiority of a democratic interpretation of providing input over the weaker notions of stakeholder theory, in which it is sufficient for decision makers in corporations or global governance institutions to imagine for themselves what people at a distance think and feel about the proposed issue. On the view here, democratic input is required, even if it often cannot take the form of full democratic participation. Later in the chapter, I consider some of the new forms of participation and representation that can facilitate this input.

Self-determination and democratic governance

The justification of democracy in terms of rights to codetermine decisions in contexts of common or joint activities, that is, as a right of collective self-determination, brings it close to the rather different notion in international relations of the self-determination of peoples. That latter notion, enshrined in international law as one of the human rights, can be said to concern "the right of the majority within an accepted

---

[8] Shue, *Basic Rights*.

political unit to exercise power."[9] It implicates issues of the constitution of the polity and also the legitimacy of secession for minority groups in ways that go beyond our current discussion. Nonetheless, we can wonder what the connection is between these similar-sounding formulations of self-determination. In addition, the principle of self-determination of peoples, along with the notion of the external sovereignty of nation-states, has helped to guard against aggressive military interventions. If globalization entails a diminution of sovereignty and instead enables an increasing degree of transnational decision-making and the emergence of cross-border communities, we can wonder what will become of the principle of the self-determination of peoples in this new context.

These are complicated questions, which I have discussed elsewhere,[10] but a few clarifications can be made here concerning the relation of self-determination to democratic governance. I think that if self-determination is interpreted as democratic self-determination, in a way suitable to newer transnational associations, it can still serve to prevent the imposition of the will of one political community on others.

James Anaya has distinguished between "ongoing self-determination," which signifies self-government, and "constitutive self-determination" as the choice by a group of its political status (e.g., whether to form an independent state).[11] A strong interrelation between democracy and self-determination has been presented by Brian Mello, who sees self-determination as a fundamental human right, interpreted as equivalent to a group's right to political participation.[12] In my own account, people's rights to freely determine their own activity necessarily takes the form of codetermination of joint activities, that is, self-determination by the collectivity of the nature and direction of the shared activity. On this approach, self-determination by a group is re-characterized as a feature of democracy itself, where the *demos* is not limited to a conception of a people resident in a given territory (although it applies there), but pertains to all institutional contexts of decision-making. In political communities,

---

[9] Margaret Moore, "Introduction: The Self-Determination Principle and the Ethics of Secession," in *National Self-Determination and Secession*, ed. Margaret Moore (Oxford: Oxford University Press, 1998), 2–3. See also Margaret Moore, "The Territorial Dimension of Self-Determination," in *National Self-Determination and Secession*, ed. Margaret Moore (Oxford: Oxford University Press, 1998), 136–7.

[10] Gould, "Self-Determination." The current discussion of self-determination draws in part on that article.

[11] Allen Buchanan, *Justice, Legitimacy, and Self-Determination* (Oxford: Oxford University Press, 2007), 332–3. citing James S. Anaya, *Indigenous Peoples in International Law* (Oxford: Oxford University Press, 1996), 81.

[12] Brian Mello, "Recasting the Right to Self-Determination: Group Rights and Political Participation," *Social Theory and Practice* 30, no. 2 (2004).

the *demos* needs to extend to everyone resident in a particular territory, and should not be limited to those of one or another nationality.

For political communities, this reframed conception of self-determination captures important aspects of the older view, but decoupled from a requirement of strong sovereignty. It would emphasize communal autonomy, or the idea that a group of people living together, with something of a common history, established practices, and an overlapping set of shared goals and cultures, have a right to codetermine the course of their projects and activities together. The view here suggests that this sort of ongoing community has to be inclusive and open to all people resident in its territory.

There are two aspects of the traditional understanding of self-determination that complicate matters here. The first problem is posed neatly in a formulation by Ivor Jennings, who writes, "On the surface, it [the principle of self-determination] seemed reasonable: let the people decide. It was in fact ridiculous because the people cannot decide until somebody decides who are the people."[13] This issue of the constitution of the *demos* is referenced in the sense of self-determination that James Anaya sets out as "constitutive self-determination," that is, as the choice by a group of its political status, as, for example, an independent state.[14] Even if we move away from the specified limitation to states and see self-determination as a possibility in any common activity, including social associations and economic institutions, it would seem that the particular common activity itself probably cannot wholly be constituted by democratic means. Although the choice of a constitutional framework for a collectivity may proceed democratically, it is unlikely that we can regard the initial formation of this collectivity as subject to democratic choice without entering into an infinite regress. In terms of actual collectivities, whether political or associative, it is unreasonable to characterize them as arising through democratic choices, although they may increasingly arise through choice itself, and such voluntariness is probably a normative desideratum for them, to the degree that it can be achieved.

Thus, my view of common activities does not see them as primarily constituted through democratic means but rather as contexts relevant for democratic decision that are given through the range of activities in which people cooperate to realize shared goals. While it is desirable that these be voluntarily constituted to the extent possible, this does not entail the circularity involved in regarding these contexts as themselves arising democratically. In addition, a substantial set of these shared contexts,

---

[13] Moore, "Introduction," 2.

[14] Buchanan, *Justice, Legitimacy, and Self-Determination*, 332–3. Citing *Ibid.*, 81.

particularly those associated with cultures, involve appropriation of traditions and histories that are initially given to us rather than created *de novo*.

Another crucial aspect of self-determination that is missing from this democratic interpretation is the connection between self-determination and territory (stressed by Margaret Moore),[15] which is especially relevant where nation-states are involved. While this is an important point that may properly set limits to the permissibility of secession in international law, it would seem to be the feature of self-determination that is most in need of revision in view of increasing global integration, particularly with the emergence of new forms of transnational localities and of cross-border regionalism. These can take the form of strong communities across literal borders or at greater distance; they can involve the devolution of political power to smaller units; and they can involve the federation of units into larger regional groupings. In some of these cases, territory itself is unimportant, for example, in the worldwide associations of scientists that have some new influence, whereas in others, the relevant territory simply shifts. Theorists like Johan Galtung have argued for the priority of municipalities within transnational democracy (though mainly on the ground that they are relatively well run compared with nation-states).[16] And again, autonomist movements have stressed that positive forms of globalization can be constructed only through a developmental process in which local groupings come to stand in solidaristic relations with others. The approach here emphasizes the deep analogy among the various associations, institutions, and groupings, whether of peoples or nation-states, all of which are susceptible to being characterized as self-determining in the relevant democratic sense. When it is recognized that these groupings are increasingly overlapping and networked, the priority of membership in just one such unit (or where there is dual citizenship, in two) will perhaps lose some of its force. While some theorists will regard this as a loss, these multiple memberships can also contribute to minimizing the exclusiveness and unfairness that besets many cases of national citizenship, and may permit addressing more squarely the requirements of global justice.

An additional strength of this reading of democratic self-determination is that it can discourage imposing democracy by force on other communities or nation-states, even as sovereignty becomes somewhat reduced in its relevance over time. It thus bears on the contemporary issue of

---

[15] Moore, "The Territorial Dimension of Self-Determination."
[16] Johan Galtung, "Alternative Models for Global Democracy," in *Global Democracy*, ed. Barry Holden (London: Routledge, 2000).

rightful forms of democratization. In the approach presented here, democracy itself has to be self-determined rather than other-determined or imposed. That is, if democracy is an expression of freedom and if it is the collective form of self-determination, the agents directly involved in the relevant community have to take the lead in implementing democratic forms of decision through their own actions. This requirement of self-directed democracy applies both to the creation of frameworks for democratic decision (e.g., constitutions specifying democratic powers, procedures, and protections), and to the use of democratic procedures and institutions within those frameworks.[17]

Democratic accountability and transnational representation: extending participation in cross-border decision-making

How can the two criteria for determining the appropriate scope for democratic decisions – common activities and all-affected – be applied transnationally? Analysts of international affairs have tended to assume that democratic participation and representation are inapplicable to international and transnational organizations, including intergovernmental organizations, international nongovernmental organizations, and, of course, transnational corporations. Even authors otherwise sympathetic to instituting greater accountability in world politics, for example, Ruth Grant and Robert Keohane (in a joint article), dismiss any claim to the relevance of democratic representation in that domain as wholly unrealistic and even undesirable.[18]

Grant and Keohane recognize a category of accountability that they call democratic accountability, understood as arising from democratic participation (optimally) and representation (secondarily). But they relegate this to the traditional domain of the nation-state, apparently for both theoretical and practical reasons. Practically, requiring democratic accountability from international organizations like the WTO, the World Bank, or the UN is regarded as too difficult and thus implausible as a demand. Theoretically, they emphasize the inherently wide scope of those affected by the decisions of these organizations and conclude that this renders democratic accountability irrelevant. They also believe it is

---

[17] I elsewhere discuss what is to be done when authoritarian governments prohibit people from operating in democratic ways. See Gould, *Rethinking Democracy*, chapter 12, and Gould, "Self-Determination."

[18] Grant and Keohane, "Accountability and Abuses of Power in World Politics."

undesirable to move in the direction of a global polity and its presumed correlate of a world government.

For Grant and Keohane, the criterion for democratic participation in decisions is a version of the "all-affected" principle: that all affected by a particular decision have a right to participate in making it. I have argued that this is too broad, because the set of all affected is very large, even larger than a polity, a feature exacerbated in the context of integrated spheres of activity worldwide. Tacitly, these authors appeal to a more delimited interpretation of the all affected principle – that those *subject to* the laws of a polity should have a role in participating and deliberating about them, either directly or through their representatives.[19] Whatever one may think about the possible advantages of "subject to" over "affected by" in the context of nation-states, the matter becomes difficult in the case of transnational or international organizations, whether in the making of regulations, policies, or individual decisions. Here, there are no established polities, or clearly demarcated *demoi* or publics for whom democratic participation and representation are relevant. Yet, the effects of decisions by the organizations of global governance, especially the WTO, the World Bank, and the IMF, are felt by those at a distance and their decisions profoundly affect the life chances of many millions, if not billions, of people around the globe.

Grant and Keohane may be hasty in concluding that democratic accountability – as including participation and representation – is inapplicable to the institutions of global governance. They see a global public or people organized into a polity – now lacking globally – as the sole context for such democratic accountability. But their argument simply rules out this accountability in advance, by wrongly insisting that democratic rights require an organized polity modeled on a sovereign state. In this sense, their argument may have a question-begging aspect, since it claims that because there is no sovereignty in global governance there can be no democratic accountability in that sense. But whether democratic accountability is possible in light of the new diminution and restraints on sovereignty posed by these institutions is what is at issue and cannot be resolved by definition.

What, then, are the implications of the democratic criteria I have proposed? For large-scale institutional contexts, the equal rights of participation and deliberation in decisions concerning common activities

---

[19] Note, however, that sometimes this criterion of "subject to" or "governed by" is distinguished from that of "being affected," as in Cohen, "Procedure and Substance in Deliberative Democracy," especially 95 and 114, fn.1.

likely require a reliance on representation rather than direct participation, whereas in smaller-scale institutions and communities, there may be a role for direct participation in addition to representative forms. Thus I would not follow David Plotke's line of argument to the effect that all valuable participation occurs only in connection with representation, or in Plotke's terms, that representation just *is* democracy.[20] Plotke supposes that participation necessarily requires that everyone eligible must actually take part in a decision (focusing his remarks on Barber's early statement of this view).[21] Instead, participation requires only that people have rights to take part, not duties to do so. A strength of Plotke's account, however, is to recognize that representation should ideally involve participative elements, even in large-scale contexts, for example, in people having two-way contacts with their representatives. Yet, representation necessarily remains second best from a participatory perspective not only in failing to give full expression to people's own agency, but because in winner-take-all systems, the minority in fact voted against the particular representative. Thus while representatives presumably strive to represent all their constituents and can be held accountable for their activities, they are only in a partial sense to be regarded as chosen by all of them.

In the approach proposed in this work, participation remains essential in the shared determination of the direction of common activities, although it is easiest to implement in small-scale institutions. We can also say that there is no barrier in principle to democracy (whether formal or substantive) in these contexts coming to embody genuinely *equal* rights of participation, although the barriers in practice are formidable, particularly where powerful economic interests have come to dominate politics and much of social life. Is participation also required in the second case, for those at a distance who are affected in their fundamental interests, or will representation suffice there? Is equal participation even possible in the global context, given that people are normally *differentially* affected by the policies of international organizations?

As previously proposed, this second principle calls for substantial input into the functioning of global governance institutions, when people are impacted in their human rights. This sort of input could partly proceed online, in terms of contributions to the deliberations over their policies. Democratic rights here are also congenial to selecting representatives, especially because of the large number of people involved and how

[20] David Plotke, "Representation Is Democracy," *Constellations* 4, no. 1 (1997).
[21] Benjamin Barber, *Strong Democracy* (Berkeley: University of California Press, 1984).

dispersed they are from the centers of power. Some direct participation is possible in giving those affected a leading role in decisions about local projects and in articulating their own basic needs and interests.

Some short- and long-term proposals

As discussed in Chapter 1, international institutions and transnational corporations can be required to prepare human rights impact assessments as a regular part of their development of policies and rules. These would be comparable to currently mandated technology assessments or environmental impact statements, but would require the development of new forms suited to the subject matter. These human rights assessments would specify likely impacts of proposed policies on affected groups, which would vary from case to case. Given the differential nature of these impacts, it may be possible to construct ad hoc representation to meet the needs of each case. This new direction would likely presuppose rights of appeal to human rights courts at both regional and more fully global contexts. Regional human rights courts, constructed through region-wide agreements, could also help to provide a framework of appeal for the cross-border associations within their domains.[22]

We have already moved to the terrain of institutional innovation. It is not possible to deduce institutional models from a concept, as it were, because we are dealing with an emerging and dynamic international and increasingly global system. We can nonetheless explore some directions for institutional innovations that accord with the two criteria for the scope of democracy.

In the relatively small-scale contexts of social and economic institutions, and in local communities, democratic rights are based on existing cooperative arrangements and reflect the growing interdependencies among the members or constituencies. In delimited contexts, where face-to-face interaction is viable, processes can ideally be deliberative and also substantive, in that they are founded on reciprocity among participants. Controversially, perhaps, this model extends democratic decision-making to firms and other economic institutions (discussed Chapter 14). It also calls for the expansion of democratic decision-making in new ecologically based communities, for example, between the northern Midwestern U.S. states and Canada. In some ways, participatory forms could be relevant

---

[22] Yet another avenue of appeal could be provided by extending the right to petition to these international institutions. See James Nickel, "Gould on Democracy and Human Rights," *Journal of Global Ethics* 1, no. 2 (2005).

on the Internet, where temporal simultaneity can replace spatial proximity as a basis for community. Internet groups, forums, or collaborative websites can sometimes exemplify features of affiliation and care, or of easy dialogue, thought to be characteristic of local communities (though they may also manifest hatred and stilted dialogue).

In broader institutional contexts, collective or joint decision-making could come to be applied to regional associations, besides the EU, in the first instance among contiguously situated nation-states. This process should not be seen as exclusively political or as confined to matters traditionally addressed by nation-states. The democratic principle advanced would also sit well with a variety of functional associations, for example, of an economic nature, where the economic associations are themselves divided by sector, with membership drawn from all those active in that particular sector, and where they cooperatively join with others from their region in decision-making.

Representation in all these spheres could either be informal, as it is now with civil society organizations, especially NGOs and INGOs, or it could become more formalized. Civil society organizations themselves could be expected to develop more democratic modes of decision-making, in order to gain fuller legitimacy in such forms of representation. The critique to which such organizations have been subject, namely, that they are wholly unaccountable, seems incorrect in the main. Some of them already incorporate democratic procedures; and the grassroots organizations especially are more accountable than the dominant international organizations. Yet it must be admitted that NGOs and the institutions of civil society could go further in introducing democratic procedures for electing representatives and permit greater participation in their decisions on the part of those for whom they claim to speak.

Beyond the multiplicity of regional and cross-border communities or other new bodies that can permit participation and representation regarding cooperative or common activities, there have been proposals for strictly political transnational representation or assemblies. Philippe Schmitter has proposed reciprocal representation in parliaments within the EU.[23] Others recommend implementing joint elections for representatives within regional political bodies,[24] and of course regional political

---

[23] Philippe Schmitter, "Exploring the Problematic Triumph of Liberal Democracy and Concluding with a Modest Proposal for Improving its International Impact," in *Democracy's Victory and Crisis*, ed. Axel Hadenius (Cambridge: Cambridge University Press, 1997).

[24] Hassan El Menyawi, "Toward Global Democracy: Thoughts in Response to the Rising Tide of Nation-to-Nation Interdependencies," *Indiana Journal of Global Legal Studies* 11, no. 2 (2004).

parties can be cultivated. We have already noted the important proposal for a "Global Peoples Assembly" within the UN, advocated by
Richard Falk and Andrew Strauss.[25] Such a more representative second
assembly within the UN, with representatives chosen at large, would be
an advance over the present situation. Yet, if it is thought to involve a
single global assembly or parliament with very substantial power, one can
worry whether it would provide sufficient space for diversity of cultural
perspectives, and also whether it would raise the possibility of a global
misuse of power, in view of human error. In this respect, the development of regional associations, particularly for the purposes of human
rights protection and fulfillment, along with new representative institutions at regional levels, might enable fuller recognition of the diversity
that currently exists globally and would constitute a more multicentric
approach to transnational representation. Regional and global directions
for democracy are compared and evaluated further in Chapter 15.

In terms of the institutions of global governance, the second democratic
criterion, which takes into account the impact of decisions on people's
fundamental human rights, would seek enhanced representation for distant people within these institutions, including economic ones, such as
the World Bank and the WTO, or within their eventual more democratic
replacements. Such representation would need to go beyond the relatively weak proposals for consultation by these international organizations
with INGOs. Beyond simply certifying these civil society organizations,
it would be necessary to work out established modes of representation for
people impacted by the various policies, rules, and regulations enunciated
by these organizations. These representatives could be either standing or
ad hoc, and the problem of assuring some measure of equality in choosing
them would be more urgent in the case of determining standing representatives. On the principle of global affectedness, the representation
of distantly affected people is of greater consequence than is the standard accountability of these organizations to the nation-states that set
them up.

This responsiveness to distant others follows from the normative priority of a cosmopolitan set of human rights in global affairs, as discussed
in earlier chapters, and specifically derives from the idea that political,
economic, and social organizations ought to be structured so that people
can fulfill their human rights through the functioning of these organizations. The democratic principle would therefore support expansive and
regularized representation for people, especially from poor and developing countries, within these organizations. It would also support ad hoc

---

[25] Falk and Strauss, "Global Peoples Assembly."

representation procedures based on specific human rights assessments of prospective policies, rules, and plans. Finally, the application of the affectedness principle globally also supports proposals for reform of the UN and its agencies, to reduce the democratic deficit that is evident in its current functioning and to make it an effective force in realizing human rights, including the economic and social ones in its purview.

14 Democratic management and international labor rights

Introduction

Across 100 countries of the world, cooperatives have over 800 million members,[1] a fact that led the UN to declare 2012 the International Year of Cooperatives.[2] Indeed, a 2008 report by the International Co-operative Alliance based in Geneva states that the top 300 cooperatives generated as much as the tenth largest economy in the world, with revenues of $1.1 trillion.[3]

Concerning a broad range of forms of worker participation in the United States, Gar Alperovitz has noted that despite growing inequality in income and wealth, an increasing number of Americans are involved in co-ops, worker-owned companies, and other alternative forms of economic organization. Alperovitz writes, "Some 130 million Americans, for example, now participate in the ownership of co-op businesses and credit unions. More than 13 million Americans have become worker-owners of more than 11,000 employee-owned companies, six million more than belong to private-sector unions."[4] He goes on to say: "If such cooperative efforts continue to increase in number, scale and sophistication, they may suggest the outlines, however tentative, of something very different from both traditional, corporate-dominated capitalism and traditional socialism." The picture that Alperovitz paints here may be a bit rosy, even in regard to worker ownership, and it does not yet centrally address the more challenging aspiration for full-scale worker democracy or worker control.

My main interest in this chapter is in fact less with ownership than with employee participation in management, or in more maximalist

---

[1] http://uncoopsnews.org/?p=159   [2] http://social.un.org/coopsyear/
[3] See www.inthesetimes.com/working/entry/5370/un_gives_nod_to_worker_co-ops_as_cle-veland_communities_embrace_model
[4] Gar Alperovitz, "Worker Owners of America, Unite!," *The New York Times* (December 14, 2011).

forms, with what has been called workplace democracy, worker self-management, or worker control. Democratic forms of management can be found throughout the world, most notably in cooperatives that combine ownership and management by workers (leaving aside the other forms such as consumer cooperatives). Worker co-ops are understood to be autonomous voluntary associations, enterprises jointly owned and democratically controlled by a group of individuals with common economic and social goals.[5]

Cases of worker self-management in corporations (with or without ownership) have persisted over the last decades, with the best-known example being the Mondragon Corporation Cooperativa in the Basque region of Spain. Mondragon is especially impressive in being the sixth largest corporation in Spain, with a wide diversity and scope in its production and services.[6] There are also important cooperative and self-management movements to be found elsewhere in Europe (e.g., in Emilia-Romagna, Italy), in Latin America (Argentina, Bolivia, and Venezuela), as well as in the United States, for example, in the plywood cooperatives of the Pacific Northwest, and in a variety of labor initiatives (e.g., among several nonprofits, medical institutions, and enterprises in the Cleveland area).[7] In the United States, however, more common than these robust cases of self-managing enterprises are the more limited sorts of participatory management promoted in business or management schools. This sort of management, in which employees have a say, especially regarding working conditions, is readily found among advanced technology firms, in professional firms such as law (which often involve shared ownership as well), and of course in universities.

With the increasing globalization of previously national economies, including corporations and the work process itself, we can ask whether such notions of democratic management or workplace democracy can plausibly be held to apply in those newly extended contexts. In addition, we can wonder whether the increasing internationalization of law and regulation could lend support to such democratic directions at work, whether in national, regional, or international contexts. Despite the interest of these questions, there has been remarkably little attention to the intersection of these issues. Instead, international labor and global justice theorists have almost exclusively focused on the more salient traditional

---

[5] www.ica.coop/coop/index.html

[6] Saioa Arando *et al.*, "Assessing Mondragon: Stability and Managed Change in the Face of Globalization," in *Employee Ownership and Shared Capitalism*, ed. Edward J. Carberry, *Assessing Mondragon* (Ithaca, NY: Cornell University Press, 2011).

[7] On the latter, see Gar Alperovitz, Ted Howard, and Thad Williamson, "The Cleveland Model," *The Nation* (March 1, 2010).

issues of eliminating forced labor, child labor, and other forms of exploitative conditions at work. They have also been centrally concerned with protecting the right to organize, and with establishing a minimum wage within states. I certainly do not want to question the importance of those crucial foci. And indeed, it is those concerns that we find primarily reflected in the existing international documents and agreements. But one is hard pressed to find any mention in the international documents or agreements of the significance of some degree of employee input into management decisions regarding their conditions of work, if not also of the desirability of more robust forms of democratic management.

Even in recent political philosophy, we can find only sporadic attention to the normative arguments in favor of introducing some measure of democratic participation to decisions taken within workplaces. Recently, some new interest has been generated by Rawls's late emphasis on what he called "property owning democracy" (though Rawls regrettably gave little attention to the democratic organization of work, per se).[8] Notions of employee participation in management have been integrated into business ethics curricula, in part under the influence of stakeholder theory, given that workers are among the main stakeholders. But the arguments for workplace democracy have not had much sway in this context, or more widely.

In this chapter, I begin by reviewing the normative basis for workplace democracy and democratic management, taking first the framework of traditional firms. The possibilities of worker-managed firms are rendered even more difficult in practice, however, by the increasingly transnational nature of contemporary workplaces, with their extended production and supply chains, and with the increased reliance on subcontracted work. I ask whether the arguments for worker participation need to take a different form in these transnational contexts. I then consider whether there is a basis for democratic management in international labor rights and also how democracy in production can plausibly be introduced or expanded in more global contexts.

In this analysis, workplace democracy is closely connected to the norm of global justice. This is so theoretically because, as I have argued in previous chapters, democracy is itself a requirement of justice, and both these concepts need to be reinterpreted in increasingly transnational, if not fully global, ways. In more practical terms, there is reason to think that at

---

[8] See, among others, Nien-He Hsieh, "Justice in Production," *The Journal of Political Philosophy* 16, no. 1 (2008); Martin O'Neill, "Liberty, Equality and Property-Owning Democracy," *Journal of Social Philosophy* 40, no. 3 (2009): 379–96; and Thad Williamson, "Who Owns What? An Egalitarian Interpretation of John Rawls's Idea of a Property-Owning Democracy," *Journal of Social Philosophy* 40, no. 3 (2009).

least in the form of cooperatives, worker-controlled enterprises can contribute directly to poverty elimination. In fact, it was this aspect, and their potential for contributing to development, that led the UN to designate 2012 as the Year of the Cooperative.[9] In addition, it can be supposed that democracy at work will produce more just outcomes, since if workers have democratic input into management decisions, they are unlikely to endorse exploitative or other unjust conditions of work. Indeed, in full-scale worker control, egalitarianism is built into the management procedures themselves, making egalitarian outcomes at least somewhat more likely as well. While existing labor law relies on collective bargaining to assure a modicum of worker protection regarding conditions of work, in this chapter I want to investigate the potential raised by fuller forms of democratic participation at work, in both national and international contexts. In all of this, I draw on, and extend, the arguments in earlier chapters.[10]

Normative arguments for democratic management and workplace democracy

Theorists have offered divergent grounds for worker self-management in firms. These range from arguments that analogize the exercise of authority within companies to political authority (Christopher McMahon) to those that call for some degree of participation in order to prevent arbitrary interference with the lives of workers, for example, by imposing unreasonable work conditions (Nien-He Hsieh).[11] Some writers argue for democratic management on the grounds that workers' interests are deeply affected by decisions at work (e.g., George Brenkert), while others stress the connection of decision-making to the autonomy of workers (Robin Archer), or to their rights of self-determination (Iris Marion Young).[12]

---

[9] http://social.un.org/coopsyear/about-iyc.html

[10] These themes were also developed in Gould, *Rethinking Democracy*, chapters 1 and 9, and Gould, *Globalizing Democracy*. The first of these contains the basic argument for democracy within firms, and the second focuses on the extension of both democracy and justice norms transnationally. Additional relevant publications include (among others): Gould, "Economic Justice" and Carol C. Gould, "Positive Freedom, Economic Justice, and the Redefinition of Democracy," in *Ethical Issues in Contemporary Society*, ed. J. Howie and G. Schedler (Carbondale, IL: Southern Illinois University Press, 1995).

[11] Christopher McMahon, *Authority and Democracy: A General Theory of Government and Management* (Princeton, NJ: Princeton University Press, 1994); Nien-he Hsieh, "Rawlsian Justice and Workplace Republicanism," *Social Theory and Practice* 31, no. 1 (2005).

[12] George Brenkert, "Freedom, Participation and Corporations: The Issue of Corporate (Economic) Democracy," *Business Ethics Quarterly* 2 (1992); Robin Archer, "The Philosophical Case for Economic Democracy," in *Democracy and Efficiency in the Economic Enterprise*, ed. Ugo Pagano and Robert Rowthorn (New York: Routledge, 1996);

My own argument for self-management or workplace democracy, originally developed especially in my *Rethinking Democracy* and suggested already in Chapters 4 and 13 of this book, is somewhat different from all of these.[13]

I see the right to participate in management by all those who work in a firm as an application of the more general right of those who are engaged in common or joint activity to codetermine the direction and course of that activity. This very general basis for democratic decision-making pertains, as we have seen, to all institutional contexts of human activity. A core aspect of the argument is an appeal to the conception of people's equal freedom. Inasmuch as collective projects or joint action with others are essential conditions for people's self-transformative activity, they need to be able to take part in them; and since they are equally agents in these contexts, none of them has the right to dominate or exploit others in this context and they must instead have equal rights to determine these activities. Since this activity is joint, this equal right must amount to a right to codetermine it. This then constitutes a democratic right to participate with others in decisions about its direction and course.

The second dimension of the argument identifies workplaces and corporations as forms of common activities. It sees them as examples of institutionalized rule-governed activities, which emerge over time and which may be more or less formally structured. They involve shared goals, which tend to be embodied within the everyday practices that characterize the functioning of these institutions, and are not always fully acknowledged by all actors. On this view, political communities are distinguished among the range of common activities by the multiplicity and complexity of the shared and overlapping goals that they aim to meet, but are not otherwise different in kind from other sorts of collectivities.

There are several things to note about this argument, which allow me to correct some misstatements of it by critics. The idea of self-development or self-transformation is not in fact a perfectionist one and the approach in this respect is consistent with liberalism (though it makes no claim to liberal neutrality per se).[14] In focusing on the development of capacities and the realization of long-term projects, this perspective remains open to recognizing a wide range of such capacities and projects. Further, the equal right to determine the course of joint activities largely follows from the equality of people's basic agency itself, that is, from the choice and

Iris Marion Young, "Self-Determination as Principle of Justice," *The Philosophical Forum* 11 (1979).

[13] See Gould, *Rethinking Democracy*, esp. chapters 1 and 9.

[14] Cf. Hsieh, "Justice in Production," 84.

intentionality characteristic of human action. This feature, along with the need to have access to the conditions for making choices and intentions effective, requires that no one be dominated in these collective situations.

The other element that may be overlooked in the argument for self-management is the social character of these individuals. As what I have called "individuals-in-relations," many of the crucial conditions for their activity are collective. Because the individuals are equal and no one has a right to dominate others, each has an equal right to determine their shared activity. Needless to say, this does not mean that all have to participate in making all decisions. They may choose managers and representatives.

The principle that serves to justify democratic management is not simply one of individual self-determination, nor is democracy required simply as a condition for self-development or for flourishing, nor simply for basic agency itself. A reliance on a principle of autonomy alone would suggest that other people outside the firm might sometimes need to participate in decisions within the firm more than do workers, if those decisions for some reason greatly impacted their possibilities for autonomy. A similar observation also afflicts interest views that see the basis for participation as residing in workers or others being affected by managerial decisions – it is indeed possible that some outsiders may be more affected than some workers.

Rather, the equal freedom principle that I have advanced, which sees decision-making as a crucial aspect of agency, is applied to the context of common or joint activities or institutions, constituted by shared goals. The additional element here thus appeals to the centrality of common activities for self-transformative agency, in that taking part in such activities cannot be traded off or eliminated in favor of more individualistic modes of self-transformation. In this social view, engaging in joint activity remains a basic condition for the development of capacities and projects. Where traditional liberal theorists have tended to make this point in regard to the state or political community, which they regard as indispensable and not susceptible to tradeoffs with individual goals that otherwise have priority, my own view extends this recognition to other forms of communities or institutions as well. It follows, then, that all those who are members of a firm have equal rights to codetermine its directions, plans, and policies, that is, to ultimate democratic rights of participation within it.

Yet another potential misinterpretation can be noted finally. Some critics of self-management emphasize that firms involve a right of exit and so the sort of voice required in politics is not needed in firms. Others, especially libertarians like Jan Narveson, believe the distinction of an economic firm from the state turns on the lack of coercion they see in the former.[15] However, what such critics fail to appreciate is that although workers can indeed leave any particular firm (if they can find another job!), they cannot leave all of them, since work is essential for gaining means of subsistence. Indeed, it is tempting to argue that this feature introduces a coercive element into the situation of workers, as our economy is presently constituted. It does not suffice, then, to say that workers can leave and find another firm they prefer to work for. Rather, given my positive argument for rights of democratic participation in firms, all of them need to be organized democratically, inasmuch as they are instances of collective activities organized around shared goals (acknowledged or not).

Before turning to the complexities for this account introduced by the increasing transnationalization and dispersal of work, we can recall some of the relations between justice and democracy on the approach advanced here, which are helpful for extrapolating to the case of global justice and transnational democracy. I have proposed that the principle of equal positive freedom, understood as (prima facie) equal rights of access to the conditions of self-transformation is the relevant principle of distributive justice and that the principle of democracy can be seen to follow from the principle of justice when taken in the essential context of collective activities. It is also the case that democratic decisions are more likely to produce just outcomes, but that is not the main justification for them. We can note that the principle of democratic participation crucially requires deliberation as well. But I do not follow strong deliberative democrats in seeing deliberation, even ideal deliberation, as the source of justification for democracy.[16]

This "common activities" account of the justification of equal rights of democratic participation provides one important criterion for the application of such democratic rights, but it is not the only criterion we need. As discussed in Chapter 13, the decisions of large collective actors – whether states or corporations or international institutions – increasingly affect people at a distance who are not members of these institutions, and may affect them in very important ways, even bearing on their possibilities of realizing basic human rights (including means of subsistence). In virtue of these significant distant effects on others, I introduced a second criterion for democratic participation, appealing to the "all-affected principle," and the interpretation I gave of this criterion can illuminate the context of transnational work.

---

[15] Jan Narveson, "Democracy and Rights," *Social Philosophy and Policy* 9 (1992).
[16] See Gould, *Globalizing Democracy*, chapter 1.

While the "all-affected" criterion is too broad for demarcating the scope of democratic participation within a given community, since some outsiders may be importantly affected by a given policy or decision, it is precisely such an all-affected principle that can help us in new global contexts. Recall that the criterion is qualified by the notion that it extends to those *importantly* affected rather than all affected *simpliciter*. Whenever distant people are affected by a decision or policy of powerful actors like corporations or states or the institutions of global governance, specifically, when they are affected in their capacity for fulfilling basic human rights, I argue that they have rights of democratic input. Especially since distant people may be differentially affected, it is plausible to call for input rather than strictly equal rights of participation, where some of the distant people or groups may in fact be more affected than the decision makers themselves. I have accordingly proposed that new methods be devised to enable broader public input into the relevant policies and decisions, including online opportunities to deliberate about the issues and to make policy recommendations. In this view, while strictly equal participation rights are restricted to the case of recognized collectivities or communities, the second principle mandating democratic "input" has considerable weight too, and cannot be satisfied by co-optation on the part of large organizations.

Modes of increasing democratic management in contemporary workplaces

One of the main problems in seeking to apply these normative requirements for democratic participation at work is that of delimiting the scope of workplaces, especially where corporations are transnational.[17] Another challenge is to figure out how each of the proposed criteria can apply to globally extended corporations, production and supply chains, and to subcontractors, and to deal with the multiplicity of alternative forms of work that can be found in contemporary economies. After briefly describing those issues, we can turn to the current formulations of international labor rights to determine their potential import for enhancing democracy at work.

The most straightforward application of the common or joint activities criterion is to firms, corporations, and other determinate economic organizations. Here the requirement is for all those working in the firm

---

[17] This problem is helpfully discussed in Yossi Dahan, Hanna Lerner, and Faina Milman-Sivan, "Global Justice, Labor Standards and Responsibility," *Theoretical Inquires in Law* 12, no. 2 (2011).

(perhaps after an initial period) to have rights to participate equally in fundamental management decisions, including concerning their own conditions of work and in the stronger case concerning the appointment of managers. This democratic principle can be extended to large corporations by combining decentralized decision-making in subunits with the representation of workers in higher-level managerial policy and decision-making. This very general characterization can apply whether or not there is employee ownership or more common forms of shareholder ownership.

However, traditional corporations, despite their enormous power, are not the only form of economic organizations and in fact employ a relatively modest share of workers worldwide. Certainly, the basic model discussed so far is readily applicable to small and large firms throughout a given economy. But the question remains how to extend democratic participation beyond clearly determined firms and corporations, and across borders. We need to consider here the broader claims of the employees of supplier firms and subcontractors, as well as of individuals working at a distance from traditional workplaces. Although some of these can be considered as members of a given corporate workforce, some cannot. In the latter case, there are two possible directions: One is to propose that if the corporations themselves become democratically managed they give the opportunity to any subsidiaries they have to themselves decide whether to introduce democratic management (and to choose some worker representatives to be included in more central corporate decision-making). Lest this sound wholly unrealistic, the Mondragon Corporation Cooperativa has, in fact, attempted to follow this model with respect to its global acquisitions and subsidiaries[18] (although it must be granted that there are features of its historical context that make Mondragon distinctive).

Another possibility is to make use of the second principle, the variant of the all-affected principle, and to propose that the corporate stakeholders who are not actual members of a firm, as well as the variety of other contemporary workers affected by powerful economic actors, should have some degree of democratic input into the relevant policies and decisions. These powerful actors would include not only global corporations but those institutions of global and regional governance that importantly regulate economic and financial activity and international trade and development (the WTO, the World Bank, the IMF; EU regulatory agencies). Although a less stringent criterion in not requiring equal participation of the members of an association, this second

---

[18] Monasterio, Jose Mari Luzarraga, Dionisio Aranzadi Telleria, and Iñazio Irizar Etxebarria. "Understanding Mondragon Globalization Process: Local Job Creation through Multi-Localization." http://community-wealth.org/sites/clone.community-wealth.org/files/downloads/paper-luzarraga-et-al.pdf

criterion is demanding as well, since the forms of democratic input that would be required are rare at present, and new forms (e.g., by way of online participation), would need to be developed.

Traditional business ethics tends to deal with these impacts on suppliers and subcontractors, as well as customers, host communities (and of course the workers), by appealing to stakeholder theory. But the latter approach counsels only that traditional corporate managers take the interests of these others into account. My proposal here, on the democratic grounds that people need to be consulted about their own needs, interests, and preferences, requires forms of consultation and democratic input that go considerably beyond this. A complication is that various economic actors are differentially impacted by corporate decisions, as well as by the economic global governance institutions. Accordingly, this second "affectedness" criterion could conceivably allow for some degree of differential input.[19]

Certainly, a requirement would follow for greater transparency in the decision-making processes of these powerful economic firms and institutions. As previously proposed, these global corporations and governance institutions could be required to prepare "human rights impact assessments" to add to the current environmental ones and other similar evaluations.[20] These assessments would not only focus on traditional human rights impacts, but centrally on economic and social ones, including labor rights that have been recognized in international law and regulations. It would also have to include an assessment of the foreseeable impacts of policies and actions on economic rights to well-being in the affected communities and on the ability of people there to fulfill their rights to education and health. In these ways, this requirement would go considerably beyond the usual emphasis on the minimal responsibility of global corporations.[21] Assessments of human rights impacts would be especially important for the economic institutions of global governance, which only barely attempt to aid in the fulfillment of these human rights, restricting their focus at best to efforts to avoid depriving people of their human rights (and often interpreting these rights mainly in civil and political terms).

---

[19] Cavallero, "Federative Global Democracy."

[20] Gould, "Structuring Global Democracy." The UN Global Compact (2011), a voluntary "strategic policy initiative," proposes a human rights due diligence process, but the human rights impact assessments envisioned here would go far beyond that both in the scope of rights covered and in the actions required of corporations. For the Global Compact statement on human rights, see http://www.unglobalcompact.org/Issues/human_rights/index.html.

[21] See, for example, Thomas Donaldson, "Moral Minimums for Corporations," in *Ethics and International Affairs*, 2nd edn., Joel Rosenthal (Washington, DC: Georgetown University Press, 1999).

Beyond this, it would be possible to open institutional and corporate deliberations to input from the wider set of workers importantly impacted by their decisions. This would likely have to take the form of online participation, perhaps coupled with occasional face-to-face discussion by delegates or representatives. Another option would be to use forms of "deliberative polling" among worker representatives. Although this polling model, advanced by James Fishkin and others,[22] has mainly been applied to public input into political decisions, there is no barrier in principle to using it to provide input in economic contexts as well. And while none of these suggestions would likely lead to strongly democratic outcomes, I think they represent an advance over the present situation.

To expand democratic input still further, another suggestion is to introduce new forms of standing or regular representation of grassroots groups of workers in the global governance institutions that regulate much of contemporary economic life. This representation (ideally based on networks of democratically managed enterprises) could initially take national forms or it could be developed in more fully transnational ways, with regard to existing regions, or by way of sectors of the economy or economic functions. Indeed, it is even imaginable to develop new representative institutions made up of these sectoral or functional economic groups that could be given some say over a set of economic regulations and policies, including those concerning labor and work, but that remains a direction for the future.

International labor rights and democratic management at work

I would like to turn finally to the question of whether international labor rights provide support for democratic management at work, and consider some possible directions for elaborating the rights in this regard. I cannot enter deeply here into the debates concerning whether labor rights should be considered human rights (as they are in fact recognized in the international agreements on human rights), but only note that my own position is squarely on the affirmative side. In my conception, human rights not only serve as constraints on states, but also importantly serve as goals for developing economic, social, and political institutions in order to make the various rights effective. Human rights taken normatively should be understood as specifying the conditions that people need for their basic life activity and for its flourishing, and thus include civil and political rights, along with economic and social ones. Among

---

[22] James Fishkin, *The Voice of the People: Public Opinion and Democracy* (New Haven, CT: Yale University Press, 1995).

the latter are the right to work and to just and favorable conditions of work, included in Article 23 of the UDHR, and articulated in Articles 6, 7, and 8 of Part III of the International Covenant on Economic, Social, and Cultural Rights.[23]

It is unfortunate, though hardly surprising, that democracy is limited to aspects of political democracy in Article 21 of the UDHR, and in fact, is not even mentioned by name there. As we saw in Chapter 4, only included are rights to take part in the government of one's country, to equal access to public service, and to periodic and free elections, with universal suffrage. There is apparently no way to interpret this article as supporting rights of democratic participation in economic or social institutions. More promising, however, is Article 23, and particularly, I suggest, its inclusion of a right to "just and favourable conditions of work." We have seen that the conception of justice implies a requirement for democratic management. More specifically, justice as equal rights of access to the conditions of self-transformation – where taking part in common activities is one of these conditions – implies a requirement to be able to codetermine these activities (on the ground of people's equal agency). On this interpretation, then, justice at work, or just conditions of work, ought to include rights of democratic management. While the account of justice here differs from the dominant Rawlsian one, I think the connection I highlight between justice and democratic participation is a strong one. As noted too, even many Rawlsians have recently come to see justice in production as presupposed in Rawls's own view and as implying democracy at work in various ways.[24] (In those approaches, the connection between justice and democratic management is not as direct as on my view, but rather tends to proceed via such notions as protection from arbitrary interference for workers, or the recognition of meaningful work as among the social bases for self-respect.)[25]

The core suggestion then is that democratic management is in fact needed to insure just conditions of work, and I propose that this specific requirement should be elaborated in further interpretations of the relevant human rights articles. Besides this, one could argue that opportunities for democratic participation are needed instrumentally in order to assure that some of the other articulated labor rights and their specifications can be met in practice. This is especially evident in regard to Article 3:3 of the UDHR, enunciating the right to just and favorable remuneration, as well as for the rights enumerated in Article 7 of the Covenant,

---

[23] International Covenant on Economic, Social and Cultural Rights. Adopted and opened for signature, ratification and accession by General Assembly resolution 2200A (XXI) of 16 December 1966, entry into force 3 January 1976.
[24] See note 4 above. [25] See Hsieh, "Rawlsian Justice"; Hsieh, "Justice in Production."

including not only fair wages and a decent living, but importantly also "safe and healthy working conditions," equal opportunities for promotions, and "rest, leisure and reasonable limitation of working hours." It is plausible to suppose that worker participation in management decisions and in setting policies would more likely ensure the fulfillment of these other rights than would traditional forms of corporate or employer management.

Interestingly for our purposes, democracy is explicitly included in international labor rights only in connection with the right to form trade unions.[26] The connection of unions to democracy is implied in the Covenant, in the notion of the promotion and protection by workers of their interests, and the restriction on limiting these rights to organize only to those necessary for security in "a democratic society." But the connection to democracy is especially highlighted in the ILO's fundamental principle dealing with trade unions, as well as in two ILO conventions, which tie the right to organize to freedom of association (Freedom of Association and Protection of the Right to Organise Convention, 1948, and the Right to Organise and Collective Bargaining Convention, 1949). The ILO also points out that the rights of association and collective bargaining themselves contribute to the achievement of decent conditions at work. In addition, the ILO states that collective bargaining promotes "peaceful, inclusive, and democratic participation of representative worker's and employers' organizations."[27]

This right of workers to freely form unions and to bargain collectively would remain important for worker-owned firms, as well as for worker-managed ones, if they were large and fell short of full worker control. This right certainly remains critical for any weaker forms of participatory management that currently exist or might be introduced. Moreover, the connection of political democracy with unions would remain even where worker-managed firms proliferated, given the abiding importance of free associations, and given the ways that common interests are standardly advanced within such political democracies.

Nonetheless, the restriction of democracy within international labor rights only to unions and collective bargaining also reflects the sharp separation between employers and workers that characterize contemporary capitalist economies, and from the normative standpoint advanced in

---

[26] It should be noted that the EU goes beyond this in recognizing a right to information and consultation with employees, as laid out in a set of Directives [http://www.worker-participation.eu/EU-Framework-for-I-C-P/Information-and-Consultation]. Needless to say, these directives fall short of calling for democratic management as argued for in this paper.

[27] www.ilo.org/declaration/principles/freedomofassociation/lang-en/index.htm

this book this restriction is unfortunate. I suggest that the existing rights remain crucial but that they need to be supplemented with explicit democratic rights of participation in management at work. As has been argued here, these new kinds of rights should maximally give all workers in a firm the opportunity to democratically determine the work process and choose managers who would be accountable to them. At the very least, and in the dispersed forms of contemporary work, the proposed rights should include requirements for strong forms of democratic input into management decisions, along with full democratic participation whenever possible. They also require that labor have delegates or representatives in the economic institutions of regional and global governance. Clearly, the further development of these labor rights in theory and practice is needed in the coming period, so that corporations, firms, and other economic actors can become responsive and accountable to those who labor in them and to workers and others who are deeply affected by their policies and decisions.

15   Regional vs. global democracy: possibilities and limitations

Introduction

Regionalism has come to the fore in recent economic and political developments and has been an important subject of attention in contemporary political science. Especially with the EU's rise to prominence over the last decades (despite the various setbacks), theorists have taken notice of the new forms of regional coordination not only there but in other parts of the world (e.g., Latin America, Southeast Asia), where these have largely centered on economic cooperation, though in some cases have involved political organization as well. Considerably less attention has been paid to the normative implications of these developments, though some theorists – especially of international law – have pointed to the regional human rights agreements that are beginning to be taken seriously, while others (especially of international relations) have commented on the democratic deficit in the EU.

Although theorists of democracy and human rights have analyzed the justifications and roles that these norms play in national contexts and increasingly even in global contexts, scant attention has been given to their potential for guiding and constraining regional political and economic development. Instead, cosmopolitan theorists of democracy and of justice often want to move the discussion directly from the level of the nation-state to that of the world as a whole, with little analysis of the emerging regionalism, increasingly recognized as important in practical affairs and public policy.

In discussions of cosmopolitan forms of democracy, what is at issue may be either full global democracy or else simply more democratic accountability in the institutions of global governance, again without attention to the normative requirements for democracy in the new regional associations. And where regionalism is considered in its implications for democracy, the discussions have tended to concern only the EU, with considerations directed to strengthening its parliament, implementing European political parties, and so on. Equally striking, insofar as regionalism is projected elsewhere and evaluated for its potential contributions for new forms of cooperation, it tends to be thought of exclusively in terms of the model provided by the EU. Yet, one of the main advantages of regionalization would seem to be the retention or enabling of a certain level of cultural diversity around the world, rather than supposing that all regions should simply follow the model of the EU.[1]

There have been noteworthy exceptions to the inattention to regions among normative theorists. Two political philosophers who have placed some weight on regionalism are Yael Tamir and Jürgen Habermas. While neither especially emphasizes regional human rights agreements, both have called attention to regions as important settings for increased transnational cooperation and regulation, particularly in regard to economic and social justice concerns. In this concluding chapter, I investigate how the development of regional forms of democracy bounded by regional human rights agreements constitutes an important new focus for normative theory. I also want to compare the arguments for such regional forms to those that have been given for more global institutions of democracy, presumably bounded by global human rights agreements and protections. A problem that characterizes many arguments for global democracy generally is the validation they continue to offer to old notions of sovereignty – by way of transposing them to the global level – and their tendency to pass over the numerous other domains in which democratic decision-making is normatively required. As we have seen, these domains include new transnational communities and interactions that crisscross these presumably orderly nested territorial frameworks, and also the quasi-public institutional contexts inhabited by corporations and other nonstate actors.

Extending regional democracy framed by human rights agreements

We can ask whether it is in fact desirable to prioritize new forms of regional democracy within human rights frameworks of regional scope. In the early 1990s, Yael Tamir offered a justification for an emphasis on regional cooperation based on the need for economic, military, and ecological coordination and planning beyond the level of nation-states. She argued that this sort of cooperation, as well as participation in decisions at that level, is required by what she calls *self-rule* rather than by considerations of *national self-determination*. The latter is best

---

[1] Michael Walzer endorses this feature of regionalism, which is an aspect of the pluralist arrangement he favors for the future. See Walzer, *Arguing About War*, 187–8.

realized by autonomous national communities below the level of nation-states that are "sheltered under a regional umbrella." On her account, "self-rule implies that individuals should affect all levels of the decision-making process," while "national identity is best cultivated in a small, relatively closed, and homogeneous framework."[2] Moreover, she goes on to argue, "Regional organizations will enable nations to cooperate as equal partners, rather than support one's nation domination over others." In Tamir's view, such a regional focus meets the need for larger-scale coordination in modern economies that goes beyond the capacities of existing nation-states and at the same time is "more likely to foster toleration and diversity than political arrangements based on oppression and domination."[3]

Tamir's notion of a regional alliance among nations suggests that the justification of a regional focus should not be framed directly in communitarian terms, where the region would simply be a larger or broader community. Rather, in her view, regions support communal concerns, practices, and traditions indirectly by potentially allowing nations more autonomy within them.

However, given that Tamir's understanding of a regional association is an ideal one in proposing nations generally smaller than existing states, we should perhaps instead look at the de facto current regions of the world and consider whether democracy within them is a plausible and appropriate normative desideratum. One difficulty is identifying what is to count as a region, and, especially if it is geographically defined, whether it encompasses an entire continent or is better understood as having a smaller extent.

Habermas advances a view that gives an important place to regionalism conceived along continental lines, for example, in the EU, which he regards as *transnational* in distinction from *supranational*, where the latter applies to fully global institutions and in particular the UN. In *The Divided West*, and his essay "A Political Constitution for the Pluralist World Society?," Habermas argues (like Tamir) for the enhanced role of regions in coordinating economic and ecological issues arising with globalization, instead of arguing for new forms of cosmopolitan democracy or world government to address them.[4] Indeed, even the institutions of global governance seem to play a secondary role in his account, inasmuch as he regards them as not strong enough to address the financial, monetary, regulatory, and redistributive requirements thrown up by economic

---

[2] Yael Tamir, *Liberal Nationalism* (Princeton, NJ: Princeton University Press, 1993), 151.
[3] *Ibid.*, 153.
[4] Jürgen Habermas, "A Political Constitution for the Pluralist World Society?" in *Between Naturalism and Religion: Philosophical Essays* (Cambridge: Polity, 2008); Jürgen Habermas, *The Divided West* (Cambridge: Polity, 2006).

globalization. Only strong continental regions can address these, he suggests, and perhaps such regions can develop new democratic legitimacy over time.

Nonetheless, Habermas seems to allow that a lot of the work of these regions can proceed by judicial and legal processes rather than strictly political means. This is even more strikingly the case for what he calls the supranational domain of the UN, which is to concern itself primarily with the maintenance of security and the protection of people against human rights abuses. Crucially, he limits the relevant human rights to the traditional civil and political ones, rather than economic and social ones. Moreover, he seems to think the former set of human rights can be protected through courts (especially a more effective International Criminal Court) as well as through a strengthened Security Council in the UN. In his view, less democracy and less politics is needed at this level, thereby defusing the criticism that democratic legitimacy is missing at this supranational level. Presumably, the situation is further aided by opening up the functioning of these institutions to deliberative input in a global public sphere. Along these lines, Habermas explains:

On this conception, a suitably reformed world organization could perform the vital but clearly circumscribed functions of securing peace and promoting human rights at the *supranational* level in an effective and non-selective fashion without having to assume the state-like character of a world republic. At the intermediate, *transnational* level, the major powers would address the difficult problems of a global domestic politics which are no longer restricted to mere coordination but extend to promoting actively a rebalanced world order. They would have to cope with global economic and ecological problems within the framework of permanent conferences and negotiating forums.[5]

In "A Political Constitution for the Pluralist World Society?" Habermas speaks more directly of a "constitutionalized world society," but explains it as "a multilevel system that can make possible a global domestic politics that has hitherto been lacking, especially in the fields of global economic and environmental policies, even without a world government."[6] Its structure is held to consist in three levels or "arenas." The first, the supranational is dominated by the UN and limited to the functions of "securing peace and human rights on a global scale." It remains composed of nation-states rather than world citizens. In order to deal with issues of global justice and even such lesser demands as the Millennium Development Goals, Habermas calls for the elaboration, in what he calls the transnational arena, of "regional or continental regimes equipped with a sufficiently representative mandate to negotiate for whole continents and to wield the necessary powers

---

[5] Habermas, *The Divided West*, 138.   [6] Habermas, "A Political Constitution," 322.

of implementation for large territories."[7] What he calls "a manageable number of global players"[8] would be needed to negotiate effective economic and environmental regulations. He believes that conflict among them could be avoided by the enhanced UN security regime he envisions. The third level in this account remains that of nation-states, which, however, require supplementation by regional alliances, to better deal with the "growing interdependencies of the global economy" that overtax "the chains of legitimation" within nation-states. As Habermas notes (in an appeal to the affectedness principle): "Globalized networks in all dimensions have long since made nonsense of the normative assumption in democratic theory of a congruence between those responsible for political decision-making and those affected by political decisions."[9]

Habermas views existing regional groupings (e.g., ASEAN, NAFTA, OAS) as generally weak and calls for strengthened alliances that could "assume the role of collective pillars of a global domestic politics at the transnational level . . . and confer the necessary democratic legitimacy on the outcomes of transnational political accords."[10] He regards the EU as the only current example of this sort of major player, although he calls for greater political integration there, with democratic legitimation, which would enable it to serve as a model for other regions. Yet, the extent of democratic decision-making within these regions is not clearly addressed here, and states (rather than the region's citizens) seem to retain many of their traditional prerogatives. Certainly, as far as interactions among the regions, Habermas envisions primarily forms of negotiation and compromise.

One of the advantages of the emphasis on regions that Habermas points to is that their development is a relatively realistic expectation in contemporary world affairs. Although their precise borders and scope remain an open question, it is evident that some degree of regionalization is taking place in regard to economic and even political matters. Thus I agree that it is plausible to argue for enhanced regional scope for democratic decision-making on the ground that it can be envisaged, as opposed to the more visionary introduction of full global democracy.

Before considering some other advantages of a regional focus, we can add an emphasis that is somewhat underplayed in Habermas's account. This is the importance of regional human rights agreements to frame increased regional democratization. Such agreements would importantly protect individuals operating in the new cross-border communities and provide a basis for appeal in connection with cross-border democratic

---

[7] *Ibid.*   [8] *Ibid.*, 325.   [9] *Ibid.*   [10] *Ibid.*, 326.

decisions about their collective activities. Moreover, these agreements have the potential not only to protect human rights but to establish these rights as goals around which social and economic development can be mobilized. Although Habermas at various points recognizes the significance of European human rights courts, his focus on guaranteeing human rights at the supranational level of the UN perhaps leads him to understate the importance of this emerging regional level of human rights agreements and jurisprudence.

Beyond its relative practicability, regional democracy has other possible advantages that can be noted, which have to do with notions of communities and with cultural issues and interpretations. Regionalization could permit greater expression of diversity in global mores and even in human rights interpretations. This would be the case only to the degree that the regions themselves, though not homogeneous, represent arenas for (overlapping) traditions and customs. Needless to say, this can only be an idealized representation because, like culture generally, the existing strands of traditions within regions are themselves very diverse. Yet, to the degree that there are overlapping shared histories and traditions, respecting these can enable some diversity not only in the forms of democratic decision-making but in the human rights interpretations that may be offered within these regional contexts.

The communitarian considerations have a similar bearing. Although quite disparate, some of the traditions and local mores are perhaps more similar to each other than they are to those in other regions. Instead of seeing the region as a single community, however, we can spell it out in a way that is consonant with the networking approach presented earlier. Like the social connections model, such an approach looks to actually existing interrelations that develop over time as serving to bring people together, not only in new collectives, but as sharing new sorts of goals and projects in relation to the economic, ecological, and political problems that they face. Further, such emerging spheres of common activity would serve to justify new domains for democratic decision-making.

A final point in favor of the regional emphasis is its connection to localities and hence to territory. Despite the virtual character of much activity by means of a global Internet, a connection to place remains significant. Of course, this territorial interpretation of regions can also be too restrictive, inasmuch as many contemporary activities and interconnected communities are truly transnational in a way that transcends regions. Even localities themselves can in a sense be transnational, as I have argued.[11] Perhaps most problematically, a region-centered approach

[11] Gould, "Negotiating the Global and the Local."

to democracy can fail to deal with the many problems that are truly global, most especially the ecological crisis posed by climate change.

Other drawbacks of the regional emphasis are normative as well as practical. In particular, we can mention the potential that these new forms of association might have for engendering conflicts between or among regions, thereby replicating and perhaps intensifying the conflicts among nation-states at this new level. In addition, it is possible that an established regionalism could reify and perhaps intensify cultural differences in the interpretation of basic international norms, including possibly weakening the force of some human rights.

As for the regional human rights agreements themselves, we can cite several problems. Only the European ones are really effective, and even there the implementation of them varies considerably and is less consistent and more difficult in parts of the continent (e.g., Turkey). The inter-American agreement is even less efficacious, and the African one almost not at all. Moreover, as James Cavallaro and Stephanie Brewer point out in their article "Reevaluating Regional Human Rights Litigation in the Twenty-First Century: The Case of the Inter-American Court" (2008), in situations where deference to the rule of law is lacking, such agreements are not respected.[12] Thus, there are two major problems with these agreements – they are lacking in most world regions, and where they exist, they are generally implemented in spotty fashion.

Extending democracy globally

We can now consider the alternative approach that emphasizes moving directly to global forms of democracy. Those who have advocated such an approach include Torbjörn Tännsjo, Raf Marchetti, and Eric Cavallero.[13] Although such global democrats may sometimes recognize principles of subsidiarity, the approach of so-called cosmopolitan democrats more explicitly argue for incorporating both regional and global perspectives.[14] I touch briefly on the role of subsidiarity in a final section in which I summarize the core elements of my own constructive view.

---

[12] James Cavallaro and Stephanie Erin Brewer, "Reevaluating Regional Human Rights Litigation in the Twenty-First Century: The Case of the Inter-American Court," *The American Journal of International Law* 102 (2008).

[13] Raffaele Marchetti, "Global Governance or World Federalism? A Cosmopolitan Dispute on Institutional Models," *Global Society* 20, no. 3 (2006); Marchetti, *Global Democracy*; Torbjörn Tännsjö, *Global Democracy: The Case for a World Government* (Edinburgh: Edinburgh University Press, 2008); Cavallero, "Federative Global Democracy."

[14] David Held, *Democracy and the Global Order* (Stanford, CA: Stanford University Press, 1995).

Raf Marchetti in a 2006 article and in his book *Global Democracy: For and Against,* and Eric Cavallero, in an article "Federative Global Democracy," have proposed robust conceptions of global democracy, understood in terms of a strong federation at the global level, which takes charge of decision-making about world affairs and operates through new global representative institutions or parliaments.[15]

Without reviewing their positions in detail here, I want to focus on a few philosophical issues that arise from their accounts and to defend and contrast the alternative view that I have presented on these matters. Earlier chapters have stressed the relevance of two criteria, which in different ways justify extensions of democracy beyond (and beneath) nation-states. We have seen that the "common activities" criterion proposes that democracy is called for in all institutional contexts where people are related in joint activities oriented to shared goals. These may also be called systems of cooperation, but that phrase may overestimate the orderly, intentional, and systematic character of these enterprises or shared activities, rather than seeing them as institutional contexts that have arisen historically or emerge in ongoing practical activities of production, social association, and governance. In all such institutional frameworks, increasingly of a transnational sort, I have argued that members of these associations have equal rights to participate in their direction. The second criterion addresses the impacts on distant people's human rights of the decisions and policies of global actors, both state and nonstate, and argues for giving these affected people input into the relevant decisions.

What lies behind the distinction between these criteria and also between notions of input and full participation is in part the critique I and others have offered of a complete reliance on an "all-affected" principle as the justification of democracy.[16] Yet, Marchetti relies on just such an "all-affected" principle in his justification for global democracy. He sees it as following from the idea that the choice bearers and the choice makers (in his terms) should be one and the same.[17] This then constitutes one interpretation of the principle of self-rule at the heart of many conceptions of democracy (cf. Tamir above). Marchetti adds the idea that this coincidence of choice bearers and makers applies to what he calls the public domain, or "public constituencies." Thus he proposes that: "A political principle has to be adopted that grants to all choice-bearing citizens as members of the public constituency in each level of

---

[15] Marchetti, "Global Governance or World Federalism?"; Marchetti, *Global Democracy.*
[16] Saward, "A Critique of Held," 37; Gould, *Globalizing Democracy,* 175–8.
[17] Marchetti, "Global Governance or World Federalism?," 289–90 and 294.

political action, including the global and trans-border, a political voice and the power to make the choice makers accountable."[18]

Despite this position's considerable appeal, two problems can be discerned in it: the first is the inherent vagueness involved in determining all affected by a given decision. Because of the widespread consequences of decisions and policies, particularly in the economic domain, it is difficult to contain the number of choice bearers or affected people. This could lead to moving nearly all decisions up to the global level, contrary to the intention of such theories to maintain some distinction among levels of decision-making. And if decisions all become truly global, clearly people's degree of input or influence on such decisions would become extraordinarily diluted. I have suggested that some notion of the important effects of decisions or policies needs to be added. Even so, we can wonder whether that will work to ground democratic decision-making, particularly if one wants to retain some notion of equal rights of participation, which would be violated by people's being differentially affected by decisions, as in fact they are.[19]

A second problem is that the demarcation of a *public constituency* remains somewhat obscure on Marchetti's account, and would have a question-begging air if it is to be used as criterial for determining who is to participate, since it is precisely in question just how a public is to be constituted, that is, who is to be included in which "public" decision-making process. We cannot assume that we know what the relevant public constituency is in advance, and it would be circular to define it in terms of those affected by a decision. Clearly, people are affected by private and interpersonal decisions as well, so it is natural that Marchetti would want to appeal to some notion of public issues or constituencies. But he would need an independent definition of those, which he does not seem yet to have provided.

A notion of affected interests shares the problem of interest views generally, inasmuch as the notion of interest is highly individual and not altogether clear in any case. Indeed, we can ask whether an individual can be adequately construed as a bundle or collection of interests; and also whether simple impact on individuals, taken apart from their social relations, can provide a sufficient basis for justifying democracy. The common activities view has an advantage is being both futural (defined by shared goals) and socially based, recognizing the diversity of arenas for collective actions and decision-making. It shares with Marchetti and others an emphasis on people's equal freedom, but understands this to require not only bare freedom of choice (which Marchetti highlights)

---

[18] *Ibid.*, 294.   [19] Saward, "A Critique of Held."

but also a positive notion of the development of people over time, in a sense that presupposes access to material and social conditions, and recognizes that people's activities can take both collective and individual forms.

Regarding the notion of impact on individuals which is central to "affected interests" approaches to justifying democracy, we can agree that such impacts are important, and perhaps especially so in regard to the exogenous effects of decisions on those who are not part of any given collectivity but importantly impacted by such decisions and policies. My suggestion has been that this gives rise to the somewhat less demanding requirement of significant input into the decision in question, and to a notion of due consideration of the affected interests rather than necessarily strictly equal rights to participate.

In a somewhat analogous way to Marchetti, Eric Cavallero uses the all-affected principle to argue for a federative account of global democracy. He specifies the principle in terms of "an analysis of relevant effects such that those relevantly affected by an activity should have a say in the democratic processes that ultimately regulate (or fail to regulate) it." He explains, "According to this interpretation, an individual is relevantly affected by the exercise of a sovereign competence if (1) its exercise imposes governance norms on her, or (2) its exercise could otherwise reasonably be expected to impose external costs on her."[20] He explains the first case by drawing on Andrew Kuper's *Democracy beyond Borders*[21] and on my *Globalizing Democracy and Human Rights*, pointing to the importance of the decisions and policies of the institutions of global governance that have decisive impacts on people's lives but in which they have no say. In this context, I have proposed devising new forms of democratic deliberation that permit democratic input into the policy making of these institutions, as well as introducing new forms of transnational representation into their functioning, initially through INGOs.

The second part of Cavallero's interpretation of this principle, the one that emphasizes external costs, is perhaps more problematic. A strength of his analysis is the detailed breakdown he gives of the types of external costs that may be relevant. With this analysis, Cavallero opposes my own proposal to specify "affectedness" in terms of important impacts on people's human rights, especially their basic human rights (which he understands in terms of "importantly affected interests"). He argues that my proposal is underinclusive. Cavallero gives the example of a river that

---

[20] Cavallero, "Federative Global Democracy," 56.
[21] Andrew Kuper, *Democracy Beyond Borders: Justice and Representation in Global Institutions* (Oxford: Oxford University Press, 2004).

two countries share, where, he argues, "it seems reasonable that citizens of the country downstream should have some say in determining what kinds and levels of pollutants are permitted to be discharged into the river upstream – even if unregulated discharges will not actually impact anyone's basic needs or human rights."[22]

In response to this objection, we can observe that many pollutants will in fact impact health, an important human right. This would support input by the affected second country into the decisions of the first regarding pollutants. Moreover, the criterion of impact on basic human rights concerns exogenous effects and does not rule out the emergence of new transnational communities that share economic and ecological interests and are organized as "common activities," which might happen in this case. More standardly, the recognition of important effects on distant people supplements the democratic rights of communities, whether these be existing or newly emerging, national or transnational. Finally, the democratic input required when people are significantly affected is designed to amplify the considerations offered by stakeholder theory rather than to replace them, and the latter considerations remain relevant to the case Cavallero cites. Even if the impacts on such stakeholders do not rise to the level of affecting their basic human rights, it would still be normatively required to consider their needs and interests in decision-making,[23] even if they are not given direct input into these decisions. Consideration of the impact on stakeholders can take the form, for example, of environmental impact assessments by the decision-makers, who should be expected to take these seriously as a guide to their policies.

On Cavallero's view, where policy decisions foreseeably impose external costs on others outside the polity in question, what he calls the "internalization condition" kicks in, which "requires that certain otherwise external costs be internalized through the constitution of composite polities comprising all who bear those costs."[24] The problem I see with this is that the external costs especially of economic policies are extremely wide-ranging and so might well drive us to fully global levels of "composite polities" too readily. Cavallero discusses this briefly by ruling out the adverse effects of macroeconomic policies that are designed to produce public goods.[25] But this exception is not adequately explained or justified in his account.

We can mention a few other difficulties with such global democracy views. One, evident in Cavallero's account, concerns its generalization

---

[22] Cavallero, "Federative Global Democracy," 56.
[23] Carol C. Gould, "Does Stakeholder Theory Require Democratic Management?," *Business and Professional Ethics Journal* 21, no. 1 (2002).
[24] Cavallero, "Federative Global Democracy," 58.   [25] *Ibid.*, 61.

of the notion of sovereignty to the global level. We can object that this would likely exacerbate the problems with sovereignty that were pointed out long ago by Harold Laski among others. As Jeanne Morefield notes, Laski argued that the notion of state sovereignty serves to obscure and maintain the underlying conflicts in society between capital and labor, and the role played by the state in upholding the power of large corporations by coercively maintaining institutions that protect unlimited private property.[26] Besides this, state sovereignty in its internal dimension has often involved the exercise of excessive coercion. It is not clear that simply expanding sovereignty to the global level will counter these problematic features.[27]

Further, global democrats like Marchetti and Tännsjö do not fully address the standard challenge that if all means of coercion were to come under the control of a world government, there would be no way to counter a tyrannical regime, if one arose. The possibility of such emergence is what can be called *the Weimar problem*. That is, it remains a possibility, though hopefully a distant one, that human error and some specific social circumstances could lead to the election of a dictator, especially if democracy is understood to consist entirely of voting and majority rule. The response that these theorists give is that tyranny is less likely with a democratic global government than without it. But this simply posits that the global government will continue to function democratically indefinitely. Indeed, according to an alternative line of argument, while the concentration of the means of coercion that such a system entails may indeed work out well, it could also function to exacerbate any anti-democratic or authoritarian tendencies that may arise and in that way eliminate freedom from a substantial portion of the populace. In short, then, while such global democratic views are appealing and have numerous strengths, they have so far been rather optimistic, and perhaps overly so, in disregarding the system defects that can arise from faulty institutional design or from human error (as well as from more malicious causes).

A multidimensional and interactive conception of democracy

We have proposed that an adequate conception of transnational democracy, attuned to the historical possibilities embedded in the present

---

[26] Jeanne Morefield, "States Are Not People: Harold Laski on Unsettling Sovereignty, Rediscovering Democracy," *Political Research Quarterly* 58, no. 4 (2005).

[27] Cavallero and other global democrats do usually propose some constraints on sovereignty in terms of human rights regimes. But the way these would work to constrain sovereignty and protect individuals is not much elaborated.

situation, should accommodate a diversity of existing forms of social organization, while still advancing more cosmopolitan frameworks of democracy, human rights, and global justice. The emphasis on beginning with the current situation suggests focusing on democratizing the functioning of global governance institutions – by enabling public input, deliberation, and transnational representation of those affected by their policies. But it also calls for turning these institutions, first, away from their contemporary deference to the interests of powerful nation-states and global corporations and, second, toward the task of minimizing exploitative economic conditions and achieving more egalitarian distributions of wealth and income, as we have seen is required by global justice. New regional forms of democracy, too, represent a potentially helpful way to manage emerging regional economic cooperation, within new or strengthened human rights agreements. Layers of global democracy are needed as well, most especially to deal with the global problems of mitigation and adaptation that are posed by climate change and for addressing its differential justice impacts, which are certain to worsen.

Yet, neither regional nor global democracy, nor even the democratization of the institutions of global governance, is sufficient for genuine transnational democracy. An additional requirement is to ensure that emerging cross-border communities – whether defined by their economic relations, ecological interconnections, or communicative networks – themselves operate democratically. Central, too, would be the intensification of opportunities for democratic participation not only in governmental contexts, but also for democratic management of firms and other smaller-scale institutions in economic, social, and cultural life.

In approaching these layers of self-rule and governance, the principle of subsidiarity, that decisions should be taken at the most local level possible, is a helpful guideline. Beginning with communities and localities as they are and emphasizing the interaction among them avoids efforts to reconstruct political communities from the top down. Still, to the degree that the present arrangement of nation-states is unjust when considered from the standpoint of the distribution of resources and historical factors like colonialism, there is much to be done to assure a measure of global justice and to begin to approach the requirement for which I have argued, namely, that of equal access to the conditions for self-development.

I have proposed that fulfilling basic human rights – as conditions for any human activity whatever – and the further rights needed for the self-transformation of people over time – constitutes a viable approach to achieving global justice in the twenty-first century. I have also argued that this process presupposes not only the recognition of all as free, as bearers of human rights, but also the amplification of democratic voice in the institutional contexts of their political and economic activity – locally, nationally, and transnationally. The proposal has been that this extension of democracy is founded on people's freedom – as individuals-in-relations – and on their need for common or cooperative activities, as well as on the requirement for their having a say when decisions importantly affect them, especially as regards their human rights. We have seen that democracy is based on the centrality of both action and interaction in social life, and necessarily also involves the intensive interaction among existing communities within a more interconnected world.

In short, I have argued for a *multidimensional* and *interactive* approach to democracy. Among the conditions needed for interactive democracy would be a human rights framework that preserves some openness for local diversity in interpretation, compatible with an overall commitment to the equality and universality of the human rights norms. These norms also need to be given more traction, as legally binding protections for individuals and minorities, including in their transnational interrelations, and also crucially as motivating goals around which social justice movements can mobilize and new institutions created for fulfilling them.

These social movements and solidarity networks are of central importance since they work to construct forms of global justice on the ground. They can also work to instantiate democratic modes of interaction among themselves and catalyze democratic transformations in existing institutions. Beyond this, a final condition is the cultivation of an active and interactive practice of democracy as a way of life, in interpersonal and institutional domains of experience. In this perspective, the recognition of the freedom of each can be seen to be fully compatible with deepening and extending their modes of cooperation in meeting the needs of all.

Works cited

Abizadeh, Arash. "Does Collective Identity Presuppose an Other?" *American Political Science Review* 99, no. 1 (2005): 45–60.

Al-Hibri, Azizah. "Developing Islamic Jurisprudence in the Diaspora: Balancing Authenticity, Diversity and Modernity." *Journal of Social Philosophy* 45, no. 1 (2014): 7–24.

"Islamic Constitutionalism and the Concept of Democracy." *Case Western Reserve Journal of International Law* 24, no. 1 (1992): 1–27.

"Islamic Constitutionalism and the Concept of Democracy." In *Border Crossings: Toward a Comparative Political Theory*, edited by Fred Dallmayr (Lanham, MD: Lexington Books, 1999), 61–87.

"An Islamic Perspective on Domestic Violence." *Fordham International Law Journal* 7 (2003): 195–224.

Allen, Amy. "Rethinking Power." *Hypatia* 13, no. 1 (1998): 21–40.

Alperovitz, Gar. "Worker Owners of America, Unite!" *The New York Times* (December 14, 2011).

Alperovitz, Gar, Ted Howard, and Thad Williamson. "The Cleveland Model." *The Nation* (March 1, 2010).

Anaya, James S. *Indigenous Peoples in International Law* (Oxford: Oxford University Press, 1996).

An-Naim, Abdullahi. "Human Rights in the Muslim World: Socio-Political Conditions and Scriptural Imperatives." *Harvard Human Rights Law Journal* 3 (1990): 13–52.

Arando, Saioa, Fred Freundlich, Monica Gago, Derek C. Jones, and Takao Kato. "Assessing Mondragon: Stability and Managed Change in the Face of Globalization." In *Employee Ownership and Shared Capitalism*, edited by Edward J. Carberry (Ithaca, NY: Cornell University Press, 2011), 241–72.

Archer, Robin. "The Philosophical Case for Economic Democracy." In *Democracy and Efficiency in the Economic Enterprise*, edited by Ugo Pagano and Robert Rowthorn (New York: Routledge, 1996), 13–35.

Archibugi, Daniele. "From Peace between Democracies to Global Democracy." In *Global Democracy: Normative and Empirical Perspectives*, edited by Daniele Archibugi, Mathias Koenig-Archibugi, and Raffaele Marchetti (Cambridge: Cambridge University Press, 2011), 254–73.

Archibugi, Daniele, Mathias Koenig-Archibugi, and Raffaele Marchetti (eds.). *Global Democracy: Normative and Empirical Perspectives* (Cambridge: Cambridge University Press, 2012).

Arendt, Hannah. *The Human Condition* (Chicago: University of Chicago Press, 1958).

The Life of the Mind (New York: Harcourt, 1989).

On Revolution (New York: Viking, 1963).

On Violence (New York: Harcourt, 1969).

Avineri, Shlomo. *Hegel's Theory of the Modern State* (Cambridge: Cambridge University Press, 1972).

Baber, Harriet E. "Adaptive Preference." *Social Theory and Practice* 33, no. 1 (2007): 105–26.

Barber, Benjamin. *Strong Democracy* (Berkeley: University of California Press, 1984).

Bartky, Sandra Lee. *Femininity and Domination* (New York: Routledge, 1990).

Sympathy and Solidarity (Lanham, MD: Rowman & Littlefield, 2002).

Bayefsky, Anne F. "General Approaches to the Domestic Application of Women's International Human Rights Law." In *Human Rights of Women*, edited by Rebecca Cook (Philadelphia: University of Pennsylvania Press, 1994), 351–74.

Bayertz, Kurt. "Four Uses of 'Solidarity'." In *Solidarity*, edited by Kurt Bayertz (Dordrecht: Kluwer, 1999), 3–28.

"Staat Und Solidarität." In *Politik und Ethik*, edited by Kurt Bayertz (Stuttgart: Reclam, 1996), 305–30.

Beitz, Charles. "Human Rights as a Common Concern." *American Political Science Review* 95, no. 2 (2001): 269–82.

The Idea of Human Rights (Oxford: Oxford University Press, 2009).

Political Theory and International Relations (Princeton, NJ: Princeton University Press, 1979).

Benhabib, Seyla. *The Claims of Culture* (Princeton, NJ: Princeton University Press, 2002).

The Rights of Others (Cambridge: Cambridge University Press, 2004).

Situating the Self (New York: Routledge, 1992).

Berlin, Isaiah. "Two Concepts of Liberty." In *Four Essays on Liberty* (Oxford: Oxford University Press, 1969), 118–72.

Beveridge, F., and S. Mullally. "International Human Rights and Body Politics." In *Law and Body Politics: Regulating the Female Body*, edited by J. Bridgeman and S. Millns (Aldershot: Dartmouth, 1995), 240–72.

Blake, Michael. "Distributive Justice, State Coercion, and Autonomy." *Philosophy and Public Affairs* 30, no. 3 (2001): 257–96.

Bohman, James. *Democracy across Borders: From Dêmos to Dêmoi* (Cambridge, MA: MIT Press, 2007).

Public Deliberation: Pluralism, Complexity, and Democracy (Cambridge, MA: MIT Press, 1996).

Brenkert, George. "Freedom, Participation and Corporations: The Issue of Corporate (Economic) Democracy." *Business Ethics Quarterly* 2 (1992): 251–69.

Brenner, Neil. *New State Spaces: Urban Governance and the Rescaling of Statehood* (Oxford: Oxford University Press, 2004).

Brock, Gillian. *Global Justice* (Oxford: Oxford University Press, 2009).

"Taxation and Global Justice: Closing the Gap between Theory and Practice." *Journal of Social Philosophy* 39, no. 2 (2008): 161–84.

Buchanan, Allen. "Human Rights and the Legitimacy of the International Order." *Legal Theory* 14 (2008): 39–70.

Justice, Legitimacy, and Self-Determination (Oxford: Oxford University Press, 2007).

Buchanan, Allen, and Robert O. Keohane. "The Legitimacy of Global Governance Institutions." *Ethics & International Affairs* 20, no. 4 (2006): 405–37.

Cabrera, Luis. *The Practice of Global Citizenship* (Cambridge: Cambridge University Press, 2010).

Calhoun, Craig. "Imagining Solidarity: Cosmopolitanism, Constitutional Patriotism, and the Public Sphere." *Public Culture* 14, no. 1 (2002): 147–71.

Caney, Simon. *Justice Beyond Borders* (Oxford: Oxford University Press, 2005).

Cathcart, Thomas, and Daniel Klein (eds.). *Plato and a Platypus Walk into a Bar...* (New York: Harry N. Abrams, 2007).

Cavallaro, James, and Stephanie Erin Brewer. "Reevaluating Regional Human Rights Litigation in the Twenty-First Century: The Case of the Inter-American Court." *The American Journal of International Law* 102 (2008): 768–827.

Cavallero, Eric. "Federative Global Democracy." In Special Issue on *Global Democracy and Exclusion*, ed. Ronald Tinnevelt and Helder de Schutter. *Metaphilosophy* 40, no. 1 (2009): 42–64.

Chadwick, Andrew. "Web 2.0: New Challenges for the Study of E-Democracy in an Era of Informational Exuberance." *I/S: A Journal of Law and Policy for the Information Society* 5, no. 1 (2009): 9–41.

Chan, Joseph. "A Confucian Perspective on Human Rights for Contemporary China." In *The East Asian Challenge for Human Rights*, edited by Joanne R. Bauer and Daniel A. Bell (Cambridge: Cambridge University Press, 1999), 212–37.

Charlesworth, Hilary. "Human Rights as Men's Rights." In *Women's Rights, Human Rights*, edited by Julie Peters and Andrea Wolper (New York: Routledge, 1995), 103–13.

"What Are 'Women's International Human Rights'?" In *The Human Rights of Women*, edited by Rebecca J. Cook (Philadelphia: University of Pennsylvania Press, 1994), 58–84.

Christman, John. "Autonomy in Moral and Political Philosophy." In *The Stanford Encyclopedia of Philosophy*, edited by Edward N. Zalta (2011).

Code, Lorraine. *What Can She Know?* (Ithaca, NY: Cornell University Press, 1991).

Cohen, Joshua. "Deliberation and Democratic Legitimacy." In *The Good Polity*, edited by Alan Hamlin and Phillip Pettit (New York: Blackwell, 1989), 18–27.

"Is There a Human Right to Democracy?" In *The Egalitarian Conscience: Essays in Honour of G. A. Cohen*, edited by Christine Sypnowich (Oxford: Oxford University Press, 2006), 226–48.

"Procedure and Substance in Deliberative Democracy." In *Democracy and Difference*, edited by Seyla Benhabib (Princeton, NJ: Princeton University Press, 1996), 95–119.

Cohen, Ted. *Jokes: Philosophical Thoughts on Joking Matters* (Chicago: University of Chicago Press, 1999).

Cook, Rebecca (ed.). *The Human Rights of Women* (Philadelphia: The University of Pennsylvania Press, 1994).

"State Accountability under the Convention on the Elimination of All Forms of Discrimination against Women." In *The Human Rights of Women*, edited by Rebecca Cook (Philadelphia: The University of Pennsylvania Press, 1994), 228–56.

Copelon, Rhonda. "Intimate Terror: Understanding Domestic Violence as Torture." In *The Human Rights of Women*, edited by Rebecca Cook (Philadelphia: The University of Pennsylvania Press, 1994), 116–52.

Cowan, Sharon. "The Headscarf Controversy: A Response to Jill Marshall." *Res Publica* 14 (2008): 193–201.

Crocker, David A., and Ingrid Robeyns. "Capability and Agency." In *Amartya Sen*, edited by Christopher W. Morris (Cambridge: Cambridge University Press, 2010), 60–90.

Crocker, Larry. *Positive Liberty* (The Hague: Martinus Nijhoff, 1980).

Crowder, George. *Isaiah Berlin: Liberty and Pluralism* (Cambridge: Polity, 2004).

Cudd, Ann E. *Analyzing Oppression* (New York: Oxford University Press, 2006).

Dahan, Yossi, Hanna Lerner, and Faina Milman-Sivan. "Global Justice, Labor Standards and Responsibility." *Theoretical Inquires in Law* 12, no. 2 (2011): 439–64.

Dahlberg, Lincoln. "The Internet, Deliberative Democracy, and Power: Radicalizing the Public Sphere." *International Journal of Media and Cultural Politics* 3, no. 1 (2007): 47–64.

Davies, Christie. "Humour and Protest: Jokes under Communism." *International Review of Social History* 52 (2007): 291–305.

Dean, Jodi. *Solidarity of Strangers* (Berkeley: University of California Press, 1996).

Devetak, Richard, and Christopher W. Hughes. *The Globalization of Political Violence: Globalization's Shadow* (London: Routledge, 2008).

Donaldson, Thomas. "Moral Minimums for Corporations." In *Ethics and International Affairs*, 2nd edn., edited by Joel Rosenthal (Washington, DC: Georgetown University Press, 1999).

Dower, Nigel. *An Introduction to Global Citizenship* (Edinburgh: Edinburgh University Press, 2003).

Dryzek, John. *Deliberative Democracy and Beyond* (Oxford: Oxford University Press, 2002).

Deliberative Global Politics (Cambridge: Polity, 2006).

Discursive Democracy (Cambridge: Cambridge University Press, 1990).

Dumas, Lloyd J. "Is Development an Effective Way to Fight Terrorism?" In *War after September 11*, edited by Verna V. Gehring (Lanham: Rowman & Littlefield, 2003), 65–74.

Durkheim, Emile. *The Division of Labor in Society*. Translated by George Simpson (New York: The Free Press, 1964).

El Menyawi, Hassan. "Toward Global Democracy: Thoughts in Response to the Rising Tide of Nation-to-Nation Interdependencies." *Indiana Journal of Global Legal Studies* 11, no. 2 (2004): 83–133.

Falk, Richard, and Andrew Strauss. "On the Creation of a Global Peoples Assembly: Legitimacy and the Power of Popular Sovereignty." *Stanford Journal of International Law* 36 (2000): 191–219.

Flynn, Jeffrey. "Habermas on Human Rights: Law, Morality, and Intercultural Dialogue." *Social Theory and Practice* 29, no. 3 (2003): 431–57.

Føllesdal, Andreas. "Subsidiarity, Democracy, and Human Rights in the Constitutional Treaty of Europe." *Journal of Social Philosophy* 37, no. 1 (2006): 61–80.

"Survey Article: Subsidiarity." *The Journal of Political Philosophy* 6, no. 2 (1998): 190–218.

Fonow, Mary Margaret. "Human Rights, Feminism, and Transnational Labor Solidarity." In *Just Advocacy? Women's Human Rights, Transnational Feminisms, and the Politics of Representation*, edited by Wendy S. Hesford and Wendy Kozol (New Brunswick: Rutgers University Press, 2005), 221–42.

Forst, Rainer. "The Justification of Human Rights and the Basic Right to Justification: A Reflexive Approach." *Ethics* 120, no. 4 (2010): 711–40.

Fox, Gregory H., and Brad R. Roth. *Democratic Governance and International Law* (Cambridge: Cambridge University Press, 2000).

Fraser, Nancy. *Scales of Justice: Reimagining Political Space in a Globalizing World* (New York: Columbia University Press, 2010).

Fraser, Nancy, and Axel Honneth. *Redistribution or Recognition? A Political-Philosophical Exchange* (London: Verso, 2003).

Frundt, Henry J. "Movement Theory and International Labor Solidarity." *Labor Studies Journal* 1, no. 2 (2005): 19–40.

Gallie, W. B. "Essentially Contested Concepts." *Proceedings of the Aristotelian Society* 56 (1956): 167–98.

Galtung, Johan. "Alternative Models for Global Democracy." In *Global Democracy*, edited by Barry Holden (London: Routledge, 2000), 143–61.

Gewirth, Alan. *The Community of Rights* (Chicago: University of Chicago Press, 1998).

Human Rights (Chicago: University of Chicago Press, 1982).

Reason and Morality (Chicago: University of Chicago Press, 1980).

Gilabert, Pablo. "Global Justice, Democracy, and Solidarity." *Res Publica* 13, no. 1 (2007): 435–43.

Gilligan, Carol. *In a Different Voice* (Cambridge, MA: Harvard University Press, 1982).

Gittler, Joseph. "Social Ontology and the Criteria for Definitions in Sociology." *Sociometry* 14, no. 4 (1951): 355–65.

Goffman, Erving. *Relations in Public: Microstudies of the Public Order* (New York: Basic Books, 1971).

Goodin, Robert. "What Is So Special About Our Fellow Countrymen?" *Ethics* 98, no. 4 (1988): 663–86.

Gould, Carol C. "Beyond Causality in the Social Sciences: Reciprocity as a Model of Non-Exploitative Social Relations." In *Epistemology, Methodology and the Social Sciences: Boston Studies in the Philosophy of Science*, edited by R. S. Cohen and M. W. Wartofsky (Boston and Dordrecht: D. Reidel, 1983), 53–88.

"Claude Lefort on Modern Democracy." *Praxis International* 10, nos. 3–4 (1991): 337–45.

"Coercion, Care, and Corporations: Omissions and Commissions in Thomas Pogge's Political Philosophy." *The Journal of Global Ethics* 3, no. 3 (2007): 381–93.

"Cultural Justice and the Limits of Difference: Feminist Contributions to Value Inquiry." *Utopia* (Athens) 21 (July–August, 1996): 131–43.

"Cultural Justice and the Limits of Difference." In *Norms and Values: Essays on the Work of Virginia Held*, edited by J. G. Haber and M. S. Halfon (Lanham, MD: Rowman & Littlefield, 1998), 73–86.

"Democracy and Diversity: Representing Differences." In *Democracy and Difference: Changing Boundaries of the Political*, edited by Seyla Benhabib (Princeton, NJ: Princeton University Press, 1996), 171–86.

"Does Stakeholder Theory Require Democratic Management?" *Business and Professional Ethics Journal* 21, no. 1 (2002): 4–20.

"Economic Justice, Self-Management, and the Principle of Reciprocity." In *Economic Justice: Private Rights and Public Responsibilities*, edited by K. Kipnis and D. T. Meyers (Totowa, NJ: Rowman & Allanheld, 1985), 202–16.

"Envisioning Transnational Democracy: Cross-Border Communities and Regional Human Rights Frameworks." In *Democracy, States, and the Struggle for Global Justice*, edited by Heather Gautney, Omar Dahbour, Ashley Dawson and Neil Smith (New York: Routledge, 2009), 63–77.

"Feminism and Democratic Community Revisited." In *Democratic Community: NOMOS XXXV*, edited by J. Chapman and I. Shapiro (New York: New York University Press, 1993), 396–413.

"Global Democratic Transformation and the Internet." In *Technology, Science and Social Justice, Social Philosophy Today*, edited by John R. Rowan (Charlottesville, VA: Philosophy Documentation Center, 2007), 73–88.

Globalizing Democracy and Human Rights (Cambridge: Cambridge University Press, 2004).

"Group Rights and Social Ontology." *The Philosophical Forum*, Special Double Issue on Philosophical Perspectives on National Identity, 28, no. 1–2 (1996–7): 73–86.

Marx's Social Ontology (Cambridge, MA: The MIT Press, 1978).

"Negotiating the Global and the Local: Situating Transnational Democracy and Human Rights." In *Democracy in a Global World: Human Rights and Political Participation in the 21st Century*, edited by Deen K. Chatterjee (Lanham, MD: Rowman & Littlefield, 2007), 71–87.

"Network Ethics: Access, Consent, and the Informed Community." In *The Information Web: Ethical and Social Implications of Computer Networking*, edited by Carol C. Gould (Boulder, CO: Westview Press, 1989), 1–35.

"Philosophical Dichotomies and Feminist Thought: Towards a Critical Feminism." In *Feministische Philosophie, Wiener Reihe Band 4*, edited by Herta Nagl (Vienna: R. Oldenbourg Verlag, 1990), 184–90.

"Positive Freedom, Economic Justice, and the Redefinition of Democracy." In *Ethical Issues in Contemporary Society*, edited by J. Howie and G. Schedler (Carbondale, IL: Southern Illinois University Press, 1995), 23–53.

"Recognition in Redistribution: Care and Diversity in Global Justice." *Southern Journal of Philosophy* 46, Supplement (2007): 91–103.

"Recognition, Care, and Solidarity." In *Socialité Et Reconnaissance. Grammaires De L'Humain*, edited by G. W. Bertram, R. Celikates, C. Laudou, and D. Lauer (Paris: Editions L'Harmattan, 2006).

Rethinking Democracy: Freedom and Social Cooperation in Politics, Economy, and Society (Cambridge: Cambridge University Press, 1988).

"Self-Determination Beyond Sovereignty: Relating Transnational Democracy to Local Autonomy." *Journal of Social Philosophy* 37, no. 1 (2006): 44–60.

"Structuring Global Democracy: Political Communities, Universal Human Rights, and Transnational Representation." *Metaphilosophy*, Special Issue on Global Democracy and Political Exclusion 40, no. 1 (2009): 24–46.

"Transnational Power, Coercion, and Democracy." In *Coercion and the State*, edited by David A. Reidy and Walter J. Riker (Berlin: Springer, 2008), 189–202.

"Transnational Solidarities." *Journal of Social Philosophy*, Special Issue on Solidarity, ed. Carol Gould and Sally Scholz, 38, no. 1 (2007): 146–62.

"Two Concepts of Universality and the Problem of Cultural Relativism." In *Cultural Identity and the Nation-State*, edited by Carol Gould and Pasquale Pasquino (Lanham, MD: Rowman & Littlefield, 2001).

"The Woman Question: Philosophy of Liberation and the Liberation of Philosophy." In *Women and Philosophy: Toward a Theory of Liberation*, edited by Carol C. Gould and Marx W. Wartofsky (New York: G. P. Putnam's Sons, 1976). Originally published in *The Philosophical Forum* 5, nos. 1–2 (fall–winter, 1973–4): 5–44.

"Women's Human Rights and the U.S. Constitution: Initiating a Dialogue." In *Women and the U.S. Constitution: History, Interpretation, Practice*, edited by Sibyl Schwarzenbach and Patricia Smith (New York: Columbia University Press, 2003), 197–219.

Gould-Wartofsky, Michael. "Here Comes the Neighborhood: The Housing Movement Goes Global in East Harlem." *The Huffington Post* (March 25, 2010).

The Occupiers: The Making of the 99 Percent Movement (Oxford: Oxford University Press, 2015).

Grant, Ruth W., and Robert O. Keohane. "Accountability and Abuses of Power in World Politics." *American Political Science Review* 99, no. 1 (2005): 29–43.

Greenawalt, Kent. "Free Speech in the United States and Canada." *Law and Contemporary Problems* 55, no. 1 (1992): 5–33.

Griffin, James. *On Human Rights* (Oxford: Oxford University Press, 2008).

Grillo, Ralph D. "License to Offend? The Behzti Affair." *Ethnicities* 7, no. 1 (2007): 5–29.

Gutmann, Amy, and Dennis Thompson. *Democracy and Disagreement* (Cambridge, MA: The Belknap Press of Harvard University Press, 1996).

Habermas, Jürgen. *Between Facts and Norms: Contributions to a Discourse Theory of Law and Democracy*. Translated by William Rehg (Cambridge, MA: The MIT Press, 1996).

The Divided West (Cambridge: Polity, 2006).

The Inclusion of the Other (Cambridge, MA: The MIT Press, 1998).

"Justice and Solidarity: On the Discussion Concerning Stage 6." Translated by Shierry Weber Nicholsen. In *The Moral Domain: Essays in the Ongoing Discussion between Philosophy and the Social Sciences*, edited by Thomas E. Wren (Cambridge, MA: MIT Press, 1990), 224–51.

Moral Consciousness and Communicative Action. Translated by Lenhardt Christian and Nicholsen Shierry Weber (Cambridge, MA: MIT Press, 1990).

"Morality and Ethical Life: Does Hegel's Critique of Kant Apply to Discourse Ethics." *Northwestern University Law Review* 83 (1988): 38–53.

"A Political Constitution for the Pluralist World Society?" Translated by Ciaran Cronin. In *Between Naturalism and Religion: Philosophical Essays* (Cambridge: Polity, 2008), 312–52.

The Theory of Communicative Rationality. Vol. 1. Translated by Thomas McCarthy (Boston, MA: Beacon Press, 1985).

Hardimon, Michael O. *Hegel's Social Philosophy: The Project of Reconciliation* (Cambridge: Cambridge University Press, 1994).

Harvey, David. *Rebel Cities: From the Right to the City to the Urban Revolution* (London: Verso, 2012).

Hass, Peter (ed.). "Special Issue on Knowledge, Power, and International Policy Coordination." *International Organization* 46, no. 1 (1992).

Hayward, Tim. *Constitutional Environmental Rights* (Oxford: Oxford University Press, 2005).

Hechter, Michael. *Principles of Group Solidarity* (Berkeley: University of California Press, 1987).

Hegel, G. W. F. *Phenomenology of Spirit.* Translated by A. V. Miller (Oxford: Oxford University Press, 1977).

Science of Logic. Translated by A. V. Miller (London: Allen & Unwin, 1969).

Held, David. *Democracy and the Global Order* (Stanford, CA: Stanford University Press, 1995).

Held, Virginia. "Care and Justice in the Global Context." *Ratio Juris* 17, no. 2 (2004): 141–55.

"Non-Contractual Society: A Feminist View." In *Science, Morality and Feminist Theory*, edited by M. Hanen and K. Nielsen (Calgary: University of Calgary Press, 1987), 111–37.

Heyd, David. "Justice and Solidarity: The Contractarian Case against Global Justice." *Journal of Social Philosophy*, Special Issue on Solidarity, co-edited by Carol C. Gould and Sally Scholz, 38, no. 1 (2007): 112–30.

Hochschild, Arlie Russell. "Global Care Chains and Emotional Surplus Value." In *Global Capitalism*, edited by Will Hutton and Anthony Giddens (London: The New Press, 2001), 30–46.

Honneth, Axel. "Recognition or Redistribution? Changing Perspectives on the Moral Order of Society." *Theory, Culture & Society* 18, nos. 2–3 (2001): 43–55.

Hsieh, Nien-He. "Justice in Production." *The Journal of Political Philosophy* 16, no. 1 (2008): 72–100.

"Rawlsian Justice and Workplace Republicanism." *Social Theory and Practice* 31, no. 1 (2005): 115–42.

Inglehart, Ronald, and Pippa Norris. *Rising Tide: Gender Equality and Cultural Change around the World* (Cambridge: Cambridge University Press, 2003).

"The True Clash of Civilizations." *Foreign Policy* 135 (2003): 62–6.

International Forum on Globalization, "A Better World is Possible!" (Report Summary, 2002, Excerpted). In *The Globalization Reader*, edited by Frank J. Lechner and John Boli (Oxford: Blackwell, 2008), 482–94.

Jaggar, Alison. *Feminist Politics and Human Nature* (Totowa, NJ: Rowman & Allanheld, 1985).

"Global Responsibility and Western Feminism." In *Feminist Interventions in Ethics and Politics*, edited by Barbara S. Andrew, Jean Keller, and Lisa H. Schwartzman (Lanham, MD: Rowman & Littlefield, 2005), 185–200.

"'Saving Amina': Global Justice for Women and Intercultural Dialogue." *Ethics & International Affairs* 19 (2005): 55–75.

Juris, Jeffrey S. "Reflections on #Occupy Everywhere: Social Media, Public Space, and Emerging Logics of Aggregation." *American Ethnologist* 39, no. 2 (2012): 259–79.

Kojève, Alexandre. *Introduction à la Lecture de Hegel*, 2nd ed. (Paris: Gallimard, 1947).

Kopelman, Loretta. "Female Genital Mutilation and Ethical Relativism." *Second Opinion* (October 1994).

Kuper, Andrew. *Democracy Beyond Borders: Justice and Representation in Global Institutions* (Oxford: Oxford University Press, 2004).

Lacsamana, Anne E. "Sex Worker or Prostituted Woman?" In *Women and Globalization*, edited by Delia D. Aguilar and Anne E. Lacsamana (Amherst, NY: Humanity Books, 2004), 387–403.

Laegaard, Sune. "The Cartoon Controversy: Offence, Identity, Oppression?" *Political Studies* 55 (2007): 481–98.

Landau, Loren B. "Can We Talk and Is Anybody Listening? Reflections on Iasfm 10: Talking across Borders: New Dialogues in Forced Migration." *Journal of Refugee Studies* 20, no. 3 (2007): 335–48.

Langlois, Anthony. "Liberal Autonomy and Global Democracy." In *Global Democracy and Its Difficulties*, edited by A. Langlois and K. Soltan (London: Routledge, 2009), 146–59.

Lindsay, Jamie. "Gewirth's Argument to the Principle of Generic Consistency," manuscript, 2011.

Loukis, Euripides, and Maria A. Wimmer. "Analysing Different Models of Structured Electronic Consultation on Legislation under Formation." Paper presented at the From e-Participation to Online Deliberation, Fourth International Conference on Online Deliberation (Leeds, UK, 2010).

Lukács, Georg. *Zur Ontologie Des Gesellschaftslichen Seins* (3 vols.). (Neuwied: Luchterhand, 1971–3).

Lukes, Steven. *Power: A Radical View*, 2nd ed. (Palgrave Macmillan, 2004).

MacCallum, Gerald C., Jr. "Negative and Positive Freedom." *The Philosophical Review* 76, no. 3 (1967): 312–34.

Macleod, Alistair. "Free Speech, Equal Opportunity, and Justice." In *Freedom of Expression in a Diverse World*, edited by Deirdre Golash (New York: Springer, 2010), 57–73.

Macpherson, C. B. *Democratic Theory: Essays in Retrieval* (Oxford: Oxford University Press, 1973).

The Life and Times of Liberal Democracy (Oxford: Oxford University Press, 1977).

Mansbridge, Jane. "Feminism and Democratic Community." In *Democratic Community: NOMOS XXXV*, edited by J. Chapman and I. Shapiro (New York: New York University Press, 1993), 339–95.

Marchand, Marianne H. "Challenging Globalisation: Toward a Feminist Understanding of Resistance." *Review of International Studies* 29 (2003): 145–60.

Marchand, Marianne H., and Anne Sisson Runyon. "Introduction." In *Gender and Global Restructuring*, edited by Marchand and Runyon (London: Routledge, 2000), 1–22.

Marchetti, Raffaele. *Global Democracy: For and Against* (London: Routledge, 2008).

"Global Governance or World Federalism? A Cosmopolitan Dispute on Institutional Models." *Global Society* 20, no. 3 (2006): 287–305.

Marshall, Jill. "Women's Right to Autonomy and Identity in European Human Rights Law: Manifesting One's Religion." *Res Publica* 14 (2003): 177–92.

Marx, Karl. "Contribution to the Critique of Hegel's Philosophy of Right." In *The Marx-Engels Reader*, 2nd edn., edited by Robert Tucker (New York: Norton, 1978), 53–65.

Grundrisse: Foundations of the Critique of Political Economy, Trans. M. Nicolaus (New York: Vintage, 1973).

Mason, Andrew. *Community, Solidarity and Belonging* (Cambridge: Cambridge University Press, 2000).

Mayer, Ann Elizabeth. "Cultural Particularism as a Bar to Women's Rights: Reflections on the Middle Eastern Experience." In *Women's Rights, Human Rights*, edited by Julie Peters and Andrea Wolper (New York: Routledge, 1995), 176–88.

McMahon, Christopher. *Authority and Democracy: A General Theory of Government and Management* (Princeton, NJ: Princeton University Press, 1994).

Mello, Brian. "Recasting the Right to Self-Determination: Group Rights and Political Participation." *Social Theory and Practice* 30, no. 2 (2004): 193–213.

Menser, Michael. "Disarticulate the State! Maximizing Democracy in 'New' Autonomous Movements in the Americas." In *Democracy, States, and the Struggle for Global Justice*, edited by Heather Gautney, Omar Dahbour, Ashley Dawson, and Neil Smith (New York: Routledge, 2009), 251–72.

Merry, Sally Engle. *Human Rights and Gender Violence: Translating International Law into Local Justice* (Chicago: University of Chicago Press, 2005).

"Human Rights Law and the Demonization of Culture (and Anthropology Along the Way)." *Polar: Political and Legal Anthropology Review* 26, no. 1 (2003): 55–77.

Miller, David. "Against Global Egalitarianism." *The Journal of Ethics* 9 (2005): 55–79.

"National Self-Determination and Global Justice." In *Citizenship and National Identity*, edited by David Miller (Cambridge: Polity Press, 2000), 161–79.

Minow, Martha. "Is Pluralism an Ideal or a Compromise? An Essay for Carol Weisbrod." *Connecticut Law Review* 40, no. 5 (2008): 1287–313.

Mitchell, Ronald K., Bradley R. Agle, and Donna J. Wood. "Toward a Theory of Stakeholder Identification and Salience: Defining the Principle of Who and What Really Counts." *Academy of Management Review* 22 (1997): 853–86.

Modood, Tariq. "The Liberal Dilemma: Integration or Vilification?" *Open Democracy* (February 8, 2006).

Moellendorf, Darrel. *Cosmopolitan Justice* (Boulder, CO: Westview Press, 2002).

Mohanty, Chandra Talpade. *Feminism without Borders: Decolonizing Theory, Practicing Solidarity* (Durham, NC: Duke University Press, 2003).

"'Under Western Eyes' Revisited: Feminist Solidarity through Anticapitalist Struggles." *Signs* 28, no. 2 (2002): 499–535.

Monasterio, Jose Mari Luzarraga, Dionisio Aranzadi Telleria, and Iñazio Irizar Etxebarria. "Understanding Mondragon Globalization Process: Local Job Creation through Multi-Localization." http://community-wealth.org/sites/ clone.community-wealth.org/files/downloads/paper-luzarraga-et-al.pdf

Moore, Margaret. "Introduction: The Self-Determination Principle and the Ethics of Secession." In *National Self-Determination and Secession*, edited by Margaret Moore (Oxford: Oxford University Press, 1998), 134–57.

"The Territorial Dimension of Self-Determination." In *National Self-Determination and Secession*, edited by Margaret Moore (Oxford: Oxford University Press, 1998), 136–7.

Morefield, Jeanne. "States Are Not People: Harold Laski on Unsettling Sovereignty, Rediscovering Democracy." *Political Research Quarterly* 58, no. 4 (2005): 659–69.

Mouffe, Chantal. *The Democratic Paradox* (London: Verso, 2000).

Nagel, Thomas. "The Problem of Global Justice." *Philosophy & Public Affairs* 33, no. 2 (2005): 113–47.

Narveson, Jan. "Democracy and Rights." *Social Philosophy and Policy* 9 (1992): 29–61.

Neuhouser, Frederick. *Foundations of Hegel's Social Theory: Actualizing Freedom* (Cambridge, MA: Harvard University Press, 2000).

Nickel, James. "Gould on Democracy and Human Rights." *Journal of Global Ethics* 1, no. 2 (2005): 211–12.

Nickel, James, and David A. Reidy. "Philosophical Foundations of Human Rights" (July 11, 2009). Available at SSRN: http://ssrn.com/abstract= 1432868 or http://dx.doi.org/10.2139/ssrn.1432868.

Norris, Pippa. *Digital Divide* (Cambridge: Cambridge University Press, 2001).

Novak, William, and Moshe Waldoks (eds.). *The Big Book of Jewish Humor: 25th Anniversary* (New York: Collins, 2006).

Nussbaum, Martha. *Creating Capabilities: The Human Development Approach* (Cambridge, MA: Harvard University Press, 2011).

"Human Capabilities, Female Human Beings." In *Women, Culture and Development*, edited by Martha Nussbaum and Jonathan Glover (New York: Oxford University Press, 1995), 61–104.

Sex and Social Justice (New York: Oxford University Press, 1999).

Women and Human Development: The Capabilities Approach (Cambridge: Cambridge University Press, 2001).

"Women and Theories of Global Justice: Our Need for New Paradigms." In *The Ethics of Assistance*, edited by Deen Chatterjee (Cambridge: Cambridge University Press, 2004), 147–76.

O'Neill, Martin. "Liberty, Equality and Property-Owning Democracy." *Journal of Social Philosophy* 40, no. 3 (2009): 379–96.

O'Reilly, Tim. "What Is Web 2.0? Design Patterns and Business Models for the Next Generation of Software" (2005). www.oreilly.com/lpt/a/6228.

Parijs, Philippe Van. *Real Freedom for All* (Oxford: Oxford University Press, 1995).

Peters, Julie, and Andrea Wolper, (eds.). *Women's Rights, Human Rights: International Feminist Perspectives* (New York: Routledge, 1995).

Pettit, Philip. *Republicanism: A Theory of Freedom and Government* (Oxford: Oxford University Press, 1997).

Phillips, Robert A. "Stakeholder Legitimacy." *Business Ethics Quarterly* 13, no. 1 (2003): 25–41.

Plotke, David. "Representation Is Democracy." *Constellations* 4, no. 1 (1997): 19–34.

Pogge, Thomas. *Realizing Rawls* (Ithaca: Cornell University Press, 1989).
   "Severe Poverty as a Violation of Negative Duties." *Ethics & International Affairs* 19, no. 1 (2005): 55–83.
   World Poverty and Human Rights (Cambridge: Polity Press, 2002).

Post, Robert. "Religion and Freedom of Speech: Portraits of Muhammad." *Constellations* 14, no. 1 (2007): 72–90.

Rao, Arati. "The Politics of Gender and Culture in International Human Rights Discourse." In *Women's Rights, Human Rights*, edited by Julie Peters and Andrea Wolper (New York: Routledge, 1995), 167–75.

Rawls, John. *The Law of Peoples* (Cambridge, MA: Harvard University Press, 1999).

Raz, Joseph. *The Authority of Law: Essays on Law and Morality* (Oxford: Clarendon Press, 1979).

Rehg, William. *Insight and Solidarity* (Berkeley: University of California Press, 1994).

Reidenberg, Joel R. "The Yahoo Case and the International Democratization of the Internet." *Fordham Law & Economics Research Paper* (published electronically April, 2001): http://papers.ssrn.com/sol3/papers.cfm?abstract_id=267148.

Rippe, Klaus Peter. "Diminishing Solidarity." *Ethical Theory and Moral Practice* 1, no. 3 (1998): 355–73.

Robinson, Fiona. "Care, Gender and Global Social Justice: Rethinking 'Ethical Globalization.'" *Journal of Global Ethics* 2, no. 1 (2006): 5–25.
   The Ethics of Care: A Feminist Approach to Human Security (Philadelphia, PA: Temple University Press, 2011).
   Globalizing Care (Boulder, CO: Westview, 1999).

Romany, Celina. "State Responsibility Goes Private: A Feminist Critique of the Public/Private Distinction in International Human Rights Law." In *Human Rights of Women*, edited by Rebecca J. Cook (Philadelphia: University of Pennsylvania Press, 1994), 85–115.

Rorty, Richard. *Contingency, Irony, and Solidarity* (Cambridge: Cambridge University Press, 1989).

Ruddick, Sara. *Maternal Thinking* (Boston, MA: Beacon Press, 1989).

Sampford, Charles. "Reconceiving the Rule of Law for a Globalizing World." In *Globalization and the Rule of Law*, edited by Spencer Zifcak (New York: Routledge, 2005), 9–31.

Sandel, Michael. *Liberalism and the Limits of Justice* (Cambridge: Cambridge University Press, 1981).

Sangiovanni, Andrea. "Global Justice, Reciprocity, and the State." *Philosophy and Public Affairs* 35, no. 1 (2007): 3–39.

Saward, Michael. "A Critique of Held." In *Global Democracy: Key Debates*, edited by Barry Holden (London: Routledge, 2000), 39–43.

Scheffler, Samuel. *Boundaries and Allegiances: Problems of Justice and Responsibility in Liberal Thought* (Oxford: Oxford University Press, 2001).

Scholz, Sally J. *Political Solidarity* (University Park, PA: Penn State University Press, 2008).

Schwarzenbach, Sibyl. "Civic Friendship." *Ethics* 107 (1998): 97–128.

On Civic Friendship: Including Women in the State (New York: Columbia University Press, 2009).

Schweickart, David. *After Capitalism* (Lanham, MD: Rowman & Littlefield, 2002).

See, Adam. "Participatory Politics and New Media: Towards a New Communitarianism." Unpublished manuscript (2012).

Sen, Amartya. "Capability and Well-Being." In *The Quality of Life*, edited by Martha Nussbaum and Amartya Sen (Oxford: Oxford University Press, 1993), 30–53.

Development as Freedom (New York: Knopf, 1999).

"Equality of What?" In *Tanner Lectures on Human Values*, edited by S. McMurrin (Cambridge: Cambridge University Press, 1980), 195–220.

"Gender Inequality and Theories of Justice." In *Women, Culture and Development*, edited by Martha Nussbaum and Jonathan Glover (New York: Oxford University Press, 1995), 259–73.

Inequality Re-Examined (Oxford: The Clarendon Press, 1992).

"More Than 100 Million Women Are Missing." *The New York Review of Books* 37, no. 20 (December, 1990): 61–6.

"Well-Being, Agency, and Freedom: The Dewey Lectures of 1984." *Journal of Philosophy* 82, no. 4 (1985): 169–221.

Shachar, Ayelet. "Privatizing Diversity: A Cautionary Tale from Religious Arbitration in Family Law." *Theoretical Inquiries in Law* 9, no. 2 (2008): 572–607.

Shelby, Tommie. "Foundations of Black Solidarity: Collective Identity or Common Oppression?" *Ethics* 112 (2002): 231–66.

Shue, Henry. *Basic Rights* (Princeton, NJ: Princeton University Press, 1980).

Singer, Peter. "Famine, Affluence, and Morality." *Philosophy and Public Affairs* 1, no. 3 (1972): 229–43.

One World: The Ethics of Globalization. 2nd edn. (New Haven, CT: Yale University Press, 2004).

Practical Ethics. 2nd edn. (Cambridge: Cambridge University Press, 1999).

Sjoberg, Laura. *Gender, Justice, and the Wars in Iraq* (Lanham, MD: Lexington Books, 2006).

Sparks, Holloway. "Dissident Citizenship: Democratic Theory, Political Courage, and Activist Women." *Hypatia* 12, no. 4 (1997): 74–110.

Stern, Robert. "Hegel, British Idealism, and the Curious Case of the Concrete Universal." *British Journal for the History of Philosophy* 15, no. 1 (2007): 115–53.

Stiglitz, Joseph E. "Globalization and Development." In *Taming Globalization*, edited by David Held and Mathias Koenig-Archibugi (Cambridge: Polity, 2003), 47–67.

Globalization and Its Discontents (New York: W. W. Norton, 2002).

Stjerno, Steiner. *Solidarity in Europe: The History of an Idea* (Cambridge: Cambridge University Press, 2004).

Stoljar, Natalie. "Feminist Perspectives on Autonomy." In *The Stanford Encyclopedia of Philosophy*, edited by Edward N. Zalta. http://plato.stanford.edu/archives/sum2013/entries/feminism-autonomy/, 2013.

Sullivan, Donna. "The Public/Private Distinction in International Human Rights Law." In *Women's Rights, Human Rights*, edited by Julie Peters and Andrea Wolper (New York: Routledge, 1995), 126–34.

Superson, Anita. "Deformed Desires and Informed Desire Tests." *Hypatia* 20, no. 4 (2005): 109–26.

Tamanaha, Brian. *On the Rule of Law: History, Politics, Theory* (Cambridge: Cambridge University Press, 2004).

Tamir, Yael. *Liberal Nationalism* (Princeton, NJ: Princeton University Press, 1993).

Tan, Kok-Chor. *Justice, Institutions, & Luck* (Oxford: Oxford University Press, 2012).

Toleration, Diversity, and Global Justice (University Park, PA: Penn State University Press, 2000).

Tännsjö, Torbjörn. *Global Democracy: The Case for a World Government* (Edinburgh: Edinburgh University Press, 2008).

Taylor, Charles. "Atomism." In *Philosophy and the Human Sciences: Philosophical Papers*, vol. 2, edited by Charles Taylor (Cambridge: Cambridge University Press, 1985), 187–210.

Multiculturalism and "the Politics of Recognition" (Princeton, NJ: Princeton University Press, 1992).

Tronto, Joan. *Caring Democracy* (New York: New York University Press, 2013).

"Human Rights, Democracy and Care: Comments on Carol C. Gould, Globalizing Democracy and Human Rights." *The Good Society* 16, no. 2 (2007): 38–40.

Moral Boundaries: A Political Argument for an Ethic of Care. New York: Routledge, 1993.

Ven, Bert van de. "Human Rights as a Normative Basis for Stakeholder Legitimacy." *Corporate Governance* 5, no. 2 (2005): 48–59.

Walzer, Michael. *Arguing About War* (New Haven, CT: Yale University Press, 2004).

Warren, Mark. "Citizen Representatives." In *Designing Deliberative Democracy: The British Columbia Citizens' Assembly*, edited by Mark Warren and Hilary Pearse (Cambridge: Cambridge University Press, 2008), 50–69.

Weinstock, Daniel. "The Real World of (Global) Democracy." Special Issue on Democracy and Globalization, ed. Carol C. Gould and Alistair Macleod, *Journal of Social Philosophy* 37, no. 1 (2006): 6–20.

Wildt, Andreas. "Solidarity: Its History and Contemporary Definition." In *Solidarity*, edited by Kurt Bayertz (Dordrecht: Kluwer, 1999), 209–20.

Willetts, Peter. "Remedying the World Trade Organisation's Deviance from Global Norms." In *Free and Fair: Making the Progressive Case for Removing Trade Barriers*, edited by P. Griffith and J. Thurston (London: Foreign Policy Centre, 2004), 131–40.

Williamson, Thad. "Who Owns What? An Egalitarian Interpretation of John Rawls's Idea of a Property-Owning Democracy." *Journal of Social Philosophy* 40, no. 3 (2009): 434–53.

Wiredu, Kwasi. "An Akan Perspective on Human Rights." In *Cultural Universals and Particulars: An African Perspective* (Bloomington: Indiana University Press, 1996), 157–91.

Wood, Allen. *Hegel's Ethical Thought* (Cambridge: Cambridge University Press, 1990).

Young, Iris Marion. "Communication and the Other: Beyond Deliberative Democracy." In *Democracy and Difference*, edited by Seyla Benhabib (Princeton, NJ: Princeton University Press, 1994), 120–36.

Inclusion and Democracy (Oxford: Oxford University Press, 2002).

Justice and the Politics of Difference (Princeton, NJ: Princeton University Press, 1990).

"Responsibility and Global Justice: A Social Connections Model." *Social Philosophy and Policy* 23, no. 1 (2006): 102–30.

"Responsibility and Global Labor Justice." *Journal of Political Philosophy* 12, no. 4 (2004): 365–88.

Responsibility for Justice (New York: Oxford University Press, 2011).

"Self-Determination as a Principle of Justice." *The Philosophical Forum* 11 (1979): 172–82.

"Violence against Power." In *Ethics and Foreign Intervention*, edited by Deen Chatterjee and Don Scheid (Cambridge: Cambridge University Press, 2003), 251–73.

Index

political societies, 21, 68, 83, 85–6, 88,
    133, 199, 210–11, 217
positive freedom, 6, 16, 39–40, 44–5, 54,
    58–64, 66–7, 71–4, 77, 89–90,
    92–3, 245
  approaches, 57, 72
  conceptions, 58, 71
  principle of equal. *See* equal positive
      freedom (EPF)
  tradition, 15, 62, 74
  See also equal positive freedom and
      freedom
Post, Robert, 169n15
power, 8, 59, 61, 152–3, 173–4, 179–85,
    187, 189–91, 193, 197, 199, 201,
    210–11, 215, 240
  democratic, 96, 235
  networking, 187
  -over, 4, 8, 59
  social, 184, 188–9, 193
  synergistic, 187
  -to, 184–5, 189
  transnational, 152, 226
  and violence, 182–3
  -with, 4, 8
protest, 8, 160–1, 171–7, 201, 215
  participatory modes of, 8, 215
public sphere, 19, 104–5, 160, 173, 175,
    207, 215, 227
  global, 197–8, 207, 259

Rao, Arati, 156n26
Rawls, John, 21, 21n32, 83, 85, 152n13,
    152, 244, 253
Raz, Joseph, 211, 211n27
reciprocity, 21, 32, 43, 54, 67, 91, 107,
    111–13, 119, 121, 125, 175, 189,
    194, 203
recognition, 4, 17–18, 22–7, 43–7, 65–6,
    68–9, 79–80, 84–5, 121–3, 131–7,
    139–41, 143–5, 147, 154–5,
    224–5
  of abstract equality, 79, 139
  equal, 121, 129, 151, 209, 223–4
  of equal agency, 76, 91, 188
  mutual, 73, 129–30, 199, 224
  the Politics of, 136
  processes of, 45–6
  reciprocal, 17, 44, 47, 53, 91, 131, 139,
      199
  solidaristic, 128, 131, 139–40, 142
  transnational, 133
  universal, 42
redistribution, 1, 20–2, 24–7, 86, 120,
    122, 127, 133–4, 137, 141
  See also distributive justice

regionalism, 30, 32, 228, 256–8, 260–2
Rehg, William, 197n2
Reidenberg, Joel R., 219n
Reidy, David, 42n12–13
relations, 4, 6–7, 42–3, 52–5, 64–5, 69–72,
    74–5, 100–4, 106, 109–10, 112,
    114–15, 126–8, 130, 176–7
  caring, 49, 184
  cooperative, 4, 106, 147
  inter-. *See* interrelations
  solidaristic, 72, 107, 112, 116, 234
  See also social relations
representation, 31, 88, 90, 94–5, 138, 154,
    156, 223, 226, 228–9, 231, 235–7,
    239–40, 250, 252
  democratic, 32, 235
  transnational, 8, 25, 32, 95, 136, 193,
      208, 228, 235, 240, 265, 268
representatives, 29, 82, 177, 211, 214, 216,
    221, 236–7, 239–40, 247, 252,
    255
  worker, 250, 252
Rethinking Democracy, 3n2, 14n8,
    16n12–13, 16n17, 17n18, 17n20,
    18n24, 32n52, 36n3, 38, 38n6, 39,
    39n8–9, 42, 59, 59n1, 63n12,
    64n15, 66n17, 72n25, 73n26,
    73n28, 82n3, 94n16, 122n8,
    131n25, 138n17, 223n12, 235n17,
    245n10, 246, 246n13
rights
  civil and political, 18
  democratic, 82, 222, 236–8, 248, 266
  economic, 24–5, 48–9, 141, 154, 191,
      219, 251
  labor, 8, 252, 255
  social, 23, 29, 35, 41, 48, 145, 192–3
Rippe, Klaus Peter, 108, 108n21–24,
    124n13
Robeyns, Ingrid, 75n
Robinson, Fiona, 100n2, 133, 134n5–6,
    141, 141n23–24
Rorty, Richard, 101, 109, 109n26, 111,
    119n3
Roth, Brad R., 25n38
Royce, Josiah, 76n34
rule of law, 198, 209–12, 262
Runyon, Anne Sisson, 149n2

Sampford, Charles, 210n22
Sangiovanni, Andrea, 121n6
Saward, Michael, 239n23, 263n16,
    264n19
Scheffler, Samuel, 121n4
Scholz, Sally J., 108n, 124n
Schwarzenbach, Sibyl, 103n7